MRS. PIOZZI'S
Tall Young Beau

MRS. PIOZZI'S
Tall Young Beau

William Augustus Conway

John Tearle

Rutherford ● Madison ● Teaneck
Fairleigh Dickinson University Press
London and Toronto: Associated University Presses

Associated University Presses
440 Forsgate Drive
Cranbury, NJ 08512

Associated University Presses
25 Sicilian Avenue
London WC1A 2QH, England

Associated University Presses
P.O. Box 39, Clarkson Pstl. Stn.
Mississauga, Ontario
L5J 3X9 Canada

The paper used in this publication meets the requirements
of the American National Standard for Permanence of Paper
for Printed Library Materials Z39.48-1984.

Library of Congress Cataloging-in-Publication Data

Tearle, John, 1917–
  Mrs. Piozzi's tall young beau, William Augustus Conway / John
Tearle.
    p. cm.
  Includes bibliographical references (p.   ) and index.
  ISBN 0-8386-3402-8 (alk. paper)
  1. Piozzi, Hester Lynch, 1741–1821—Correspondence. 2. Authors,
English—19th century—Correspondence. 3. Conway, William Augustus.
1789–1828—Correspondence. 4. Actors—Great Britain—
Correspondence. I. Piozzi, Hester Lynch, 1741–1821. II. Conway,
William Augustus, 1789–1828. III. Title. IV. Title: Mistress
Piozzi's tall young beau, William Augustus Conway.
PR3619.P5Z88   1991
828'.809—dc20   89-46415
[B]   CIP

No more examining the Postman's Hand,
Nor fond Initials traced upon the Sand,
Nor empty Projects idly plann'd,
At Weston super Mare.
But Resignation, Hope and Joy
By Turns possess, by Turns employ
L'Amie Octogenaire.

—Hester Lynch Piozzi to William Augustus Conway, 1819

Contents

Illustrations

William Augustus Conway, by George Henry Harlow, 1815. *From the RSC Collection, with the permission of the Governors of the Royal Shakespeare Theatre.*

Hester Lynch Piozzi, drawn by J. Jackson for the Cadell series of portraits, 1810. *Reproduced by permission of the Trustees of Dr. Johnson's House.*

Preface

SOME years ago I set out to explore the careers of two English actor-managers who toured extensively in Britain and the United States in the last quarter of the nineteenth century. It was the heyday of a theatrical dynasty which had begun with William Augustus Conway in the reign of George III and ended with Godfrey Tearle, who died just after the coronation of Elizabeth II. While in America in 1883, Osmond Tearle had married the actress Marianne (Minnie) Conway and returned to England, where they bought up their sons in their touring Shakespearean company. One of them, Conway Tearle, later settled in America, where he appeared on Broadway, and became one of the earliest film stars, predating Rudolph Valentino as the highest-paid actor in Hollywood. His step-brother Godfrey had appeared on the cinema screen even earlier, as Romeo in a film of a London stage production in 1907. Godfrey Tearle was a fine Shakespearean actor who enjoyed a distinguished career on stage and film, and later in television, and was knighted in 1951 for services to the theatre. That year an article appeared in *Theatre Notebook* entitled "Oral Tradition in the Theatre," describing an incident at a rehearsal of *Julius Caesar* at His Majesty's Theatre in 1932, when Tearle, as Brutus, was astonished to learn that the death speech which he had just delivered, and had known ever since he was a boy, was a corrupt version. Many years later I found the same text in a copy of the promptbook that Osmond Tearle used at the Shakespeare Birthday Festival of 1889 at Stratford-upon-Avon, and was then able to trace its origins to John Philip Kemble, who had introduced this unShakespearean interpolation in 1812. Since then all four generations of the family had adopted it. William Augustus Conway was the first to hear those lines when he played Mark Antony to Kemble's Brutus in 1813, and his greatgrandson Godfrey Tearle must have been the last actor ever to have committed them to memory.

This story brought me into contact with Professor John Ripley of McGill University, who had just written a comprehensive stage history of *Julius Caesar,* and it was he who encouraged me to extend my researches to the enigmatic but neglected Conway, an unlikely founder of a theatrical family, having apparently been so morbidly sensitive to criticism that he was driven to suicide. He left few traces of his career, let alone his background and personality. Contemporary sources of information were scarce, and he remained a shadowy figure until I came across *Love Letters of Mrs. Piozzi, written when she was eighty, to William Augustus Conway,* published in 1843, which opened up fresh avenues of research. I discovered that the relationship between my quarry and the former Mrs. Thrale had puzzled the literary world for generations, and now my curiosity about *her,* of whom I knew even less, spurred on the chase.

I soon found that I was not the only hunter in the field. Indeed, two seasoned professionals, Professors Edward and Lillian Bloom of Providence, Rhode Island had been working on some Piozzi correspondence for many years, and in "A Portrait of a Georgian Lady" in the Bulletin of the John Rylands University Library of Manchester had offered a taste of their forthcoming edition of letters. Glenise Matheson, keeper of manuscripts at Manchester put me in touch with the Blooms, who told me where to find the few Piozzi/Conway letters that were known to exist, scattered thinly over several collections in the United States; they shared my enthusiasm for unearthing Conway, and welcomed me wholeheartedly to the field. Through Jean Preston, curator of manuscripts at Princeton University Library, another major source of Piozzi material, I approached Viscountess Eccles, the former Mary Hyde, author of *The Impossible Friendship: Boswell and Mrs. Thrale* and *The Thrales of Streatham Park,* and an important collector of original material. She too was delighted to learn that someone was working on Conway's story, and offered me every encouragement.

From then on I realised that to finish the task it would be necessary to consult manuscript material which had been disseminated throughout the United States of America, far away from its birthplace, and often broken up into meaningless parcels. In the event chagrin gave way to pleasure at being carried almost door to door by "Amtrak" to see these treasures in the magnificence of their new homes. What better way could there be of visiting Philadelphia (for the Historical Society of Pennsylvania and the Theatre Collection in the Free Library), Princeton (where Lady Eccles most kindly placed some of her Hyde Collection at our disposal); New York City (for the Pierpont Morgan Library to meet Herbert Cahoon; and the Library of the Performing Arts at Lincoln Center); New Haven (for Yale), and Boston, for the newspaper library in Logan Square, and Harvard.

I acknowledge with gratitude the permission to publish extracts from manuscript material in the Beinecke Rare Book and Manuscript Library at Yale University, the Rare Books and Manuscripts Library at Columbia University, New York, the Harvard Theatre Collection, the Hyde Collection, Somerville, New Jersey, the Pierpont Morgan and the Princeton University libraries, the Special Collections of the Charles Leaming Tutt Library at Colorado College, and the Simon Gratz Autograph Collection at the Historical Society of Pennsylvania. Nearer home I have consulted the John Rylands University Library of Manchester, and gratefully acknowledge their permission to quote from Piozzi correspondence in their possession; the reference libraries of Bath, Bristol and Birmingham, and the subscription library at Penzance: the British Library, the British Library Newspaper Library, the University of London Library and the Library of the Society for Theatre Research then housed above it in the crowded tower of Senate House, the Westminster Central Reference Library, and, by kind permission, the library of the Garrick Club.

I am especially grateful to John Ripley, who generously shared with me the fruits of his own Conway researches and encouraged me to go further, to Lady Eccles and to Edward and Lillian Bloom for their moral support throughout the "Piozzi" stages of my work, and to all of them for their invaluable advice on the manuscript.

Finally, my thanks go to my wife, who has acted as secretary and research assistant, collaborator, and critic, with unflagging patience.

MRS. PIOZZI'S
Tall Young Beau

Introduction

Hester Lynch Piozzi, the former Mrs. Thrale, needs no introduction to students of English literature—for as James Clifford wrote in a definitive biography which is still in print,[1] "of the many women who have made a place for themselves in English literary history, perhaps none has been more often the subject of controversy than Hester Lynch Piozzi, the friend of Dr. Johnson, the rival of Boswell, the sprightly, irrepressible mistress of Streatham. In her own time she was a well-known figure in London society, with steadfast friends, and a host of bitter enemies." He said that more than a century after her death, Mrs. Piozzi continued to arouse either "ardent admiration or intense dislike," but it was Clifford himself who laid the foundation for a more rational assessment of her character and talents; and it is largely due to him, and to his contemporary, Katharine Balderston,[2] and to later biographers who built on their foundations, that opinions about Mrs. Piozzi are now less polarised than they were.

Mrs. Thrale's public image, as the sought-after hostess, the friend of writers, artists, actors, and politicians, and an aspiring Bluestocking in her own right, suffered its first injury in the glare of adverse publicity that followed the death of her first husband, Henry Thrale, owner of a brewery in Southwark and former MP for the borough. It was generally assumed that Samuel Johnson, who had been a more-or-less-permanent guest of the Thrales for sixteen years, would continue to enjoy the hospitality of Streatham House for the rest of his days, and some even thought that he would take Thrale's place as de jure head of the household, though he was then over seventy, and Mrs. Thrale thirty years younger. Instead, after three turbulent years, during which she was accused of turning the great man out of house and home, and the papers speculated about more likely suitors who might share her wealth, she outraged her daughters, her friends, and society in general by marrying Gabriel Piozzi, who was not only a mere musician, but a foreigner and a Catholic. Mrs. Piozzi was by now only too aware that she was surrounded by "Lovers and Haters, Friends and Foes," and that in the world at large she had more detractors than supporters.

Within a few months of her remarriage, Johnson was dead: abandoned, neglected, and driven to his grave, as some alleged, by his former friend.

The new Mrs. Piozzi then had the temerity to publish her *Anecdotes of the Late Samuel Johnson, LL.D.*, and her *Letters to and from the late Samuel Johnson, LL.D.*, before her rival could finish his famous biography. Even worse, Boswell thought that in both of her works Mrs. Piozzi had set out deliberately to play down his importance in Johnson's world and to exaggerate her own. He eventually got his own back with a skilful character assassination in his *Life of Johnson*, and established Mrs. Piozzi's reputation as a weak, foolish, disloyal, and untrustworthy woman, which was to persist throughout the nineteenth century. Edmund Malone branded her "that despicable woman," and traces of that image may be discerned even today in Johnson's House in Gough Square, where a printed guide asserts that "she was robust, vivacious and well educated, but congenitally inaccurate;" and that "perhaps the most revealing commentary on her character is that the man who was once Mrs. Thrale's 'Friend, Father, Guardian and Confidant', became to Mrs. Piozzi 'the yoke which my husband laid on me.' "

The success of the *Anecdotes* and the *Letters* encouraged Mrs. Piozzi to write on topics that owed nothing to her association with Dr. Johnson, beginning with *Observations and Reflections on a Journey through France, Italy and Germany,* and ending, in 1801, with her ambitious *Retrospection*. Her breezy, colloquial style found few admirers in the literary world, and the many errors in the latter work confirmed the prejudices of those who doubted her veracity. But by this time the Piozzis had retired to Wales, out of public view, and were left to enjoy their lives in relative peace. Twenty-five years of happy marriage ended in Piozzi's death in 1809, and in her second widowhood, Mrs. Piozzi retired to Bath. She died in 1821, at the age of eighty, having outlived nearly all her friends and enemies of former years.

Apart from her published writings and diaries, she left a legacy of thousands of private letters which were written not only to entertain but, as she frequently reminded her readers, to be kept for posterity, knowing that they would provide a fascinating commentary on her life and times. She asked Sir James Fellowes, whom she met in Bath in 1815, to be an executor of her will, and to be "careful of my literary fame,"[3] and she encouraged her friends to return her letters to him after her death. They were preserved so diligently that James Clifford was able to read at least twenty-five hundred letters in her own hand, as well as over two thousand letters written to her, in libraries and in private collections in Britain and the United States. The first major edition of the letters is in the course of publication.[4]

One set of letters which Clifford did not investigate for himself was that between Mrs. Piozzi and the actor William Augustus Conway. Some of these were published in 1843 and sparked off fresh controversy about her character, providing ammunition for a new generation of detractors and puzzling her admirers, right down to the present day. John Russell Smith, of Old Compton Street, Soho, printed a small pamphlet entitled *Love Letters of Mrs. Piozzi, written when she was eighty, to William Augustus Conway,* purporting to show that "Mrs. Piozzi was in love and that she wished to be loved again by the object of her affection." The idea was so ludicrous that many readers rejected the letters as scurrilous forgeries, but in Bath, where older residents could recall seeing the tiny Mrs. Piozzi and the tall leading man of the Theatre Royal walking together almost every day, the local *Journal*[5] found nothing untoward in the publication. "This is a literary curiosity whose title will no doubt gain it access to thousands of libraries; but in Bath, where the parties were well known, and where, by so many, they are held in remembrance, it will be in very general demand. It is a very interesting little pamphlet."

Rumours of an improbable liaison had also reached London, according to James Winston, who noted in his diary on 4 February 1820 that "Conway, whose real name is Rugg, was expected about this time to be married to Mrs. Piozzi, whose income exceeded £7,000 a year, and whose age is upwards of 80."[6] But the Reverend Edward Mangin, who had already written his *Piozziana*[7] in 1833, recorded his view that

> Mrs. Piozzi's letters to Mr. Conway are not only authentic but highly characteristic, extremely well written, and most obviously the letters of an aged, warm-hearted, large-minded person, to a youthful, friendless gentleman, endowed by nature with an engaging exterior, considerable talents, much professional ambition, and acute feelings, sore with disappointments and oppressed with the frowns of fortune! . . .
>
> All the love to be discovered in this meagre pamphlet is confined to the preface, and the preface-maker's well-devised title, "Love Letters", dexterously applied to stimulate vulgar curiosity.[8]

The *Athenaeum*[9] also rejected the claim that Mrs. Piozzi had been in love with Conway, but in less charitable terms than Mangin had used:

> We have not exactly come to this conclusion; though certainly if we lay aside all consideration of the ages of the parties, the letters may be fairly enough called Love Letters. We doubt, however, whether Mrs. Piozzi was ever in love—she had not heart enough—she was a weak, vain, foolish woman, who loved excitement; a far cleverer actor than Mr. Conway, and in the scene before us she played her part to perfection.

The first major biography of Mrs. Piozzi did not appear until the spring of 1861, when Abraham Hayward edited the *Autobiography, Letters and Literary Remains of Mrs. Piozzi (Thrale),* a well-intentioned but disorganised work in two volumes, based largely on his subject's own writings, including some autobiographical notes[10] she had prepared for Sir James Fellowes, her literary executor. Hayward tried to raise her reputation as a woman and a writer to some degree of respectability, but his efforts were greeted by derisive opposition and did little to change the entrenched opinions of the literary establishment, who preferred to see Mrs. Piozzi through the eyes of Boswell and Macaulay.[11] As to the "love letters," he was convinced that they were out-and-out forgeries and beneath contempt. However, the controversy that followed his biography flushed out some unpublished material which suggested, at least, that the last word had not been said on her relationship with Conway, and Hayward was obliged to rush out a second edition within months of the first.

Charles Elliott Norton, one of America's foremost scholars, friend of Ruskin, and reputed to be a leading exponent of the art of biography, wrote an article[12] based on some notes found in a copy of Mrs. Piozzi's two-volume *Observations and Reflections,*[13] which Mrs. Piozzi had presented to Conway in 1819. Inside the volumes she had inserted a long manuscript in which she set out to tell Conway the story of her life, as if to ensure that her latest friend should have a firsthand account of the more controversial events of her past. It was, according to Norton, "as lively, as entertaining, and as rich in autobiographic illustration" as any of the material in Hayward's book; but he regretted that "one of the most marked and least satisfactory expressions of Mrs. Piozzi's character during her later years was the fancy she took to Conway. . . . She treated him with a most flattering regard—with an affection, indeed that might be called motherly, had there not been in it an element of excitement which was neither maternal nor dignified."

Fresh evidence as to the extent of Mrs. Piozzi's affection for the actor had also come to light in the *New Monthly Magazine* for April 1861, when an unnamed reviewer, whom Hayward recognised as "a distinguished man of letters," recorded that Conway had shown Charles Mathews (the actor whose "At Homes" had made him the most popular entertainer of the day) a letter from Mrs. Piozzi offering marriage.

Hayward mentioned both of these articles in his second edition, but he still held to the belief that the love letters were forgeries, and it was not until the following year that their provenance was revealed, when a Mrs. E. F. Ellet disclosed to the *Athenaeum*[14] that she owned "a hundred or so" letters written by Mrs. Piozzi to Conway, among them the few that had been published. She insisted, however, that the controversial letters had been reproduced without her knowledge and consent, and that the punctuation had been altered and the typography selected so as to distort their intended meaning. From the letters in her possession, she was convinced that Mrs. Piozzi's relationship to Conway was no closer than that of a doting mother to a son.

Her playful compliments and endearing expressions are not in bad taste when her age and his profession are remembered. Persons of lively imagination rarely separate the idea of an actor from his great personations, and are ready to bestow on him the exaggerated praises half due to the poetic creation which he embodies. These letters of Mrs. Piozzi show her heart full of ardent piety, pervading all her actions and her views of life; they show her old age enriched with mental treasures, and accompanied by "honour, love, obedience, troops of friends." They are valuable not only as rare literary curiosities, but as illustrating the sunny close of blameless life, irradiating and softening all things in its mellow light, and melting into the "clear hyaline of heaven." Truly, the writer deserved better than to have her countrymen receive the anonymous slander as truth.

The *Athenaeum*[15] followed Mrs. Ellet's intervention with a long article, quoting from about fifteen of the letters, in random, scrappy, and often undated extracts. Its author agreed with Mrs. Ellet's contention that the 1843 publication had grossly distorted the nature of the correspondence, and declared that while Mrs. Piozzi had many detractors in her lifetime, even they "never breathed against her name the accusation of female frailty. This scandal has been reserved for our own day."

Almost a generation later, the *Gentleman's Magazine*[16] ran a twelve-page article with the promising title of "Mr. Conway and Mrs. Piozzi," but this, unfortunately, shed no new light on the relationship. The author had not seen the *Athenaeum* revelations and was still debating the forgery theory. The story surfaced again another generation later, with the publication in 1914 of *The Intimate Letters of Hester Piozzi* and *Penelope Pennington, 1788–1821,* in which Conway featured frequently. This correspondence revealed, according to the editor, Oswald G. Knapp, that the two ladies were almost equally devoted to the charming young actor, and, apart from trying to advance his career, they were concerned about his infatuation with a young lady they both thought unworthy of him. Knapp believed that the most emotional of Mrs. Piozzi's letters to Conway had been grossly misinterpreted and had been written to console him when the young lady turned him down.

The letters were next mentioned in the Introduction by S. C. Roberts, to a new edition of Mrs. Piozzi's *Anecdotes,*[17] and he, too, concluded that they were genuine enough, but he held out no hope of ever understanding them.

How can we discover or define the motives of a sentimental and vivacious old lady writing to a handsome young actor? Is an exact meaning to be attributed even to a passage like this?

"This is Preaching . . . but remember how the Sermon is written, at three, four, and five o'clock by an octogenary pen . . . a Heart (as Mrs. Lee says) 26 years old: and as H.L.P. feels it to be; ALL YOUR OWN."

It might be thought that by this time the last word had been said on a subject of ever-diminishing importance, but academic interest died hard, and in 1927 the Harvard University Press published a slim, 350-copy edition of *The True Story of the so-called Love Letters of Mrs. Piozzi: "in defence of an elderly lady"*, by Percival Merritt. In fact, Merritt's principal contribution to the controversy was to identify Mrs. Ellet as an American writer who was too young to have been the original purchaser of the letters. His other contribution was to discover in a New York bookshop a letter written by Mrs. Piozzi to Conway dated 5 January 1820, which fell between the third and fourth of the published letters. Its style and content convinced him that the others must also be authentic; but his case for the defence of Mrs. Piozzi's reputation was based entirely on the *Athenaeum* article of 1862 (which he reprinted in full) and on the conclusions that Knapp had drawn from the Pennington letters.

Merritt took the view that Mrs. Ellet had said all there was to be said about the matter, though her intervention in the debate had come too late to undo the damage that had already been done. "The poison," he said, "has been thoroughly disseminated." He dismissed the "no smoke without fire" theory and said that once the smoke had been cleared away, there would be no fire to see. He predicted, however, that "the next writer who touches on Mrs. Piozzi, or the next auction sale or book catalogue which lists a copy of the pamphlet, will send forth the usual cloud of smoke."

In that respect he was wrong. The next writer to follow Merritt was James Clifford, and he merely referred the reader back to Merritt himself "for the complete evidence in regard to this diabolical fabrication." He added, however, that "the canard still is believed by many casual students of the eighteenth century. . . . Readers have preferred to believe a salacious lie, rather than the less sensational truth." Unfortunately, Clifford devoted only four or five pages to the last two years of Mrs. Piozzi's life, and he played down Conway's part in it.

Since then, both Mary Hyde[18] and William McCarthy[19] have discussed the friendship between Mrs. Piozzi and Conway without getting involved in the controversy over the letters: Mary Hyde, whose warm affection for her subject shines through all her work, thought that Mrs. Piozzi's attachment to Conway was "inspiriting, effusive, and somewhat silly, but platonic," while McCarthy saw Conway as an all-embracing son, father, uncle, tutor, and hero—a Perseus to her Andromeda, rescuing her from stagnation.

So nearly a century and a half has elapsed since the publication of the "love letters," during which time opinions about the relationship have moved between two extremes, all based on conjecture and very limited evidence. Clifford relied on Merritt, and Merritt relied on Ellet for an interpretation of the letters in her possession. Unfortunately, although

Mrs. Ellet was a prolific writer about women in history, she never wrote about Mrs. Piozzi, and she made no attempt to edit her collection on her own account. Merritt does not appear to have known that Mrs. Ellet earned some notoriety herself in the 1840s with her flirtatious poems to Edgar Allan Poe, and was threatened with action for libel after circulating rumours of an improper relationship between him and her rival poetess, Fanny Osgood.[20] Her reliability as a witness to Mrs. Piozzi's character might be open to question.

Conway's name seems to have made its first appearance under Mrs. Piozzi's hand in a red leather-bound book entitled "The Daily Journal, or Gentleman's, Merchant's and Tradesman's Annual Accompt-Book for the Pocket or Desk, for the Year of our Lord 1815, the fifty-fourth of the Reign of King George III, and the sixty-third of the New Style used in Great Britain."[21] The pages headed "Memorandums, Observations and Appointments" were crammed with the names of her morning callers and other "droppers-in," engagements for dinner (usually midday), afternoon tea, supper, concerts, the theatre, or just cards and conversation. The record of letters written and received spilled over onto the opposite page with her household accounts, the state of which was a constant source of worry, and every week began with a "black," "grey" or "white" Monday, as appropriate. The last entry on each page usually recorded a visit to Laura Chapel, with a terse comment on the sermon. And on 30 September "Saw Mr. Conway in Alexander [the Great]. He speaks like Mrs. Siddons a little." They were not to meet until three years later, but from then on he was to become the dearest person in her life.

In contrast to Mrs. Piozzi, *of* whom and *by* whom so much has been written, there can be few people who have been as much in the public eye as William Augustus Conway once was, who have left so few traces of their existence—whose birth, life, and even death are shrouded in mystery. His professional career has been neglected by theatre historians, and the reference books are not to be relied on. When he appeared in London, he was hounded by Hazlitt and harried by Hook, but the provincial engagements which brought him to Mrs. Piozzi's notice have slipped into obscurity. He was reputed to be the natural son of Lord William Conway, whose father was the first marquess of Hertford, and his portrait, which now hangs in the Picture Gallery at the Royal Shakespeare Theatre, Stratford-upon-Avon, would certainly not be out of place alongside other Conways in the Hertford seat at Ragley Hall in Warwickshire. This likeness was to become one of Mrs. Piozzi's most treasured possessions, and *he* was to become her "tall young beau," her "chevalier," her "noble-blooded friend," the "incomparable Conway," whose cause she espoused and whose talents she championed. After she died, Conway sailed for America, where the critics were more sympathetic than those in London,

9 Monday	Angelo better, I may say well. Mr Lunell called,	I finish'd my Journey Book for poor Conway, & wrote to him by the Post... & Bessy. James gone a Pleasuring to Cardiffe.
10 Tuesday	I had a bad Night—took Sir James Fellowes's Tinct. and Chicken Broth to day: no Dipping.	I wrote to Sir John Salusbury Drenk Tea & walked with Mr Prior He gallantee me home at about 10 oClock.
11 Wednesday	A better Night; but ter- rible Dreams of Mr Moore somehow — waked myself with	crying. Got a good Dip, and eat a bit of Rabbit and was better. wrote a Letter with my Book.
12 Thursday	Packed up James again with a fine Salmon for Birmingham, & the Book	& the Letter full of tender Reproaches a nice cool day for sending Fish I had a good Night, only such horrid Dreams — of Babies.
13 Friday	Fierce News about the Radical Reformers, & a Sad Story of a Miss Horseman	I feel stupid & sleepy. Mr Prior looked in my Books — saw Prior the Poet quoted, & thought it had to what a Fool! do with her Husband.
14 Saturday	I sent the Prior some Mulberries — They came to me & spoil	the Evening. I read Erskines Speeches They are really very Eloquent. I got a Dip today. No James returned
15 Sunday	Church Mr Scott very good Sense, & very good Ser	=mon. I do not know why it was not Mr Jenkins that preached, — He the favorite, & I suppose deservedly.

A page of Mrs. Piozzi's diary, actual size. *Reproduced by permission of the John Rylands University Library of Manchester.*

Account of Monies.	Received.			Paid & Lent.		
	£.	s.	d.	£.	s.	d.
Bessy's Book, Bathing included	—	—	—	4	17	9
There was an odd Phenomenon at Night, a sort of Mirage.						
Took from Fry 50ᵗ Paid all over him	—	—	—	26	0	0
I eat Salmon for Dinner; felt as if I was dining with Con: =way: — It was the same Dish.						
Prior came in the Evening. The Lady said her Husband was in Love with me, I replied I was very glad of it.						

and he appeared in New York as Hamlet, Coriolanus, Romeo, and Othello, "with great success," according to the *Oxford Companion to the Theatre*. "An actor in the style of Kemble, Conway seemed on the threshold of a brilliant career; but he was morbidly sensitive to criticism, and, his morbidity increasing with age, he threw himself overboard while on the way to Charleston and was drowned."

In his cabin was a trunk full of books, papers, press cuttings, playbills, and letters, including Mrs. Piozzi's "Journey Book" and annotated copies of her *Letters to and from Dr. Johnson,* her *Retrospection,* and her *Anecdotes,* Johnson's *Lives of the Poets,* Wraxall's *Historical Memoirs,* a French translation of Johnson's *Rasselas,* and a Bible.[22] His effects were shipped back to James Buchanan, the British consul in New York, who, being aware of the allegation of suicide which was circulating in some quarters, went through the papers in the hope of shedding some light on the late actor's state of mind. He was so fascinated by the picture that emerged of a "truly amiable and unfortunate man" that he was moved to write at length to the newspapers in praise of someone he had never been fortunate enough to meet. It was with some reluctance that he restrained himself from becoming Conway's biographer, "rather than the protector of his memory."

Buchanan was probably the only person, apart from the recipient himself, to have seen Conway's collection of Piozziana, and was certainly the last person to have studied it before authorising its sale by auction in July 1828. The consul retired in March 1843, and there is just a chance that he could have heard about the publication in London that year of *Love Letters of Mrs. Piozzi,* but evidently he did not read it; for, being uniquely qualified to put the letters into proper perspective, he would assuredly have jumped to the defence of both parties.

The collection of letters, which was still intact in 1861, was dispersed later, probably after Mrs. Ellet's death in 1877, and today only small blocks of the autograph letters are to be found, in the John Rylands University Library of Manchester, in the Pierpont Morgan Library in New York, the Historical Society of Pennsylvania in Philadelphia, and the Tutt Library in Colorado Springs. Mrs. Piozzi kept a tally of her letters to and from Conway in her pocket diaries, from which it is possible to estimate how many are missing. Some of the printed extracts published by the *Athenaeum* can now be dated and put into context, and together with the seven "love letters," they account for about a third of the number that Mrs. Ellet claimed to own. Only a handful of Conway's letters to Mrs. Piozzi has survived.

In addition to the letters and autobiographical notes written *for* Conway, Mrs. Piozzi often wrote *about* him to her other friends, and fortunately most of the relevant manuscript letters have survived. Those between Mrs.

Piozzi and Mrs. Pennington, now in Princeton University Library and at Rylands, reveal more about Conway than their editor did; her letters to Fellowes, more than one hundred of which were quoted by Hayward, and are now widely dispersed, and her letters to Miss Williams, at Rylands, all contribute to the story.

Altogether, then, in spite of the "disappearance" of contemporary manuscript material which might have contained vital evidence, sufficient remains to finish the task that eluded Buchanan and to do justice to the memory of both Mrs. Piozzi and her "tall young beau."

1

Mr. Conway

ALMOST all that is known about the first eighteen years of the life of William Augustus Conway is to be found in a biographical sketch in the *Theatrical Inquisitor* for May 1814, written toward the end of his first season at Covent Garden. This reveals that he was born in Henrietta Street (now Henrietta Place), off Cavendish Square, London, in 1789. The day and month were not mentioned, but other evidence suggests that the event took place in late January or early February, at about the same time that Mrs. Piozzi was celebrating her forty-eighth birthday two or three hundred yards away in Hanover Square. He was sent as a child to Barbados, where he was educated under the supervision of the Reverend William Maynard Payne, rector of Saint Andrews, Bridgetown, and chaplain to the House of Assembly. In 1807 he returned to England, "for the recovery of his health, which had suffered considerably from the nature of the climate," and was taken to see a play at the Theatre Royal, Bath, where he "instantly imbibed that passion for the stage which neither the advice nor the remonstrances of his friends had the power to remove, and for the gratification of which all the plans previously laid down for his career were abandoned." He knew no one in the theatrical profession and had never been behind the scenes in any theatre, but somehow he persuaded William M'Cready,[1] lessee and manager of the new Theatre Royal, Manchester, to give him his first chance, and in a leading role at that. Perhaps the only surviving record of this debut is the announcement in the *Chester Chronicle* that "This present evening, Friday 13 November (1807) Their Majesties' Servants will perform the celebrated Tragedy of THE REVENGE. The part of Zanga by a Gentleman, being his first appearance on any stage." M'Cready had been trying out a new company in Chester before opening in Manchester, where the newcomer was given two more anonymous billings, as Rolla in Sheridan's *Pizarro*. When he appeared on the stage for the fourth time, on 21 December, the playbill revealed that the part of Zanga would be filled by "Mr. Conway, the young gentleman who had played Rolla," and he was rewarded with a twelve-month contract.

M'Cready played the low-comedian roles himself and believed in giving his patrons good value for money, putting on three or more plays every night, from Sheridan (then a contemporary playwright) to Shakespeare, including rarities like *The Winter's Tale, Cymbeline, Richard II*, and *Julius Caesar*, and many more trivial pieces whose titles would mean nothing to theatregoers today. Conway's height[2] and aristocratic bearing, even as a young man, fitted him for the dashing officer and gentleman roles, and after his first season, during which he performed perhaps fifty different parts, he was promoted to leading man. Shortly afterward, the overoptimistic, Micawber-like M'Cready went bankrupt, and his son William Charles,[3] then only sixteen, left Rugby School and, with all the self-confidence of youth, saw his father off to Lancaster jail, rescued the stranded company, and took them through the snow to an engagement at Newcastle. He recalled that adventure in his (posthumously published) *Reminiscences*,[4] after scaling and holding the commanding heights of the profession himself for thirty years. "Poor Conway" (he could never mention the name without the epithet), "then a very handsome young man, with a good voice, great ardour in the study of his art, and evincing very considerable promise, was its hero, performing Hamlet, Othello, Jaffier, etc. to very good houses. He was the great favourite, and as the leading actor of a country theatre, deservedly so."

When M'Cready senior was released after several weeks in jail, he was so impressed with his son's competence in running the company that he urged him to try the boards himself. The boy was reluctant at first, feeling that he could never compete with Conway's "beauty of person, commanding stature, and physical power." But in June 1810, at the Theatre Royal, Birmingham, he went on as Romeo, billed, of course, as a "young gentleman," and discovered that he could move an audience. From then on he never looked back, appearing regularly on the bills as "Mr *Wm* M'Cready," to distinguish him from his father (the spelling "Macready" was to come later). He applied himself diligently to the study of his craft and lost his awe of Conway.

There was no room for two young leading men in the company, and inevitably it was Conway who left: in October 1811 he joined the Theatre Royal in Crow Street, Dublin, where he played for the first time opposite Eliza O'Neill, a rising star who had been born into the theatre and was also making her debut in the Irish capital. She was tall enough not to be dwarfed by the new leading man, and good-looking enough to match his own "beauty of person." "A young actress has burst suddenly and unexpectedly on the town," proclaimed the *Irish Dramatic Censor*, "who appears to be gifted by nature with every rich requisite necessary to place her at the head of her profession. . . . Her voice is rich, powerful, melodious;—her delineation of character is correct (far beyond her years). No studied inflection—no artificial pauses—Not one tragic scream has grated on the public ear." At twenty, she was the youngest Juliet to have been seen in Dublin, and it would not be surprising if, as the *Dictionary of National Biography* asserts, Conway should have formed a "violent but unavailing passion" for her. His acting, however, was less mature than hers, as he had more than a tendency to rant, but he was so *gentlemanly,* onstage and off, that one critic urged his readers to "Be to his faults a little blind / Be to his virtues very kind."

In their second season together Conway and O'Neill attempted *Macbeth* and *Venice Preserved,* in which Conway played Pierre to O'Neill's Belvidera for the first of many times, and later, when John Philip Kemble visited Dublin in the course of a long provincial break from Covent Garden, they shared the stage with him in *Coriolanus, King Lear,* and *Julius Caesar.* Kemble was followed by another star, the comedian and mimic Charles Mathews, who took a liking to Conway, and recommended him to Covent Garden. It is not known whether the engagement was approved by Kemble, but on 4 October 1813 the playbill for that theatre announced the appearance of "Mr. Conway from the Theatre Royal Dublin" in the title role of *Alexander the Great,* and the *Annals of Covent Garden* recorded the arrival of the "tall, earnest, handsome, but ungainly Conway from Ireland." Thus was born the myth, repeated in many reference books, that he was Irish.

It was a quiet beginning to the season, lacking Sarah Siddons, who had retired, and Kemble, who had not returned after his tour. It fell to Conway to share the leading roles, including Othello to Charles Young's Iago and Jaffier to Young's Pierre in *Venice Preserved,* and to assume three title roles: Romeo, Henry V, and Coriolanus. Kemble made a welcome return to the cast before the end of the year and, in January 1814, appeared as Cato, supported by Conway as Juba. That was followed by *Julius Caesar,* in the version that Kemble had honed and polished to his own liking over a number of years.[5] He was the Brutus, and Charles Young the Cassius, while Conway took over Charles Kemble's role as Mark Antony. In the opinion of the *Morning Post,* this revival showed the powerful Covent Garden company at its best, and the young man from the provinces could hardly complain about a review which said that his Mark Antony added much to the effect of the tragedy. In May the *Theatrical Inquisitor* took the view that he had now "passed the fiery ordeal of a London audience, and if we may augur from his youth, genius, and unremitting application, we may look forward to his attaining an excellence which has seldom been exceeded."

Up to this time, Conway had scarcely been noticed by William Hazlitt, whose imagination had just been set alight by the first appearance in London of Edmund Kean. He burst on the Drury Lane stage with a sensational portrayal of Shylock as a fiery villain instead of the traditional

red-wigged comedian; and followed it with the wickedest *Richard III.* The
public flocked to see this new phenomenon, and Covent Garden was hard
pressed to keep up. For weeks the rival theatres traded blow for blow,
competing with each other in *Richard III, Hamlet,* and *Othello,* sometimes putting on the same play on the same night. The Lane could not
match the Garden's *Julius Caesar,* nor did Covent Garden attempt to
compete with *The Merchant of Venice.* Hazlitt thrilled at Kean's Richard,
but "of Mr. Conway's Richmond it would be too painful for us to speak as
we think." And Conway's Othello to Young's Iago was milk-and-water
compared with Kean's Othello at the other place the following night.

Covent Garden badly needed both a counterattraction to Kean and a
replacement for Sarah Siddons and, after much haggling, secured Miss
O'Neill's services over the next three seasons for fifteen pounds a week,
rising to seventeen. Fortunately, she was an instant success, and Hazlitt
was lavish in praise of her Juliet; but

> of Mr. Conway's Romeo we cannot speak with patience. His acting is a nuisance
> to the stage. The tolerating of such a performance in principal parts is a disgrace
> to the national character. We saw several foreigners laughing with mischievous
> delight at this monstrous burlesque of the character of Romeo. He bestrides the
> stage like a Colossus, throws his arms into the air like the sails of a windmill,
> and his motion is as unwieldy as that of a young elephant. His voice breaks into
> thunder on the ear like Gargantua, but when pleased to be soft, he is 'the very
> beadle to an amorous sigh' [Shakespeare wrote "humorous," but Hazlitt rarely
> checked his quotations.] Mr. Coates's absurdities are tame and trifling in com-
> parison. There is, we suppose, no reason why this preposterous phenomenon
> should not be at once discarded from the stage, but for the suppressed titter of
> secret satisfaction which articulates through the dress-boxes whenever he ap-
> pears. Why does he not marry?

The relevance of that question may have been obvious to contemporary
readers, if not to today's, but it was clearly intended to be as insulting as
the comparison with Coates. This popinjay was a wealthy amateur who
had rented a theatre in order to promote his own acting and was dubbed
"Romeo" Coates after playing the part in red pantaloons, a blue spangled
cloak, full-bottomed wig, and a tall hat. Off stage, in London as in Dublin,
Conway was accepted, as the *Theatrical Inquisitor* put it, in "the best and
first society of the kingdom," which was not given to the usual run of
actors and may have predisposed the radical Hazlitt against him. However,
in spite of Hazlitt's hostility, Conway continued to play Romeo, and Jaffier
to Young's Pierre and Miss O'Neill's Belvedira; and he shared the stage
with Kemble, as Juba in *Cato,* Mark Antony, Falconbridge, Alonzo in
Revenge, and Macduff. Of his Henry V, the *Inquisitor* wrote "we do not
think that there is a finer exhibition, taking it in all its parts, than his
personation of Henry. We are happy to bear this testimony to his merits,

as on former occasions he justly challenged our severity." Hazlitt asserted that

> Mr. Conway topped the part of Comus with his usual felicity, and seemed almost as if the genius of a maypole had inspired a human form. He certainly gives a totally new idea of the character. We allow him to be 'a marvellous proper man', but we see nothing of the magician, or the son of Bacchus and Circe in him. He is said to make a very handsome Comus: so he would make a very handsome Caliban; and the common sense of the transformation would be the same.

Nevertheless, Covent Garden retained Conway for a third season and gave him permission, in the recess, to make the brief appearance in Bristol and Bath, where he was to attract the attention of Mrs. Piozzi.

Meanwhile, Macready was making steady progress in the provinces, wisely biding his time before entering the capital. Mrs. Piozzi, who regarded herself as an authority on the stage, had already picked him out as a promising young actor when he appeared for a season at Bath earlier that year, and she saw him again in a return visit in *Much Ado about Nothing.* (Her diary for 9 December recorded "Went to the Play with the Lutwyches, Benedick and Beatrice.") A few days later Mrs. Piozzi and Macready were both guests at the home of Dr. and Mrs. Gibbes, and the encounter made such an impression on the young man that he recalled the occasion in his *Reminiscences,* (1:109–10), leaving us with this vivid pen-picture of the lady and her foibles in her seventy-sixth year.

> The party was select and very agreeable, but rendered especially interesting by the announcement in the evening of "Mrs. Piozzi". It seemed almost as if a portrait by Sir Joshua had stepped out of its frame when the little old lady, dressed *point device*6 in black satin, with dark glossy ringlets under a neat black hat, highly rouged, not the end of a ribbon or lace out of place, with a faltering step, entered the room. And was this really "the Mrs Thrale", the sage monitress of *The Three Warnings*?7—the indefatigable tea-maker of the Great Insatiable? She was instantly the centre on which every eye was fixed, engrossing the attention of all. I had the satisfaction of a particular introduction to her, and was surprised and delighted with her vivacity and good-humour.

She entertained the distinguished company with a reading of *Paradise Lost,* "enunciating with studied and elaborate distinctness each of the physical ills 'that flesh is heir to.' " Then, on the stroke of ten she took her leave with "Cinderella-like abruptness," which, according to Dr. Gibbes, was her invariable custom. Macready's first impression of Mrs. Piozzi was tarnished a few days later when they met again at the Twisses'. Francis Twiss, an editor, theatre critic, and Shakespearean authority, helped his wife, Fanny (Sarah Siddons's younger sister), run a boarding school for young ladies. On this occasion the company consisted of "not more than five or six elderly persons, and a bevy of young girls, most, or all, with

strong theatrical leanings. The consequence was that after a brief conversation with the lively little lioness, the younger people clustered together at the farther end of the drawing room talking about plays, from
Shakespeare to the 'Italian Lover.'" Shortly afterward, Mrs. Piozzi rose
and took her leave with a cold good-night, long before her usual hour. "I
then learned that, accustomed and expecting to be the attraction of the
evening wherever she might be invited, she could never conceal her
chagrin if disappointed in receiving the homage of the circle she might be
in. Here was the ruling passion cherished to a degree of weakness that
excited compassion from one so stricken in years, to whom unhappily
they had not proved the 'years that bring the philosophic mind.'"

Macready went too far in quoting Wordsworth's "Intimations of Immor-
tality" against her (that judgment probably came from Francis Twiss, who
was no admirer of Mrs. Piozzi), though she may well have taken umbrage
at being ignored by a bevy of young ladies chatting about plays and
players, perhaps unaware that this little old lady, now living in two rooms
at the lower end of the town, had once entertained in splendour the leading
playwrights and actors of the day. But the incident went unnoticed in her
diary, which recorded only "Evening at Mrs. Twiss's." Macready never
met Mrs. Piozzi again, but forty years later he still remembered her, and
particularly her connection with Conway, whose "admiration for her
talents awakened in her a lively interest for him, and cemented a friendship between them which was variously canvassed by the many."[8]

On his return to Covent Garden, Conway found that John Kemble's
brother Charles had rejoined the company to reclaim his former roles,
leaving Conway to strike new ground, but Hazlitt was not impressed by
either actor. He admired Miss O'Neill's Monimia in *The Orphan:* "we
never wish to see it acted otherwise or better," but "we liked Charles
Kemble not much, and Mr. Conway's Polydore not at all. It is impossible
that this gentleman should become an actor, unless he could take 'a cubit
from his stature.'" Hazlitt could not resist attacking Conway even when
he was not involved in the performance under review: at the Haymarket,
he described a Mr. Meggett as "a very decent, disagreeable actor, of the
second or third rate . . . a Scotch edition of Conway, without his beauty,
and without his talent for noisy declamation."

The *Theatrical Inquisitor* was more constructive in its criticisms:

We have frequently been impelled to the disagreeable task of commenting on
the faults of Mr. Conway's acting. It is now with a much greater degree of
satisfaction that we feel able to compliment him on the manner in which he
played Theseus. We have seldom seen him sustain a character with such propriety; and we are happy to perceive he feels that an actor who means to excell
must possess diligence and application, have a mind open to conviction, and
never be so opinionated in his judgment as not sometimes to admit the correc-

tions of a candid observer. It is by pursuing this plan that Mr. Conway will attain excellence.

But soon he would have to pursue that plan elsewhere, as the season and his contract drew toward their close. On 23 April 1816, when the company celebrated Garrick's, as well as Shakespeare's, birthday with a Grand Pageant of scenes from the classics, Conway appeared as Henry V; but he was not in the cast the following month, when Sarah Siddons came out of retirement to play the Queen in *Henry VIII* for the benefit of Mr. and Mrs. Charles Kemble. Conway made his last appearance at Convent Garden on 9 July in the long but unrewarding role of Posthumus, and after three seasons of diminishing fortunes and relentless ridicule by Hazlitt, his prospects of further employment in the metropolis, at any rate for the time being, were slight. Macready, timing his entry to London to perfection, was to make his debut at Covent Garden in September, while Kean still held sway at Drury Lane. The only other London theatre licensed by Letters Patent to perform "straight" plays was the Haymarket, which opened only during the summer, and there was no alternative for Conway but to return to the provinces. In October, Robert Elliston,[9] intent on building up the reputation of the Birmingham Theatre Royal and making his own name as an impresario, made great play of his prowess in securing the services of Eliza O'Neill before she returned to Covent Garden for her third season. After the event his mouthpiece, the *Birmingham Gazette,* asserted that "in the memory of the oldest inhabitant of this town no event in our theatrical history has occasioned a sensation so remarkable as the performance of Miss O'Neill. . . . Mr. Conway will take his benefit this evening—being the only remuneration for his valuable services." The prima donna did not deign to stay to support him.

After several other provincial engagements, Conway made a brief appearance in Bath and Bristol in the spring of 1817, apparently unobserved by Mrs. Piozzi but scrutinised closely by the *Bath and Cheltenham Gazette*.

> Nothing is more conspicuous amongst the false refinements of our present actors than the affectations of elaborate art. Mr. Conway is full of it; he appears to have tried the bow of the great tragic Ulysses, Kemble, but . . . he has only betrayed his weakness by an attempt superior to his own strength, and ill-adapted to his faculties. It is true he caught the grosser parts of Mr. Kemble's excellence: he speaks sensibly, and stands finely; he evinces talent, but throws no ray of genius on the object of his efforts. . . . In Joseph Surface, however, he deserves considerable praise; he portrayed the smooth, steady, undeviating hypocrisy of the character with powerful effect.

That criticism was fair enough, but the box office was the best judge of public response, and Conway was marked down for a return engagement.

In the meantime Elliston rewarded him for his generous support of Miss O'Neill by giving him star billing for several weeks during the summer, and shared the stage with him and the up-and-coming Miss Somerville. From Birmingham Conway moved to Liverpool, where Kean had just finished a summer engagement, and opened with *Hamlet*. Two weeks later, after a display of the best of his repertoire, he took his benefit as Coriolanus, and travelled to Bath, where he was to share the leading business with James Prescott Warde of the resident company, and was once again to play opposite Miss Somerville.

Mrs. Piozzi was not at the theatre on the opening night of the season, 22 November 1817, to see Warde as Jaffier, Conway as Pierre, and Miss Somerville as Belvidera, but a week later she noted in her diary: "Went to the Play with Miss Willoughby, Isabella[10] and Don Juan.[11] I was very much entertained." There was no need, apparently, to remind herself that the Don Juan was William Augustus Conway, whom she was soon to adopt as her protégé, and in retrospect Mrs Piozzi recognised that Conway had entered her long life at a propitious moment. "I wonder if you recollect asking me once," she was to remind him later, "if I should like to lead my life over again: such a *happy* one, as you then thought it. Poor H:L:P.! a *happy* life!" And then, as if to remove any impression of self pity, she added: "Yet few, if any have been more so, I believe." A few months later she explained herself more fully in a private autobiography which she entitled "The Abridgment."

2

"The Abridgment"

MRS. Piozzi's story began with an explanation:

A Lady once—'twas many Years ago—asked me to lend her a Book out of my Library at Streatham Park. A Book of Entertainment, said I, of course. That, I don't rightly comprehend, was her odd Answer; I wish for an Abridgment. An Abridgment of what? *That* you must tell *me,* my dear, for I am no Reader, like you and Dr. Johnson; I only remember that the last Book I read was very pretty, and my Husband called it an Abridgment . . . And if I give some Account of myself here in these few little Sheets prefix'd to my "Journey thro' Italy etc.", you must kindly accept

"The Abridgment"

My Descent as far as Katherine de Baraygne, Cousin & Ward of our Queen Elizabeth may be easily deduced from marginal Notes to the two qto. vols.[1]

Hester Lynch Salusbury was proud of her pedigree, owing her name to the Sir John Salusbury, who married Katherine de Beraine, the so-called Mam Cymru—Mother of Wales. She was born near Pwllheli, in Caernarvonshire, on 16 January 1740/41 (Old Style), and like many of her contemporaries, never came to terms with the new calendar, which was introduced when she was eleven,[2] since when 27 January 1741 became her official date of birth. But until the end of her life, she always regarded 16 January as her real birthday, and what is more, she would confuse her friends, if not herself, by counting the day she was born as her first birthday, on which basis she was to celebrate her *eightieth* with a Grand Gala on 27 January 1820.

She admitted to being a precocious child, reading well in French at the age of seven and in Latin at the age of ten, and her doting parents believed that their only child had unusual talents as a writer. She stopped growing when she was an inch under five feet tall and was attractive, though no beauty.

She expected to inherit the family estates in Flintshire, as well as Offley Park in Hertfordshire, home of her widowed uncle Sir Thomas Salusbury, in return for which he demanded a say in the choice of a husband. When he nominated Henry Thrale, her father "protested his scorn of Mr. Thrale's low birth and flashy dress, his fashionable manners too, wearing Miss Hart's portrait outside his snuff-box, and boasting of gallantries my father knew too much of to approve in a son-in-law."[3] But after a blazing family row, he collapsed and died, and less than a year later, on 11 October 1763, Hester Lynch Salusbury and Henry Thrale were married. Until that night she had not spent more than five minutes alone with him, nor had she ever seen Streatham House, Thrale's establishment in a one hundred-acre estate in what was then the countryside, until she arrived there with the wedding guests for the reception. In exchange for a dowry of ten thousand pounds, Thrale settled half his Oxfordshire rents on his bride and got a wife who was willing to spend her winters in a house at the brewery at Southwark. Less than a month later, Sir Thomas married the Honourable Mrs. Sarah King and deprived his niece of her prospects of inheriting Offley.

Married life was dull at first, with a husband who worked many hours a day at Southwark, and was out on the tiles at night.

"Dear, dear Dr. Collier[4] dismissed; he was they said, so eccentric he would put such Notions in the Girl's Head; Theatre proscribed, young Wives should take their Pleasures at Home, mine consisted in holding my Head over a Bason 6 Months in the Year, 3 of which I was permitted to pass at Streatham Park, and one at Brighthelmstone—the Rest at Deadman's Place, Southwark, listening for Mr. Thrale's Carriage at 2, 3, 4 o'clock in the Morning."

He was very much the master of a household that he had run as a bachelor. His wife, though well trained in domestic skills, was not allowed in the kitchen and never knew what was for dinner until she sat down at the table. The first child was on the way almost immediately, and Mrs. Thrale lived in an almost permanent state of pregnancy for the next fifteen years. Their first child, Hester Maria, was only a few months old when the playwright Arthur Murphy—one of Henry Thrale's less raffish friends— introduced them to Samuel Johnson, and all their lives were to be transformed.

The Johnson Years

Mrs. Piozzi had evidently given Conway some account of her life with Johnson in her annotations to the *Anecdotes* and the *Letters,* and wrote little about this period in "The Abridgment." In 1765 Johnson was at the peak of his fame: he had met James Boswell and had founded the Literary Club, along with Reynolds, Burke, Beauclerk, Goldsmith, and others. He had just completed his edition of Shakespeare's plays and was working on the Preface. He soon became a regular guest at the Thrales' dinner table, and when he fell into one of his black depressions, accepted their invitation to move to Streatham House, where Hester helped to nurse him back to mental health. From then on, for the next fifteen years, he was accepted as one of the family, having a room of his own above the library at Streatham and another above the countinghouse at the brewery.

Streatham Park, with its new star, became the centre of a celebrated literary circle. Mrs. Thrale was a brilliant conversationalist who could hold her own in the cut and thrust of friendly disputation, while her husband enjoyed provoking a war of words and sitting back to enjoy the debate. Johnson's personal shortcomings as a houseguest are a matter of legend, but he was ever grateful for the blessings the Thrales bestowed on him. He collected books for the library at Streatham, gave Mrs. Thrale Latin odes to translate, and took to baby Hester as though she were his own child; she was his "Queen Hester," shortened to "Queeney," by which he always knew her, and he helped enthusiastically with her education.

Only four of the children grew to adulthood—Queeney, Susan, Sophia, and Cecilia—and they never got on well with their mother. She found no love in her marriage, either, and once confessed that she knew her husband no better than any other gentleman who visited their house. There was a much closer rapport, and a strange interdependence, between Johnson and Mrs. Thrale, for apart from their shared interest in almost all branches of learning, he revealed to her a private person unseen by the world. Quite early in their acquaintance he encouraged her to keep a note of everything interesting she might hear, and some years later she began to transcribe her jottings into the first of six calf-bound notebooks that her husband gave her, each embossed in gold with the word *Thraliana*. This became her major diary, which she kept up until the death of her second husband. In its pages she wrote of the secret, "far dearer to him than his Life," that Johnson had entrusted to her (and, as she thought, to her alone). "Such is his Nobleness, & such his Partiality, that I sincerely believe that he has never since that day regretted his Confidence." Nor did she commit to paper his fear of insanity but hinted at his dependence on *her* when she wrote; "how many times has this great formidable Doctor Johnson kissed my hand, ay & my foot too upon his knees!"[5]

He had been an honorary member of the family for four years before he introduced Boswell, who told Mrs. Thrale that one day they would become "rivals for that great man." He envied her the close association with the scholar, which he could enjoy only on brief visits to London. It was not until 1773, when they set off on their famous journey to Scotland, that Boswell could observe his idol at close quarters for weeks on end. Mrs. Thrale was not sorry to lose Johnson's company, which earlier that year had become burdensome. She was pregnant for the ninth time, her mother was dying of cancer, her four-year-old daughter, Lucy, fell seriously ill, Thrale was depressed by business worries, and Johnson himself had cried out for attention during another bout of mental illness. As soon as he was well enough, she urged him to undertake that long-projected Hebridean journey.

While he was away Mrs. Thrale survived the birth of a weakling son only to see her beloved Lucy die, and there was no more grief left in her heart to spare on the death of her Uncle Thomas: only bitterness at the loss of "the almost certain Hopes of an ample Fortune, in the full expectation of which I had been bred up from twelve Years old."[6] So long as he was alive, there was always the possibility that the second Lady Salusbury might die first, and eventually her dream of possessing Offley Park would come true. It was a symbol of a happy youth and a future independence, and the only consolation was that the Welsh estates now passed to her, and thence, by the laws of the day, into her husband's hands. Two years later, the Thrales suffered their most tragic loss when their son Harry died suddenly, at the age of nine. Mrs. Thrale prized him above all her children for his loving nature, and he had been the heir who would have carried on the business.

Thrale's business worries receded, and improvements were made to Streatham House. Joshua Reynolds began a series of portraits of the family and their friends to adorn the library walls; and Johnson embarked on the last of his great works, his *Lives of the Poets,* sharing his opinions with Mrs. Thrale, who acted as his amanuensis for some of the essays. Fanny Burney paid her first celebrated visit to Streatham Park, to become a pet of Johnson's and an intimate friend to Mrs. Thrale and to Queeney, and Fanny's father, Dr. Charles Burney, was welcomed to the circle—not least because he would stay up late with Johnson and allow his hostess to get to bed.

In 1779 Thrale suffered a stroke, and a stillbirth finally dashed their hopes for a son to carry on the name. After more trouble at the brewery, Henry sought refuge in overindulgence at the table, which brought on another stroke the following year, from which he recovered sufficiently to visit Bath, with his wife and Fanny Burney, to recuperate. Mrs. Thrale had now enjoyed the longest period free from pregnancy in her married life and began to appreciate her emancipation, relaxing in the company of other visitors to the spa, who were eager to listen to the friend of Samuel Johnson; among them, Sophia Weston (the future Mrs. Pennington), and Mrs. Montagu, "Queen of the Bluestockings," whom Mrs. Thrale was anxious to cultivate. At the theatre they saw Mrs. Siddons, who was a friend of Miss Weston's, as Belvidera in *Venice Preserved.*

When Thrale lost his parliamentary seat that autumn, he agreed to move out of their winter quarters at the brewery into a house in Grosvenor Square, where the doctors could attend him more readily, and where Mrs.

Thrale could entertain her widening circle. A Signor Piozzi, engaged on Dr. Burney's recommendation to teach Queeney music, became one of the attractions of her salons. The fourth volume of *Thraliana* began in February 1781 at her new address, where

> I have set up Piozzi's Concert quite completely: we go every Fryday so prettily, & have such an elegant Room, & so select a Company, & he sings so divinely: all does well with *this* Project, & I got him 34 Subscribers at 5 Guineas each by my own personal Interest. A pretty good Stroke this to collect 180£ for a musical Professor in Times like these.

A room was provided for Johnson, but Mayfair was far too grand for him; he much preferred his old quarters at Southwark, or the disorder of Bolt Court. As for Thrale, he had lost interest in everything apart from his mistress,Sophia Streatfeild, and overeating and drinking; rejecting all pleas for moderation, he seemed positively to invite the stroke that killed him that April. Johnson had just completed the *Lives of the Poets* and feared that life with the Thrales was virtually over, too.

A Turbulent Widowhood

"The Abridgment" took up the story once more. With five underage daughters to bring up (the youngest, Harriet, was not yet three and was to die within two years), a prosperous business, as well as properties in Brighton, Streatham, Oxfordshire, and Wales to oversee, Mrs. Thrale had much on her plate. Thrale had appointed Samuel Johnson, a cousin, Henry Smith, and his friends John Cator and Jeremiah Crutchley to assist his widow as joint executors, cotrustees, and guardians of the children, and he left her a life interest in his properties, the Welsh estate reverting to her under the terms of their marriage settlement. A sum was set aside for the daughters' upkeep, and each of them was to receive twenty thousand pounds on coming of age.

After some debate, the trustees agreed to sell the brewery, which was acquired by the Barclay family in partnership with John Perkins, Thrale's manager, for £135,000, of which Mrs. Thrale received £30,000, and the remainder went in trust to the daughters. So ended a period of her life when her "fate was bound up with the old Globe Theatre, upon the Bankside," the "remayns" of which were still visible, "hexagonal in form without, tho' circular within."[7]

Streatham's heyday was over, but Dr. Johnson, in spite of his advancing age and failing health, would have willingly taken Thrale's place as head of its household; as a trustee of the estate and guardian of the girls, he would in any case expect Mrs. Thrale to accept his advice on family and domestic matters. Indeed, so long as he continued to live *en famille,* he would be seen as the father of the family, if not actually husband of the mistress. Mrs. Thrale was trapped: Johnson was becoming increasingly difficult to live with, his emotional dependence on her was suffocating, and she was afraid that she might be saddled with him until he died. For his part, he just *hoped* that things would go on much as before, and his friends assumed that Thrale's widow would at least continue to provide food and shelter as Thrale had done for many years. There were some, Boswell was one, who even thought she should marry him. He had circulated a poem, in execrable taste, the day after Thrale's funeral, entitled "Ode by Samuel Johnson to Mrs. Thrale, on their supposed approaching nuptials." Her concern was how to extricate herself from a heavy responsibility without giving pain to the one who was still her "Friend, Father, Guardian, Confidant." It was in reality, impossible.

She moved from Grosvenor Square to Harley Street and then to Argyll Street, where "dearest Piozzi was so constant a visitor, and our mutual passion so perceptible, the newspapers became insolent, and the *Ladies*[8] outrageous." As a wealthy, and still vivacious widow, she had already received several proposals which she had scornfully rejected, though she realised that remarriage, to the right man, would solve many problems. To the consternation of friends and family, she began to look at the protective Piozzi as a possible husband. Queeney's fierce independence had been in evidence from childhood, and now, at the age of eighteen, she had grown into a formidable character. To her, the very idea of her mother's remarrying at the mature age of forty was embarrassing enough; to have a Roman Catholic, a foreigner of not very high birth, an entertainer, *her own music teacher,* as a stepfather was appalling. Mrs. Thrale was well aware that such a union might damage her daughters' own marriage prospects, and knowing, without asking, what Johnson's advice would have been, dared not consult him. Gossip reached such proportions that Fanny Burney urged her either to marry the man, or send him away for good. Queeney, who was equally close to Fanny, was cold and noncommital, and Mrs. Thrale decided that for once her own happiness came first. She wrote in *Thraliana* that she had given Piozzi some hope.

However, when the guardians Crutchley and Cator took a hand, threatening to put the daughters in chancery to protect them from a Catholic stepfather, Mrs. Thrale's resolve was broken. "We could not therefore marry without making ourselves uneasy—and though the Parting half crazed him and broke my Virgin Heart, for such it was, we did agree on a Separation. He gave up all my Letters, all my Promises, into [Queeney's] hands, who turned her Back on him, and never mentioned his Name to me nor I to her, till a very distant Day."

A bewildered Piozzi went back to Italy, and Mrs. Thrale took herself and the girls to Bath, where Johnson could not reach her. He was only half aware of the Piozzi affair, and when he suffered a stroke in June (1783), he expected Mrs. Thrale to rush to his side as she would in former days; he was deeply wounded when she did not, and could not understand what he had he done to deserve her indifference. In fact, he had become the innocent target of her resentment at her own fate: if she could not have Piozzi, she was determined not to be a slave to Johnson. Both were consumed with self-pity; his health deteriorated further, and she went into a decline. Eventually the girls were so concerned that a doctor was called in, who advised that Piozzi was the only cure.

Many months went by before Piozzi ventured back to England, reluctant to make the journey without firm assurances that he would not be humiliated again. Fanny and Queeney were convinced that he had gone forever, but on 2 July 1784 *Thraliana* recorded: "The happiest day of my whole life, I think—*Yes* quite the happiest; my Piozzi came home yesterday & dined with me." She wrote to all the other guardians to announce her decision to marry him, and with some trepidation enclosed a personal letter to Samuel Johnson begging his pardon for "concealing from you a connexion which you must have heard of by many. . . . I could not have borne to reject the counsel it would have killed me to take, and I only tell you now because all is irrevocably settled and out of your power to prevent."[9] Johnson was devastated, and replied savagely:

Madam, if I interpret your letter aright, you are ignominiously married; if it is yet undone, let us once more *talk* together. If you have abandoned your children and your religion, God forgive your wickedness. If you have forfeited your fame and your country, may your folly do no further mischief. If the last act is yet to do, I who have loved you, esteemed you, reverenced you, and served you, I who long thought you the first of womankind, entreat that, before your fate is irrevocable, I may once more see you. I was, I once was, Madam, most truly yours,

Sam: Johnson

July 2 1784

Her reply was firm and dignified.

Sir,

I have this morning received from you a rough letter in reply to one which was both tenderly and respectfully written, that I am forced to desire the conclusion of a correspondence which I can bear to continue no longer. The birth of my second husband is not meaner than that of my first; his sentiments are not meaner, and his superiority in what he professes acknowledged by all mankind. . . .

To hear that I have forfeited my fame is indeed the greatest insult I ever yet received. My fame is as unsullied as snow, or I should think it unworthy of him who must henceforth protect it. . . . Farewell, dear Sir, and accept my best wishes. You have always commanded my esteem, and long enjoyed the fruits of a friendship never infringed by one harsh expression on my part during twenty years of familiar talk. Never did I oppose your will, or control your wish; nor can your unmerited severity itself lessen my regard; but till you have changed your opinion of Mr. Piozzi, let us converse no more.

Johnson replied straightaway, penitent as always when he knew he had gone too far, and she responded affectionately, but they never corresponded again. He was a broken man, and told Fanny Burney a few months later that he had put Mrs. Thrale out of his mind and had burned all her letters. It was a tragic end to a famous friendship. Within a week or two, another friendship came to an end, when Mrs. Piozzi realised that Fanny Burney had played a double game all along, acting as her confidante while urging Queeney to oppose the marriage. From that time on, Fanny was "l'aimable traitresse." Queeney's feelings for her mother also bordered on loathing, and she never forgave her for deserting her family for Piozzi.

The press made merry at the unseemly romance between these two "middle-aged" lovers, and Mrs. Montagu was convinced that Mrs. Thrale had gone mad.[10] The new Mrs. Piozzi was too happy to care what they all thought, as they prepared for a honeymoon on the Continent. A carriage was built for the journey, equipped with every possible convenience, with a portable forte-piano for him and writing desk for her, a full service of china and silver, her *Thraliana* and a new set of notebooks in which to record their travels. Piozzi urged his wife to take enough tea and books to read, but when he saw her packing a Bible he said "that book is prohibited you know, my dear, be careful how you carry it."[11]

They sailed away from Dover on 4 September, and Mrs. Piozzi's heart "rejoyc'd when I saw the shores of England receding from my View.

> Boldly to venture on a Land unknown.
> It could not use me worse than this had done.

Now read the preface."

3

Mrs. Piozzi

THE preface which Mrs. Piozzi urged Conway to read next was another long manuscript introducing "the printed account of our very interesting journey, from scraps written in the carriage or at bad inns." They arrived in Naples on 10 December, three days after the death of Samuel Johnson, the news of which did not reach them until the English newspapers arrived, "full of gross insolence to me."[1] The Bluestockings were convinced that Mrs. Thrale's imprudent marriage had shortened his life, and an anonymous article[2] alleged that Thrale's death, brought about by his own intemperance, had led to the disgrace of his wife, who had then "raised an obscure and penniless fiddler into sudden notoriety." Mrs. Piozzi jumped to the conclusion that James Boswell was the author; and when a London bookseller wrote begging her to let Johnson's executors have her personal recollections for inclusion in a biography, her husband urged her to publish them on her own account. Enlisting the aid of Samuel Lysons, a young law student whom she had met in Bath, she offered her story to another bookseller, Thomas Cadell, and, relying only on memory and *Thraliana,* she began to put together her reminiscences, writing "from milestone to milestone," until they reached Florence, from where, in September, she sent her manuscript to London.

The first printing of her *Anecdotes of the late Samuel Johnson, LL.D* was sold out on publication in March 1786 and was immediately attacked by the literary establishment, which resented Mrs. Piozzi's candid portrait of their hero. Boswell in particular was incensed, partly at having been beaten to the press by his rival and partly because he thought, with some justification, that Mrs. Piozzi had set out deliberately to belittle his importance in the great man's life. She had also allowed the unhappiness of the past few years to colour her account of their association over the longer period; given more time for reflection, she might have omitted to say that after Thrale's death:

I found it convenient to retire to Bath where I knew Mr. Johnson would not follow me, and where I could for that reason command some little portion of time for my own use; a thing impossible while I remained at Streatham or at

London, as my hours, carriage, and servants had long been at his command, who would not rise till twelve o'clock perhaps, and oblige me to make breakfast for him till the bell rung for dinner, though much displeased if the toilet was neglected. . . . The original reason of our connection, *his particular disordered health and spirits,* had long been at an end, and he had no other ailments than old age and general infirmity. . . . Veneration for his virtue, reverence for his talents, delight in his conversation, and habitual endurance of a yoke my husband first put on me, and of which he contentedly bore his share for sixteen or seventeen years, made me go along with Mr. Johnson, but the perpetual confinement I will own to have been terrifying in the first years of our friendship, and irksome in the last, nor could I pretend to support it without help.

The Piozzis continued their tour, ignorant of the storms that the *Anecdotes* had created. The wealthy English signora was flattered by the attentions of the Italian nobility but was disconcerted to find that her husband, a mere professional, was not always accorded the same warm reception; in fact, he was sometimes persona non grata. It was some compensation that he was accepted on equal terms by the English men and women, mostly literati whom they met on their travels. But perhaps the greatest impact that Italy made was the response of the Church to her religious beliefs, which Piozzi had only hinted at before they left England: every priest they met wanted to convert this highly articulate, extremely literate, dedicated Christian to the "one true Church." She was appalled at the arrogance of the "Romanists"—she would not call them Catholics—who regarded her Protestant faith as heretical, and she stood up vigorously to their arguments, to the great embarrassment of her husband. "When dear Mr. Piozzi was tired of my pedantry he would say sometimes 'I will indeed get my wife a little puilpit [*sic*]—and she shall preach like a predicateur.'" He had known all along that life would be far more tolerable for them in her country than in his. And when Cadell urged Mrs. Piozzi to publish Johnson's letters, the time had come to head for England.

London Life

Another ten pages of "The Abridgment" sped through the next thirty-two years of Mrs. Piozzi's life, from her return to London in March 1787 to her second widowhood and the beginnings of her friendship with Conway. She recalled that on their first evening in London they went to see Sarah Siddons as Imogen in *Cymbeline,* and shortly afterward set up home in Hanover Square, "which we opened with music, cards &c." As the *World* put it, "Mrs. Piozzi, if not again admitted to the Blue Stockings, will probably establish a similar meeting of her own." She was determined to resume her position in London society and to assert her husband's rank at the same time. Piozzi had managed their European expenses very well, and their joint assets of about sixty-five thousand pounds would enable them to live in style: the Greatheeds[3] introduced them to a new circle of friends, which included Sarah Siddons, now at the peak of her fame,[4] in partnership with her brother, John Philip Kemble, at Drury Lane. The "leaden idol" that Mrs. Thrale had dismissed at Bath was to become the star attraction at her salons and one of her closest friends.

The "Miss Thrales," so called by their mother, greeted her politely but distantly and stayed ostentatiously away from her social gatherings. While the Piozzis were abroad, Queeney had come of age and had taken ten-year-old Cecilia away from the school where her mother had left her. Mrs. Piozzi now insisted that Cecy should live under *her* roof, and the ensuing tug-of-war merely added to the list of disputes between mother and daughters, some of which kept the lawyers busy for years. Family problems apart, Mrs. Piozzi's main preoccupation on her return was the editing of the letters, assisted, once more, by Samuel Lysons. Astonishingly, she found herself pregnant again, for the fourteenth time, but that ended in a miscarriage early in the new year, and shortly afterward the *Letters* appeared, to another chorus of controversy.

Theatricals

Mrs. Piozzi also broke into the theatre in a minor way, with an epilogue to Bertie Greatheed's tragedy, *The Regent,* which the Kembles put on at Drury Lane in 1789. That was followed by invitations to assist in amateur theatricals at the duke of Richmond's, where to her relief and gratification, her husband was accepted on equal terms. "We were now thinking of plays and prologues and theatres, day and night,"[5] so different from her years with Johnson, who disliked the performing arts. Mrs. Piozzi impressed her hosts by dashing off a lyric to open the tragedy of *Theodosius,* which she recalled in "The Abridgment":

> Vain's the Breath of Adulation,
> Vain the Tears of tend'rest Passion
> While a strong Imagination
> Holds the wand'ring Mind away.
>
> Art in vain attempts to borrow
> Notes to soothe a rooted Sorrow,
> Fix'd to die—and die tomorrow
> What can touch her Soul today?

There was now no stopping her ambition to succeed as a dramatist, and the Kembles gave her some encouragement when they agreed to consider

The Two Fountains, based on Johnson's *Floretta;*[6] but they turned it down after keeping it for two years. She also wrote a distinctly autobiographical comedy, *The Adventurer,*[7] in which a rich widow falls in love with an adventurer of lowly occupation—"Oh that he were a Gentleman by Blood, as he is by Sentiment! What low Profession could then taint his Honour?" When he turns out to be the illegitimate son of Lord Harry Forrester, and therefore a "Gentlemen by Blood," her friends approve their marriage, and all's well.

Mrs. Piozzi was delighted when her husband fell in love with Wales at first sight, and they began to divide their time between her Welsh estate and London, making Bath one of their ports of call en route, where the Theatre Royal in Orchard Street[8] was one of their pleasures. Sarah Siddons had begun her career there when William Wyatt Dimond[9] was the leading man. He was still there, as manager, and the Dimonds and the Piozzis became close friends. In London all the Siddons family were frequent guests at Hanover Square, and later at Streatham Park, which the Piozzis restored in 1790 in Italianate style and furnished with treasures from their tour. Sarah Siddons, suffering from a nervous depression at that time and unable to act, stayed there right through the renovations and was ministered to by Mrs. Piozzi, who was not inexperienced in nursing the mentally ill. A grateful Mrs. Siddons told Sophia Weston,[10] "I fear my heart will fail *me* when *I* fail to receive the comfort and consolation of dear Mrs. Piozzi. There are many disposed to comfort one, but no one knows so rationally or effectually how to do it as that unwearied spirit of kindness."

Brynbella

Eventually, the Piozzis decided to build a home in Wales, where they could retire from the eighteenth-century rat race—and where, unlike Streatham, Piozzi could remain if she were to die first. For three or four years they travelled between Streatham, Bath, and Flintshire where they watched their dream-home grow on a fine site, at the top of a hill in the grounds of Bach-y-Graig, "which I am dying to show dear Mr. Conway." From there they would enjoy views across the Clwyd valley, and eight miles to the north, the sea: "Brynbella," a Welsh-Italian hybrid for "beautiful hill," was to be its name. Sadly, though, these years were marred by Gabriel's recurring attacks of gout, and by disputes with the "Miss Thrales," relieved for Mrs. Piozzi by research for another literary project.

About this time Sophia Weston had married William Pennington, a former colonel in the British army who saw service in North Carolina and became master of ceremonies of the Clifton Hot Wells in 1785. The

Penningtons lived in Dowry Square, just off the Hotwells Road from
Bristol, where the Piozzis were to be frequent guests on their journeys
between Wales and London. All four got on well until they fell out in 1804,
and the Penningtons went unmentioned in "The Abridgment."

The eldest three "Miss Thrales," having attained their majorities, had
collected their fortunes but had no suitors. In fact, it was the youngest,
Cecilia, who married first, eloping to Gretna Green with John Mostyn
when they were both underage. They settled in Segroid, near Brynbella,
where the Piozzis busied themselves about the house and garden, taking
walks and getting to know their neighbours. The nearest, and with whom
Mrs. Piozzi was to correspond at great length, were Sir John and Lady
Williams, who lived at Bodylwyddan, across the valley, beyond Saint
Asaph; and not too far distant, Eleanor Butler and Sarah Ponsonby, the
eccentric "Ladies of Llangollen."[11]

Streatham House remained empty, managed by her steward, Alexander
Leak, until the summer of 1798, when the Piozzis made a journey to
London to find a tenant, and while there, Mrs. Piozzi published anony-
mously her *Three Warnings to John Bull*. She also made start on a most
ambitious *Retrospection*—an overview of history since the birth of Christ;
and then it was back to Brynbella and the social round of Flintshire, where
life was by no means dull. Writing to Mrs. Pennington a few months
later:[12]

> I am appointed Queen of our County Assembly, with Lord Kirkwall who is King
> consort. We take it by quarters here, and *our* quarter expires next Thursday
> sennight—the full moon—'tis our third and last night, and I shall come home at
> five in the morning,—change my dress and drink my coffee, and set out for the
> famous cottage of Llangollen Vale, where dwell the fair and noble recluses of
> who[m] you have heard so much. . . . Well! we spend two days with them, and
> then away to dear Miss Owen at Shrewsbury. . . . On the 3rd therefore we start
> from her to you, from Shrewsbury to Bristol, and I suppose Wednesday or
> Thursday will see our meeting. We must stay a week, no longer, for I really want
> Bath waters. . . .
>
> I hope you will come to Bath, and that sweet Siddons will meet us there. . . .
> and that will be too much felicity: to see her where I saw her first with
> admiration [!], and see her now again, with beauty unimpaired; see her in *your*
> company, and call her friend!! Oh, then I *should* say the tide was turned, of
> private as of public affairs.

Mrs. Siddons, Mrs. Pennington, and Mrs. Piozzi enjoyed a perfect
triangular friendship, kept up more by correspondence than by contact.
Mrs. Siddons had been nursed by Mrs. Piozzi, and Mrs. Pennington had
nursed Siddons's daughter Maria through to a lingering death from tuber-
culosis. "Was ever woman blessed with *two such friends*?" she asked Mrs.

Pennington, and answered her own question: "No, never; but yours, dear soul was the greater tryal, and by so much the deeper is my sense of gratitude."

John Salusbury Piozzi

The Piozzis had invested twenty thousand pounds in Brynbella and had restored the little parish church at Dymerchion, where they built a vault to be their final resting place. It now represented not only her Welsh heritage but her union with Piozzi, and Mrs. Piozzi vowed that it should never go to Miss *Thrales*, three of whom had never accepted him, and who would merely sell it and add to their considerable wealth. She needed a male heir who would keep it in the family, and on 17 January 1798 she noted in *Thraliana*

> Italy is *ruined,* and England *threatened.* I have sent for one little Boy from among my husband's Nephews. He was christened John Salusbury; he shall be Naturalized and educated, & then we shall see if he will be more grateful & rational, & comfortable than Miss Thrales have been to the Mother they have at length *driven to Desperation.*

The little boy was John Salusbury Piozzi, the son of Gabriel's younger brother, Giambattista, who had been impressed by Gabriel's marriage to a wealthy widow and had flattered her by giving the baby her name. He had even suggested that they should adopt the child, but this was not taken up until the family was made homeless by the Napoleonic occupation and it was thought that his mouth would be one less to feed. "He must be a scholar," she told Lady Williams, "& we will try very hard to make him a very good one." That responsibility was first entrusted to the Reverend Reynold Davies of Streatham, and his adoptive parents saw little of young Salusbury, as they called him, except at holiday time.

Her *Retrospection* was nearing completion, and a letter to Mrs. Pennington one day in May 1800 described her daily routine: "'Tis five o'clock in the Morning. I was up at four, shall call the Men and Maids at six, send away this Scrawl at seven, jump into the bath at 8, breakfast at 9, work on the book till 1, walk till 3, have dined by 4, fret over Gillon's Despatches and Piozzi's misery all the rest of the day; a pretty biographical Sketch of your literally poor H:L:P." Gillon's "despatches" were concerned with Queeney's threatened lawsuit contesting her mother's entitlement to the rents on the Crowmarsh estate in Oxfordshire.[13] Eventually she was persuaded to withdraw her action, but the affair did nothing to improve relations between mother and daughter.

Retrospection was published early in 1801, full of typographic and factual errors, and apart from a short pamphlet, it was to be her last published work. She never stopped writing, though, nor lost hope of seeing other books in print, but the next few years were to be marred by Piozzi's recurring attacks of gout. The snows of Wales drove them to winter in Bath, and they saw a good deal of the Penningtons until 1804, but after a quarrel, the two Mrs. Ps did not meet again for fifteen years. Mrs. Piozzi's attitude to broken friendships was unbending, as she explained to her nephew some years later, when writing of Mme D'Arblay, the former Fanny Burney. "When Connections are once broken, 'tis a foolish Thing to splice and mend. They never can (at least with me) unite again as before. Life is not long enough for *Darning* torn *Friendships;* and they are always a Proof however neatly done, that the *Substance* is worne out. A new Dress can be better *depended* upon."[14]

Mrs. Siddons and her husband were about to obtain a legal separation (on friendly terms, it must be added), and he had taken lodgings in Pulteney Street, Bath, close to the Piozzis' winter quarters. William Siddons was devoted to his former Streatham friends, though Mrs. Piozzi was not overfond of him: she firmly believed that Sarah's earlier disorders were due to "the P—— given by her husband,"[15] but his crippling rheumatism and Piozzi's gout, not to mention marriage to famous women, made common cause between the two men. They saw a good deal of each other in 1805, both in Bath and at Brynbella, where William spent several weeks. In the next few winters they shared an interest in the theatre and the friendship of William Dimond and his wife, Matilda. John Palmer, the man who "invented" the mail coach and was joint lessee and manager of the Orchard Street theatre, sponsored the building of a new theatre in Beaufort Square, which William Siddons, on his return from Brynbella in the autumn of 1805, described in a "thank-you" letter to the Piozzis: " 'Tis very handsome indeed, and to all appearances very commodious both for performers and spectators. They expect something of a riot here this evening on account of there not being a Shilling Gallery which they have been always used to."[16]

William Dimond, "a well-bred and pleasing Creature," as Mrs. Piozzi described him to Conway, transferred to the elegant new Theatre Royal as joint lessee and manager, and in private "did the Honour of his House & Table with a particular Grace indeed."

Soon, as "The Abridgment" lamented,

Piozzi's fine Hand on the organ & Pianoforte deserted him. Gout such as I never knew fastened on his fingers, distorting them into every dreadful Shape, and filling them with solid and liquid Chalkstones almost without example. . . . For the last two or three Years even Composition grew unpleasant to him; he could not try how it would succeed. When Life was gradually but imperceptibly closing around him at Bath in 1808 I asked him if he would converse with a Romish Priest—we had full opportunity there. "By no means", was his reply, "call Mr. Leman of the Crescent." . . . Mr. Piozzi received the Blessed Sacrament at his Hands; but he recovered sufficiently to go home and die in his own House.

Before they left Bath, they saw Sarah Siddons make her last appearance in the town, when "she played Calista to Dimond's Lothario,[17] in which he looked so like Garrick it shocked us all three, I believe, for Garrick adored Mr. Piozzi, and Siddons hated the dear little great man[18] to her heart." Mrs. Siddons had made that appearance in Bath especially to be near her husband, whose health was also failing, and he died shortly afterward. Almost exactly a year later, Mrs. Piozzi sadly recorded in *Thraliana:* "No Birthday kept, no Pleasure, no Comfort: poor Piozzi seems merely kept alive by Opium & Brandy; if we leave *them* off—Spasms & Sickness ensue: if we follow them up, Something dreadful will I fear ensue——*Must Ensue.*" And on 30 March she wrote: "Everything most dreaded *has* ensued, all is over; & my second Husband's Death is the last Thing recorded in my first Husband's Present! Cruel Death!"

Relations with her daughters had been maintained at arm's length during the Piozzi years. She was not invited to Sophia's marriage to the banker Henry Merrick Hoare in 1807, nor to Queeney's the following year—she was forty-four, the same age as her mother had been when she married Piozzi. Her husband was a sixty-three-year-old widower, Admiral Lord Keith, Nelson's commander during the Napoleonic Wars, who had made his fortune out of prize money and was one of the wealthiest men in England. Cecy was widowed and had three sons; Susan was still *Miss Thrale,* and she fell in love with a married man, the artist William Frederick Wells, and set up home with him.

4

Bath Cat

MRS. Piozzi was alone, for the first time in twenty-five years of companionship with her beloved Piozzi. Friends, and even daughters, rallied round, and gradually the pattern of her second widowhood emerged. The focus of her attention was now young John Salusbury Piozzi and his development as a "scholar, a Christian, and a gentleman"; in the background lurked the spectre of Streatham Park, Henry Thrale's dubious legacy.

She kept a close eye on her nephew's education, which was now in the hands of Thomas Shephard at Enborne Cottage, near Newbury; after a year's cramming in Greek, he matriculated at Oxford in April 1811. Then, thanks to a good deal of lobbying by Mrs. Piozzi, he was admitted to Christ Church the following term as a Gentleman Commoner, a rank filled with the younger sons of the nobility, with whom he shared a distinctive gown and a cap with a golden tassel, and dined at the same table in Hall. Unfortunately, he did not share his aunt's love of learning: "he spent me above 700£ per annum, and kept me in continual Terror lest the bad Habits of the Place should ruin him, Body, Soul & Purse."[1] Indeed, after only three terms she was more relieved than sorry when he begged to be allowed to leave the university and live the life of a country gentleman in Wales. His only ambition was to marry Harriet Pemberton, the sister of a school friend, as soon as he came of age, and Mrs. Piozzi came to the conclusion that "marriage alone could save him from destruction."

Having finally conceded that her nephew would never be a *scholar,* she was determined that he would at least be accepted as a *gentleman;* but the name Piozzi, which she was fiercely proud to hold herself, was an obstacle in that path, and Harriet was not enthusiastic about becoming another Mrs. Piozzi. In 1813 deeds were drawn up permitting him to bear the name and arms of the Salusbury family, and shortly afterward his aunt rewrote her will leaving to the newly styled John Salusbury Piozzi Salusbury her Welsh estates and all her goods and chattels. Finally, and against all advice, she made the estates over to him on the occasion of his marriage in November 1814, and thus deprived herself of a home and a source of income.

In 1811 Streatham had become vacant again: its latest tenant had gone bankrupt, leaving the house and furnishings in disarray, and Mrs. Piozzi's daughters, through Lord Keith and Merrick Hoare, refused to contribute to its repair or to take off her hands an estate that would be theirs by right before many years were out. She had no choice but to spend a good deal of money on it and either live there herself or seek another tenant, but a few months' residence, shared for a time with Mrs. Siddons, soon convinced her that the place was too expensive for her to live in permanently. After spending sixty-five hundred pounds on it, she leased the property to Count Lieven, the Russian ambassador, and took lodgings in "a nutshell here at Bath, where I used to live gay and grand in Pulteney Street."[2] As she wrote in her "Abridgment," "retirement to Bath with my broken Heart and Fortune was all that I could wish or expect."

Her "nutshell" consisted of two rooms at 17 New King Street, two doors away from the house (now a museum) where Sir William Herschel, the astronomer royal, once showed her the moon through his telescope. She had only herself to blame for being so confined. Piozzi, who had restrained her rasher instincts and did not approve of the way she spoiled his nephew, would have been alarmed at her folly in giving up Brynbella while lavishing so much on the white elephant of Streatham. By the end of the year her own doubts began to surface, as she opened her diary for 1815 with the entry:

My Resolution is to serve God better than last year, to thank Him Night and Day for bringing me to see this year. My Daughters rich & I suppose happy. My Grandchildren well provided & prosperous. My protégé married & of Age, and I trust living the life he likes with the People he loves. Myself, tho' cast off by *him* and by *Them;* not despised by *others,* but respected in my ragged Gown, and inhabiting the Parish of Walcote, Bath.

On the next page she calculated that her immediate debts would absorb three hundred pounds of her January dividends, leaving two hundred pounds to live on, confident that "we shall do that very well if it please God, and save a little tiny Trifle to add to the April dividends." For the first time in her life she had to count the pennies, and the state of Bessy Jones's housekeeping book[3] each Monday determined whether the day was "white," "black" or intermediate shades of "gray." On 1 January: "A beautiful Sermon at Laura Chapel, a good and pious beginning of I hope a happy New Year. I dined at Lutwyches, met an agreeable Sir James Fellowes,"[4] who was as delighted to meet the celebrated Mrs. Piozzi as she was to meet a man from so different a world. He was an entertaining raconteur himself, as well as an attentive listener to her own stories, and became a constant companion and trusted friend.

She had already met another Bath resident, the Reverend Edward

Mangin[5] whose latest book, *A View of the Pleasures arising from the Love of Books,* had caught her eye, and he shared her love of the theatre. The gloomy prospect of impoverished widowhood in Bath began to brighten, as a new chapter opened in the long story of her life. The pages of her diary were crammed with the names of older friends and acquaintances, too numerous to mention here, except Margaret Williams, sister of Sir John Williams of Bodylwyddan, who lived in Upper Park Street, above the Royal Crescent, and who was a constant companion; the Lutwyches, who lived in Marlborough Buildings; Mrs. Stratton and the Twisses, of Camden Place; and Matilda Dimond, now widowed herself. Her husband had "lived respected and died regretted . . . in full Possession of Beauty, Talent and Reputation beyond Hope of Man."[6] Matilda and their son William had taken over the management of the theatre in partnership with John Palmer, and whenever Mrs. Piozzi was upset by family and domestic problems, Mrs. Dimond would bid her forget her worries and sit in her box at the theatre. On 18 February the diary recorded: "went to the Play & admired Macready acting Mr Luke"[7] on the last night of his first season in Bath.

Another page turned in the Streatham story when Count Lieven wrote to say that such was the pressure of these dreadful times (Napoleon had escaped and was on the march) that he could no longer enjoy her beautiful place and wanted to quit without penalty, after only six months of a three-year tenancy. Mrs. Piozzi's carefully worked-out plans to pay off the builders and furnishers were in jeopardy, and Salusbury realised, perhaps for the first time, what a drain Streatham was on his aunt's resources and, therefore, on his own future inheritance. The daughters were unhelpful and unsympathetic, declining once more to take Streatham off her hands, and on 17 May she "sate at home in the Evening & pitied poor Mrs Piozzi— squeezed and despised between two rapacious Families." Salusbury urged her to give up the search for another tenant, to sell her life interest in the property, and instead of buying an annuity for herself with the proceeds, to give him the money. "Charming Boy," she observed to her diary.

Sir James Fellowes, the only man she could turn to for practical, disinterested advice, offered to visit Streatham and advise her what to do. He had already established himself firmly in Mrs. Piozzi's favour by showing great interest in her life and times, responding to her anecdotes and shaping up to become a Boswell to her Johnson; Mangin was her second favourite, and often escorted her to the theatre, where, as he was to acknowledge in *Piozziana* (p. 222), she was "a most entertaining companion: . . . I was highly pleased to have my taste sanctioned by a person such as she was."

The theatre was doing well, in spite of the unsettled times: Master Betty—the Young Roscius—was the star attraction that May.[8] He called

on Mrs. Piozzi several times during his engagement, and one day took her
for a drive round the town and the surrounding country. "Incomparable
Coachman" was her verdict. A week or two later her headline news was
"Paris taken—Went to see Kean as Shylock. Whitbread[9] committed suicide." She told Lady Williams that

> We forget even Wellington and Blucher when Mr. Kean appears. I have seen him
> now in Shylock, Macbeth and Richard, and nothing can exceed the Applause he
> gains or the Crowds that follow him. There are so many devices now to obtain
> Notice—we must not wonder if Faults are found in some of them—but old
> Macklin used to say the Treasurer of the house is the best Critic—and if so Kean
> is the best Actor. Our theatre here is said to hold only £300, and there was £309
> paid here last night.

Mangin was curious to know whether Kean reminded her of Garrick.
"In some respects, yes," she thought. "Kean is for ever energetic and
often natural, which Garrick was *always;* and then, he is short and
sprightly; and like Garrick's his little frame seems constantly full of fire."
Mangin was amused by the comparison, and observed that Mrs. Piozzi
was really too kindhearted for the "ungracious duties of criticism; yet she
could occasionally apply the laws in such cases made and provided, with
calmness and discrimination."

The next star to visit Bath was Conway, making his first appearance
there "by permission of Covent Garden," and making his first, favourable,
impression on the "too kind-hearted" Mrs. Piozzi. A few weeks later she
was to meet Macready at the Gibbeses' and the Twisses', where she
apparently took umbrage at being ignored. She was still sensitive about
her reduced circumstances, telling Fellowes that the "wretched State you
found me in" was caused by her concern for "the Child whose Situation in
Life I now felt responsible for."

> Finding my Fortune circumscribed in a Manner wholly new to me, no Doubt
> remained of all Celebrity following my lost Power of entertaining Company,
> giving Parties, &c; and my Heart prepared to shut itself quite up, convinced
> there existed not a Human Creature who cared one Atom for poor H : L : P now
> she had no longer Money to be robbed of.

As 1815 drew to a close, and Fellowes added his weight to those who
advised her to sell her life interest in Streatham, she could look forward to
being freed of that burden. She signed off her autobiography with a
quotation from *Paradise Lost:*

> Thus have I told you all my State; and brought
> My story to that Sum of earthly Bliss
> Which I enjoy: and since at Length to part,
> Go; sent of Heaven, angelic Messenger,

Gentle to me, and affable hath been
Thy Conversation, to be honour'd ever
With grateful Memory.

In her diary she acknowledged that a year "passed in two small Rooms with two Maids only, has been sweeten'd by the Indulgence of Heaven prospering my honourable Intentions of denying myself the trappings which my Life has been accustomed to carry & for the Sake of paying my Debts & delivering my Successors from all Disputation and Inconvenience. The Friendship and Partiality of dear Sir James Fellowes & his Family have been much my Consolation and will prove in the End seriously advantageous—I am sure it will—to their obliged H: L: Piozzi."

Farewell to Streatham

Within the next six months, Mrs. Piozzi was to be deprived of the undivided attentions of her new gentlemen friends. Fellowes was about to marry Elizabeth James, heiress to Adbury, a small estate just south of Newbury, and in March Mrs. Piozzi made sure of his permanent attachment to herself by naming him as joint executor, with Salusbury, of her will, his task being to look after her literary remains. And by way of reward, Fellowes and his bride spent their honeymoon at Streatham Park among her treasures before they were dispersed forever. Mangin, who had been widowed for many years, married Mary Nangreave in July and remained in Bath.

The sale of the effects of Streatham House realised nearly £4,000, and the empty house and grounds were disposed of for the remainder of her life for £260 per annum, on a full repairing lease; thirty-five years of worry came to an end. Mrs. Piozzi could now leave her nutshell and resume her place as a hostess, hesitating, as she told Fellowes, "between a convenient house on the Queen's Parade, or pretty No. 8 Gay Street, which is particularly inconvenient for the servants below stairs." The pretty Gay Street house won, and by August her brass plate was on the wall.

Gay Street was a fashionable address, between Queen Square and the Circle: the sedan chairmen sat awaiting custom in their little twin pavilions just below, in Queen's Parade. Farther south, across Queen Square, Princes Street led to Beaufort Square and the Theatre Royal, and to the north, beyond the Circle, lay Camden Crescent and Camden Place. While her new home was being redecorated, Mrs. Piozzi paid a visit to Brynbella to see John Salusbury and his babies and was saddened by what she found. "*No* newspapers," she told her diary, "and *no* companions, *no* books and *no* conversation. Sun never shines." She was glad to get back to Bath, and tell Dr. Gray, one of her long-standing correspondents:

Number 8, Gay Street, Bath.

8 Gay Street, Bath, 27 Sept 1816

I have got a pretty neat house and decent establishment for a widow, and shall exist a true Bath Cat for the short remainder of my life, hearing from Salusbury of his increasing family, and learning from the libraries of this town all the popular topics—Turks, Jews, and Ex-Emperor Buonaparte, remembering still that now all my debts are paid, and my income set free, which was so long sequestered to pay repairs of a house I was not rich enough to inhabit, and could not persuade my daughters to take from me—

> 'Malice domestic, foreign levy,
> —nothing can touch me further'

as Macbeth says of Duncan when he is dead. Things will at worst last *my* time, I suppose.

Her income was now £2,500 a year and she had £3,000 in the 3 percent Consols, which, as she told Fellowes, "ought to be enough for any single woman." Shopping for silver and linen for her new home was a justified extravagance, after which anything she could save would go toward the £6,000 she "owed" Salusbury, in place of Piozzi's bequest to his family, which she had been unable to raise at the time of his death. She kept Fellowes informed about her progress toward that goal and about her activities in general: "Mrs Dimond offers me a place in her box tonight, whence will be seen Maddinger's horrible 'Sir Giles Overreach' played by Mr. Kean. If he can stretch that hideous character as he does others, quite beyond all the authors meant or wished, it will shock us too much for endurance, though in these days people do require mustard with everything."[10]

As usual, on the last page of her diary Mrs. Piozzi summed up the past year and looked forward to the next. 1816 had been "a happy one to me, getting me out of *Distress,* yet seems somehow particularly long: but I have lost those who sweetened 1815, & I have lost some Health & much Activity. Well! It was a great mercy that I sold Streatham Park as I did— another Year's Penance in New King Street would have destroyed my Faculties. . . . I hope when my Divds. come in I shall have left enough to pay all my Debts—& go quietly forward to July—If it should please God I live so long. I hope so."

In her next letter to Fellowes she reported that Kean had played Sir Giles Overreach "very finely indeed. A clear Voice and dignified Manner are not necessary to the Character, and personal Beauty would take off too much from one's Aversion. I was well entertained, and caught no cold at all." Kean was followed by Kemble, on a farewell tour before retiring:

Bath, 16th January 1817

On the seventy-sixth Anniversary of my life, according to your good Father's Reckoning, the first thing I do after returning God Thanks, is to write to dear Sir James. Kemble is here, and has called on me; I was shocked at the Alteration in his Face and Person. Poor Fellow! But the Public were, or rather *was* very contented, and huzzaed his Coriolanus gallantly. I was glad for twenty reasons; Brutus and Sicinius being precisely the Hunt and Cobbett of 2000 years ago, it was delightful to hear how they were hissed.

Hunt and Cobbett, like Carlile and Paine, were her real-life villains, and she was doing her best to preserve the old order against the threats from the radicals. Her nephew had, with her influence, established himself firmly in the Welsh squirearchy, as High Sheriff of Flintshire, in which capacity he was about to present a loyal address to the Prince Regent and, for a due consideration, was to receive a knighthood. He made a quick visit to Bath to beg two hundred pounds for incidental expenses, and later returned as "Sir John Salusbury." Shortly afterward, when James Cathrow, the Somerset Herald who had dealt with Salusbury's change of name, hinted that a certain duke might use his influence at Carlton House to procure a baronetcy, and thus perpetuate the title that her nephew had just acquired, Mrs. Piozzi responded with alacrity; but the "consideration" that the duke had in mind was 5,000 guineas, and quite beyond her reach, since she had barely £4,000 in stocks (worth less than £3,000) and £885 at the bank. However, the sponsor dropped his figure so quickly to 3,000 guineas that a bargain seemed to be within reach. This was the money she was saving up for Salusbury, but if he preferred the honour instead, that was his affair.

On 17 August Mrs. Piozzi set off for London for further negotiations, having waited, as she told Fellowes, until London was empty enough. "I will not go to encounter Invitations and Parties on the one hand, Slights and cold Looks on the other." The excursion afforded an opportunity for her to stay with Sir James and Lady Fellowes at Adbury, a mile or two off the Bath Road, and a convenient halfway house on the journey to London. She arrived at Blake's Hotel in Jermyn Street on the evening of the twentieth, "just as the lamps were lighting." Within a few days she was able to dispose of her business with Cathrow—terms were agreed on a "no result–no pay" basis, and she was free to relax with the few old friends she cared about, among them Lady de Blaquiere and her daughter Lady Kirkwall, and Mrs. Siddons and her daughter Cecilia, who had been named after Cecilia Thrale. Even Lady Keith was sociable, and drove her round the new sights, which she reported on to Sir James:

London is most embellished since I saw it last, but the Regent's Park disappoints me: had it been, as I fancied, a Place appropriated to the Regent, with Rangers, &c., the Boundaries of London northward would have been ascertained, and a beautiful Spot, like Hyde Park, have contributed to the Health and Ornament of the Metropolis; but Buildings there are, it seems, hourly increasing, and it will end in an irregular Square at last, of which there are enough already. The Bridges are very fine, and will make my old Habitation, Southwark, a gay Place in due Time, I dare say. . . .

I actually passed through Southwark—the Borough I canvassed three Times, and inhabited thirteen Years—without knowing where they had carried me any more than if I had been found in Ispahan. The Gas-lights and Steamboats, and new Bridges[11] are all incomparable. . . . But Adieu! I must dress to dine at what I call out of Town, the Top-house in Baker Street.

That was Mrs. Siddons's house at 27 Upper Baker Street (now obliterated by Baker Street station), overlooking the new Regent's Park. They had much to talk about, not having met for two or three years and exchanging only the occasional letter. The theatrical event of the year had been the retirement of John Kemble at Covent Garden when Sarah had come out of her own retirement to support him. Her histrionic outlets were now confined to readings at her parties, and her main preoccupation was the search for a successful match for Cecy, who feared she might end up "on the shelf." A less happy conversation piece for the two old friends was a book which had just appeared, entitled *The Sexagenarian, or the Recollections of a Literary Life,* by William Beloe,[12] which included a chapter about "Mrs P******, whose great characteristic was vanity."

. . . acute, ingenious, and variously informed she undoubtedly was; but there was a pert levity about her which introduced a perpetual suspicion of her accuracy, and an affectation also which it seems wonderful that Dr. Johnson could ever had endured. . . . No person seems better to have understood this lady's character than Boswell.

There was nothing new in that, but never before had Mrs. Piozzi been accused of denying her daughters their birthright in favour of an "Italian mountaineer who had turned up, calling himself the nephew to a never-enough-to-be lamented musician."

He was educated first at an expensive school, and afterwards at the University; and upon him, and his heirs for ever, are the estates and honours of one of the oldest families of Cambrian origin irrevocably vested and settled. . . . The old family mansion, forsooth, was not good enough for his Italian Highness. This was accordingly pulled down and a new and splendid structure erected for his Honour, at an expence of not much less than twenty thousand pounds. To carry the jest as far as it will possibly endure to be carried, this paragon of mothers and widows, constantly carries her dear boy's miniature picture in her bosom, and exhibits it on all occasions with the most unnatural and preposterous exultation.

The fact that the author had died just before his book was published only poured fuel on Mrs. Piozzi's impotent rage. She appealed to Fellowes: "Can you tell me what's good for the Bite of a dead Viper's Tooth? Oyl, I trust, and Emollients; yet 'tis a slow Remedy. I feel ashamed to think how much the posthumous Poyson has disturbed me. Write a Word of Consolation, and Adieu." Back in Bath she urged Fellowes, "Don't buy the Book, dear Sir. That Method only propagates the Mischief." She continued to grumble to Fellowes, and to her commonplace book, about Beloe's unwarranted attack, but he was gradually pushed into the background by a succession of events, happy and unhappy, at the tail of the year.

There was the visit of the queen, who was attended by Dr. Gibbes, later knighted for his services, the tragic death in childbirth of the popular Princess Charlotte and her son, the birth of a handsome baby to Bessy (who had married George Bell, Mrs. Piozzi's coachman, earlier that year). He was christened Angelo George, his first name being a punning salute to "the dear, dear master" *Gabriel*. There was a letter from Cathrow with good news about the baronetcy, the departure of the Mangins for a prolonged visit to Ireland, and the arrival of William Augustus Conway for an engagement of several weeks.

5

Patroness

THE Miss Willoughby who accompanied Mrs. Piozzi to see Conway as Don Juan was, she told Edward Mangin, "the only companion I could ever entice into the theatre. Going to the theatre with her was a pleasure, because no flirtations hindered one's minding what passed on the stage." She was the natural daughter of the late Whig leader, the Honourable Charles James Fox,[1] whose parents were Lord Holland and the former Lady Caroline Lennox, daughter of the duke of Richmond. Miss Willoughby was therefore very well connected, although she shared her father's political outlook, which Mrs. Piozzi certainly did not; but she preferred her company at the theatre to that of her less gifted friend Margaret Williams,[2] who was "so diligent at translating and explaining matters to her beau [Mr. Wickens] that it breaks and fritters away all my attention."

At home the new baby was also something of a distraction, taking the place of the grandchildren her own daughters had never allowed her to fondle. There was excitement, too, when Cathrow confirmed that the baronetcy would be approved, and bitter disappointment when Salusbury said he did not want the honour after all. Considering the efforts she had exerted on his behalf, her reaction was remarkably restrained. "I praise him *not*," she wrote in her dairy, "but wish to oblige no one against their will." When Mrs. Dimond asked her to write an epilogue for *Fazio*, a new tragedy which was to be performed in January, she was not in the mood to take it on. "So ends the year 1817, poorly, poorly *indeed*, but I hope not guiltily spent—yet scarce innocently either—if without mental improvement by H:L:Piozzi."

The new year opened with "annual congratulations" from Lady Keith and letters from her other daughters (Cecy was in Rome), news of the death of Dr. Burney, and the birth of a grandson at Brynbella. She read a "frightful new Romance, *Frankenstein*, horrible Impropriety," and heard from a friend about "poor *Fazio*, how wicked it is! I saw no Wickedness in it"—meaning, presumably *in the text*, as she was not present at the performance. Nor, apparently, did she go to the theatre again during Conway's engagement, but she kept in touch with the gossip through her

Theatre Royal, Bath, Beaumont Square. 1805 facade by Palmer and Dance. The theatre was gutted by fire in 1862 and was rebuilt with a new front facing Sawclose.

friends and the newspapers. This was Conway's longest engagement since his flight to the provinces, and the local newspapers were eager to compare their judgments with those of the London critics. They were also at war among themselves, accusing each other of bias for or against individual members of the resident company. The *Bath and Cheltenham Gazette* assured its readers loftily that it judged them all on merit, "and we have little time and less inclination to notice the pseudo-critics who dart the impotent stings of their little malice at us through the columns of contemporary prints." It cited the "turgid bombast of the writer [in the *Bath Journal*] who beplasters Mr. Conway with the gross flattery that 'he is decidedly, and without exception, the best Petruchio we have ever seen.'" However, the *Gazette* itself was highly entertained by his "excellent performance" as Mr. Oakley in *The Jealous Wife,* and asserted that his Don Giovanni and his Hardiknute in *The Knight and the Wood Daemon* "excelled any other we have hitherto seen of either character." On the debit side, "Mr. Conway's Macbeth if inferior to that of Kemble, Young, Macready, etc., is nevertheless respectable, and at times he soared considerably above mediocrity." And to balance that, his Bassanio "powerfully convinced" the same critic of the "superiority of his claims as an elegant and gentlemanly performer; to the softer passions of the lover and friend he adds a grace which, flowing with an unbounded facility, imparts to the whole a vigour and colour, warmth and life, not easily paralleled."

With reviews like that, it is not surprising that Conway was in great demand in the salons of Bath, though he did not meet Mrs. Piozzi during this engagement, either at Gay Street or elsewhere. Sickness kept her indoors for a week or more, although she was well enough to accept some invitations and to celebrate her birthday twice (once on the sixteenth with "dinner for only ten," and again on the Friday after the twenty-seventh with "14 Friends to Dinner; 66 in the Evening, to hear Catches & glees very well executed indeed"). Conway who lodged in nearby Princes Street, was not one of the guests, but was at least aware of Mrs. Piozzi's existence before he left Bath; her name had cropped up when he was a guest at 13 Camden Place, and he had remarked to Mrs. Stratton that he "could be happy in a prison with dear Mrs. Piozzi and her Anecdotes."[3] And after his benefit at the end of the month in the title role in *Pizarro*, she showed that she had been following his progress when she reported to Edward Mangin in Dublin (this letter in Princeton University Library).

Bath 4 Feby. 1818

What a comfortable Letter you have written to me my dear Sir, what a friend I have lost out of my Sight since you took Wing for Ireland—so many unpleasant Reasons, and some agreeable ones too have I had for wishing you back again. . . . The Weather has kept me within so long, I lose all but the quite prominent Stories of the Times: for even Miss Williams has been snowed up for this long while and Coaches cannot travel to the Parties any how. Mr. Conway has had a flaming Night of it, however. I dare not venture the Crowd; but he must have gained as much as Barry or Mrs. Cibber used to do in my young days. The Theatre is rather larger—is it not said to be? than old Drury Lane, but then they need to build the Stage up with Scaffold for Favourites.

As Mrs. Piozzi's health and the weather improved the theatre began to feature once again in her diary. She saw Charles Young twice during his customary Easter engagement, and "Betty the Roscius" both onstage and off, when he called on her several times for a chat. Meanwhile, Conway moved on for a short engagement at Bristol with Eliza O'Neill, a combination which the *Bristol Journal* said had been "a powerful attraction" (they acted *The Apostate, Romeo and Juliet,* and *Fazio*). "As to Mr. Conway, we can truly say that his abilities and exertions rendered Miss O'Neill's performance doubly interesting." Hazlitt was about to put his own, less oblique, criticisms of Conway into permanent form in *A View of the English Stage,*[4] or more correctly of the *London* stage, a collection of his notices of the past four years which had seen the metropolitan debuts of Kean, O'Neill, and Conway, the retirement of Kemble, and the occasional reemergence of Sarah Siddons. In the book Hazlitt omitted some of the

Playbill, Theatre Royal, Bristol, 23 March 1818. *Reproduced by permission of the Trustees of the British Library.*

more savage references to Conway that had appeared in his newspaper articles, but he defended with equal vigour his disparagement of the one debutant and his exuberant support of the other, whose "original" style of acting had been subjected to "illiberal opposition" from the old guard.

> Though I do not repent of what I have said in praise of certain actors, yet I wish I could retract what I have been obliged to say in reprobation of others. . . . Those who put themselves upon their trial must, however, submit to the verdict; and the critic in general does little more than prevent a lingering death, by anticipating, or putting into immediate force, the sentence of the public. . . .
>
> What I have said of any actor has never arisen from private pique of any sort. . . . To Mr. CONWAY and Mr. BARTLEY my apologies are particularly due: I have accused the one of being tall, and the other of being fat. I have also said that Mr. YOUNG plays not only like a scholar, but like a 'master of scholars'; that Miss O'NEILL shines more in tragedy than in comedy; and that Mr. MATHEWS is an excellent mimic. I am sorry for these disclosures, which were extracted from me, but I cannot retract them.

That explanation fell far short of the apology which Conway's friends thought he deserved, and Hazlitt issued a further statement in a letter to the *Theatrical Inquisitor:*

> Some expression in my View of the English Stage relating to Mr. Conway, having been construed to imply personal disrespect for that gentleman, and to hold him up to ridicule, not as an actor, but as a man, I utterly disclaim any such intention or meaning, in the work alluded to, the whole of what I said there being strictly intended to apply to his appearance in certain characters on the stage, and to his qualifications or defects as a candidate for theatrical approbation.
>
> W. Hazlitt May 24 1818

Hazlitt neither withdrew nor explained the relevance of the question "Why does he not marry?" and his protestations of impartiality did not convince the *British Stage,* writing about the "fearful dispute which the work has given rise to":

> All this, it must be confessed, is pitiful enough, and reflects disgrace only on the writer. His enmity to Conway indeed is apparent throughout, and scarcely ever does he let slip an opportunity of having a hit at him. Even in his remarks on performances at Drury Lane and the Haymarket, with which the question of Mr. Conway's merits has no very apparent connection, we still find his name introduced for the sake of ridiculing the misfortune (or rather crime) he labours under of being six feet high. To this crime we are persuaded Mr Conway owed much of the obloquy and abuse he laboured under while on the London boards; but if we might be allowed to offer an opinion unbiassed either by friendship or spite, we should say that few actors have more strenuously endeavoured to earn the good opinion of the town, or better deserve it. Mr. Hazlitt certainly cuts no very enviable or dignified figure in the above business, but it is invariably the

case that those who are blustering and arrogant in their attacks are the most ready to recant or apologise when attacked in return. The truth of the matter is, Mr. Conway is a tall man, and Mr. Hazlitt knows it.

It is difficult to understand why Hazlitt should have devoted so much attention to an actor who, in his estimation, was so inferior; it may be that having seen off Kemble, whose style he deplored, and seen the advent of Kean, who had broken the mould, he could not tolerate anyone who might perpetuate the older school. It would be surprising if his book and its aftermath had not been discussed in Bath theatrical circles and it may well have been the bite of this "viper's tooth" that inspired Mrs. Piozzi to offer her friendship and patronage to Conway, a gesture which, as we shall see, must have been made about this time. He was about to make a brief return to support Eliza O'Neill, whose first appearance in Bath had been announced, and Mrs. Piozzi may have sent him a note of encouragement on that occasion. Her letters showed, however, that she was more interested in Miss O'Neill, and was eager to judge for herself whether she was fit to wear the mantle of Mrs. Siddons.

"Miss O'Neill," she told Fellowes "will be visible here with the naked eye . . . on the 13th June. I shall make her panegyric an excuse for another letter. The first debut on these boards is Belvidera, which I have seen Siddons play to Dimond's, Brereton's, and to Kemble's Jaffier, well recollecting how she spake and acted every passage, particularly her soft but striking 'Farewell! remember Twelve!' which was sure to electrify the house.'" She wrote in similar vein to all her absent friends. "It will be pretty to compare her," she suggested to Mangin, "with dear Siddons whose every accent and action in Belvidera is familiar to my mind and alive in my remembrance"; and in her next letter said she had been unwell, "but there shall be a Rally to go & see Miss O'Neill. Poor Mr. Warde I suppose is not a Renault or a Jaffier *fine enough* so she brings beautiful Mr. Conway for a partner. It will be a melting Scene of Distress to us all." In fact Conway was to play Pierre.

The occasion warranted a trip to the market to buy "a Cap for the Play without Feathers or Ribbons that they may see over my Head. Saw Miss O'Neill in Belvidera—very fine. I thought the Play well acted throughout. Mr. Conway's Pierre admirable." She sat at her desk afterward to write her criticisms for the benefit of absent friends. "Our Ladies are all in Hysterics," she told Fellowes, "our Gentlemen's hands quite blister'd with clapping, and her Stage Companions worn to a Thread with standing up like Chairs in a Children's Country Dance, while she alone commands the Attentions of such Audiences as Bath never witness'd till now. The Box-keepers last Night said that the Numbers Kean drew after him were Nothing to it." Her letter to Mangin revealed that "Miss O'Neill has fascinated all Eyes; no Wonder; she is very fair, very young, and innocent looking; of gentlest Manners in Appearance certainly, and Lady-like to an Exactness of Imitation. The Voice and Emphasis are not delightful to my old-fashioned Ear; but all must feel that her Action is quite appropriate. . . . My aristocratic Prejudices, too, led me to think she under-dressed her Characters; one is used to fancy an Audience entitled to Respect from all Public Performers; and Belvidera's plain black Gown, and her fine Hair twisted up, as the Girls do for what they call an old Cats' Card-party pleased me not." Mangin did not agree with her censure of Miss O'Neill's dress, but kept his views to himself until, in *Piozziana* (p. 92), he pointed out that black was not only fashionable in Venice but symbolised Belvidera's sorrow at Jaffier's failed fortunes. "Anything gaudy in her attire would appear to me infinitely more out of place."

Mrs. Piozzi reported to Miss Willoughby, who had gone to stay with the Honourable Mrs. Fox at Saint Anne's Hill, Chertsey, that

> She is a charming Creature without doubt, and charms as it should seem, without intending it, calling in no Aid from Dress, or Air, or studied Elegance . . . but like Dryden's Cleopatra,
>
> > She casts a look so languishingly sweet
> > As if, secure of all Beholders' hearts
> > Neglecting, she can take them.
>
> Comparing such an Actress with Mrs. Siddons, is like holding up a Pearl of nice Purity, and asking you if it is not superior to a Brilliant of the finest Weight and Water. . . . Well! I do hope your Favourites the Wardes will rise in the Profession. He is indefatigable & tho' I felt him feeble & sinking in some Parts—some Scenes I mean—of that never-ending Jaffier: he sustained many Scenes admirably. The one with Renault was inimitable: and 'tis so long indeed since I have seen such a beautiful Pierre as Conway. Mr. Warde is so correct, too so-never-wrong. The Poet has always Justice done him by a scholar-like Speaker: on the whole I was very well entertained.

She turned down a ticket for Miss O'Neill's benefit, "because my Curiosity was satisfied. She is a very fine Actress." Conway had returned to Birmingham, for what was to be Robert Elliston's last season as lessee, and opened in *Fazio* on 29 June. He was welcomed back by the *Gazette,* which asserted "that the long acquaintance we have had with this gentleman, his justly acknowledged abilities as an actor, his highly respectable conduct and deportment have deservedly stamped him as a general favourite."

Meanwhile, Mrs. Piozzi had checked the state of her finances (£5,000 in 3 percent Consols, and a bank balance of £500) and spent several days taking leave of all her friends before setting off, with George Bell at the reins and Bessy inside, for a long-planned visit to Wales for the christening of her first great-nephew.

Farewell to Brynbella

They took a leisurely five days over the journey, spending two nights in Worcester, where she visited the cathedral; in Coalbrook Dale she admired Telford's Iron Bridge; and at Chester she walked two miles round the walls, for the first time since she had been there with Samuel Johnson. Salusbury sent his own carriage to Holywell to take her the last ten miles to Brynbella, allowing George and Bessy to stay behind to visit their families. She was soon "devour'd by beggars"—old employees and villagers who had enjoyed the Piozzis' handouts but found the new squire less than generous.

By happy coincidence, the christening took place on the anniversary of her marriage to Piozzi—"our gay Day—always the happiest Day of my long Life." She was pleased to meet old friends and neighbours, but otherwise she found Brynbella depressing. She was unhappy at the way Salusbury was running the estate—"poor old Bach-y-Graig stript stark naked"—but had to accept that it was no longer any of her business. She "looked out poor old *Thraliana*," which had been locked away at Brynbella, but "could not sleep after. Felt disposed to lament over Distresses of 46 years ago." Salusbury, fearing that the volumes might reopen old controversies, advised her to burn them, and she, fearing that they might not be safe if left in his charge, packed them up to take back to Bath. Then, after a stay of seven weeks, she took her farewell of Dymerchion church, "probably for the last Time of my Life," realising that Brynbella would never be the same again for her. She was not to return until she was carried there to lie beside her beloved Piozzi.

On the last day of August they left Brynbella, not for Bath, but to make a dash for London after a night in Holywell, where Bessy took leave of her friends. Then there was "distress upon distress" when "kicking Horses and broken Springs" forced an overnight stay in Nantwich, but they made up lost time by running the ninety miles from Lichfield to Dunstable in less than eleven hours. There they bought "playthings in straw"[5] for the Brynbella babies and finished their journey at Blake's Hotel on 4 September. After a good night's sleep she "dropp'd cards at Lady Coventry's, Lady Keith's, Mrs. Hoare's, Mrs. Siddons', and dear no. 7 Weymouth St. [Lady de Blaquiere's]," and spent a happy week chatting to old friends, visiting exhibitions, shopping for dresses, laces, and china. She "paid 40£ for a Patent alarm watch—Viner's best," which she was to treasure for the rest of her days, called at Hammersley's, and noted that she could find another £500 for Salusbury toward her goal of £6,000.

On the way home they "drove to Windsor by way of a Frolic" instead of keeping to the Bath road through Salt Hill, and went to Divine Service at Saint George's Chapel. After a night at Reading and another at "dear Adbury," they arrived safely at Gay Street, relieved to find Angelo none the worse for their absence. The diary for the next few weeks showed Mrs. Piozzi to be in fine fettle: all the old droppers-in were welcomed, and their calls returned: "Mrs. Twiss to cry and Mrs. Stratton to laugh," the Mangins back from Ireland, Miss Willoughby from Surrey, and even "Lysons, Sammy Lysons!!!" There was much talk, too, with Mrs. Dimond.

But what the diary did not disclose was that after her return to Bath she had sent her footman to Birmingham with her portrait, and that he had returned bearing Conway's response: "Oh, if your lady but retains *her* Friendship; oh, if I can but keep *her* Patronage, I care not for the rest."[6]

There is no hint in Mrs. Piozzi's diary as to when that friendship and patronage was first offered, but in a letter to Conway some months later[7] she reminded him that "your Fancy in a happy Hour prompted you to court Acquaintance with Thrale's Wife more than Piozzi's Widow." This was perhaps an allusion to his conversation with Mrs. Stratton about Mrs. Piozzi and her *Anecdotes*. It would have been entirely within character for her to respond to his interest by offering her hospitality when he next played in Bath. That opportunity soon presented itself, when he returned to his lodgings at No. 6 Princes Street, which joins Queen Square on the opposite corner to Gay Street, and is only few yards from the theatre where he was billed to appear on 31 October as Don Felix in *The Wonder.*[8]

Unfortunately, Mrs. Piozzi was unwell and was not in Mrs. Dimond's box to greet him, nor did Conway call to pay his respects to his new patroness. She did not venture to the theatre until Miss Willoughby dined with her a week later and "we went to the Play. A new Melodrama [*Bellamira*]. Conway incomparable in Manfredi—Warde good too & a Girl",[9] but as yet there was no contact between patroness and protégé. Perhaps neither knew how to proceed. She was still unwell, and worried about her own affairs. George Bell had given in his notice, apparently abandoning Bessy and their child, and Salusbury was once again dunning her for money. The estate which four years earlier had been a source of income as well as a home for Mrs. Piozzi evidently did not provide enough to support her nephew and family, and he continued to make demands on her meagre resources, while she was still scrimping and saving to build up capital for him. But as she usually gave him what he asked for, he doubtless assumed there was plenty more to be had. She sent him two hundred pounds.

When Conway did eventually meet Mrs. Piozzi, he had been in Bath for six weeks, and even then he had, apparently, asked Miss Willoughby to accompany him to Gay Street. The date which she would in future call "our Anniversary" was highlighted in the margin of her diary with a pointing finger:

Saturday 12 December Mr. Conway called so late yesterday, I could not see him; not half well today, but he came again & I was very glad. The O'Biernes came too, & Dr. Browne Mill & Miss Willoughby.

The week before Christmas brought another star to Bath, Conway's friend Charles Mathews, who failed to get a mention in the diary: "Miss Willoughby to Dinner & the Play—The Hypocrite. Conway's Col. Lambert charming!" Mathews played the part of Maw-worm, one of his best impersonations. Sir James Fellowes was in Bath, too, and spent several days listening to Mrs. Piozzi's readings from the volumes of *Thraliana* that she had rescued from Brynbella. She counted her blessings at the end of yet another year, signing her diary off with a broad flourish: "& who is so happy as H:L:P. at the Close of the Year 1818?" And then, "I *open* my new Red Book for 1819. but how will the book close!?"

She threw herself into her self-appointed task as Conway's chief promoter, selling tickets for his benefit and swelling with pride over his press notices. The *Gazette* was impressed by his "animated portrait of the virtuous Abbot" in *The Orphan of the Castle* and enraptured by his Coriolanus:

In whatever light we view the Coriolanus of Mr. Conway, pleasure and approbation are the result. He appears to have investigated the mind of the noble Roman, not only as it refers to every surrounding circumstance, but with the most minute attention to all the natural propensities of humanity. His occasional suppression of rage, his sudden bursts of passion, and his expression of ambition, evince a grand combination of executive skill.

After much more flattery, the reviewer concluded:

Mr. Conway is peculiarly fitted for the personification of the Noble Roman: he possesses a fine, commanding countenance, and is 'in person rather taller than the common size'; with a mellow, extensive, and not unpleasing voice: his figure is of heroic stature. . . . He was greeted throughout with the most unequivocal and enthusiastic plaudits.

On 23 January *The Hero of the North* and *Comus* were presented for Conway's benefit, and the *Gazette* thrilled: "it was with so much pleasure that we witnessed so elegantly attended a house," and "it is not too much to assert that no theatre in the kingdom could possibly surpass the excellence of this presentation." Mrs. Piozzi told her diary that "Conway acted incomparably & Mr. Warde spoke the Attendant Spirit to perfection.

Conway's voice when he praises the sweet Echo was *so* tender, *so* affecting I could scarce keep my seat." She enlarged on those impressions in her commonplace book:

> *Spirit:* The beautiful Verses Milton put into the mouth of the Attendant Spirit in Comus were never surely so incomparably, so faultlessly pronounced as by Mr. Warde, an actor on our stage here. Mr. Mangin says he spoke them too well, meaning with pedantic care to shew he understood them, but I do not recollect that he forgot the Actor in his Declamation—it was altogether excellent—and his grave Rebuke—severe in youthful Beauty added Grace invincible—but I think our stage is very well supplied. Conway and Warde, both fine fellows in their way. Comus last night deserved great applause from the many, and from the few, much sober Approbation.

In the margin she wrote: "I hate to see Comus—I have some odd peculiar Reasons—and it makes me ill too."

She celebrated yet another birthday with "a sweet Concert & a gay Assemblage of Company. Too great a Crowd was the only fault. *Conway* staid them *all out*." From that day forward, as Mrs. Piozzi was to remind him,[10] they were *Friends*.

6

"Transcendant Conway"

MRS. Piozzi was delighted to claim this Adonis as her property, to add prestige to her parties, regretting only that other hostesses like Mrs. Stratton and Miss Willoughby had claimed him first. However, *she* could offer not only her table and her talented friends but her personal recollections of the Johnson days. And from her knowledge of language and literature, of history and mythology, of dramatists, actors and actresses, she could illuminate every play in Conway's repertoire. She might even be able to exert some influence on his behalf with the theatre management.[1] In return, Conway could entertain her guests with stories of the theatre, at least one of which found its way into her commonplace book.

> Lady Caroline Lamb[2] asked Mr. Conway why they never play'd King Lear now. "Oh, Madam! Your Ladyship must be well aware of the Cause of our Forbearance when you recollect our Sovereign's Situation."[3] "Why, dear me," was the Reply. "You yourself act the Libertine[4] every Week, tho' the *Regent* has the executive Power in his Hands!"

Warde had no part in *Don Giovanni,* and Conway did not appear in Warde's favourite *Guy Mannering.* They shared the leads in *A Tale of Mystery,* but as there were always two items on the bill, they were rarely called on to appear together in the same play. Then Conway did not act at all for four weeks, leaving the field to Warde and the visiting Miss Kelly. The resident leading man, Miss Willoughby's protégé, had been with the company since his novitiate five or six years earlier, and had married, and found many friends in the town. He had ably supported all the visiting stars, including John Kemble on his farewell appearance, the wild Kean, the rising Macready, and the exciting Miss O'Neill. Immediately after her departure, he had made his London debut at the Haymarket, and he and his supporters looked askance at the engagement of another (and more handsome) actor to share the leading roles, not just for a few nights, but for a long season. Problems were bound to arise on both sides of the curtain, testing the loyalties of patrons, critics, and hostesses alike and in Bath, hotbed of gossip and social rivalry, people began to take sides.

Indeed, the "faction-fights which rent theatrical Bath in 1818–19," Mrs. Piozzi leading the supporters of " 'Handsome' Conway against those of Warde,"[5] have passed into legend. The story, which first appeared in a biography of Charles Kean[6] and was later enshrined in theatrical history in *The Bath Stage*,[7] claimed that each of these actors had "a patronising dowager who sat in opposite stage boxes and led the applause for their respective protégés."

> The red and green factions of the crews at Constantinople in the reign of Justinian, or the feuds of the Orsinis and Colonnas during the middle ages at Rome never raged with greater intensity than the 'Vereker' and 'Piozzi' parties which divided British Baiae[8] in support of their respective favourites of the buskin.

The name of Vereker does not appear in Mrs. Piozzi's diary, although there was a Mrs. Vereker in Bath at that time, and the name still exists there.

> In private life the performers were pursued by a sort of biassed enthusiasm, an infatuated admiration. . . . Ladies giving tea-parties wrote upon their card of invitation, "Mr. Conway will be present". . . . When Mr. Warde found himself in bondage to the suit of an obdurate creditor . . . eleemosynary turkeys, fowls, and rounds of beef were supplied by his friends. . . . When Mr. Conway fell sick from over-exertion upon the stage, three physicians were despatched daily to his door . . . anxious enquiries were made hourly as to his state . . . turtle soup, venison, and pineapple were poured in upon him.

It was a grossly overdrawn picture, based, perhaps, on an element of truth—Mrs. Piozzi's unreserved support of Conway on stage may well have drawn counterfire from the other camp. However, as far as Mrs. Piozzi was concerned, her admiration for Warde was undiminished by her patronage of Conway, and socially they were both equally acceptable in her circle. "Tea at dear delightful Mrs. Strattons with Warde and Conway," and "Warde called with tickets for his benefit" bore witness to that.

The management not only suffered headaches over the allocation of parts between the two leads but were also under fire on account of the length of the programs. In March the *Gazette* complained that the final curtain rarely came down before 11:30, and sometimes it was after midnight, and "in consequence many families missed the exquisite gratification of witnessing the double attraction of the representation of the works of Shakespeare and Milton upon the same evening." If there was any truth in Dr. Gibbes's assertion that Mrs. Piozzi never stayed out late, she had to change her habits now, and did not leave early from that recital of the words of her favourite authors by her favourite actors. Warde played the King, and Conway the Prince, in *Henry IV, Part 1*, which she thought was "very well done indeed. Conway looked like Guido's Angel,"[9] but as to the *Comus,* she confessed to Conway a few months later that his voice and manner affected her so strongly that she "pretended engagement after the play, and ran." The *Gazette* was not so easily overcome with emotion, but did go so far as to doubt whether the evening as a whole could have been surpassed by either of the metropolitan theatres. However, they were still dissatisfied with management's time keeping, and they intended to publish in future the time that the curtain fell each night, as told by the Pump Room clock.

By now Conway had been in Bath for over four months, and had secured a special place in Mrs. Piozzi's affections; on 12 March she wrote "Charming Conway came home with me from Hetling Court, & sate a happy hour; & thanked me *1000* Times: I shewed him my Shakespeare." But the following day he broke the news gently that he might be leaving Bath at the end of the season. Alfred Bunn,[10] a young man of about twenty-two, had taken over the management of the Birmingham Theatre Royal from Robert Elliston and wanted Conway to join him as stage manager and leading man. In one of the few notes of Conway's that has survived, he sought Mrs. Piozzi's advice. This, and the others quoted below, are in the John Rylands Library.[11]

The dawn is overcast, the morning lours, and heavily in clouds brings on the day.[12] Nothing is *yet* determined: I am in possession of a *proposal* from them, which shall be communicated to *you* during the course of the morning. My answer will require much deliberation. The Ides of March are come, but not *gone.*

That evening (it was actually the *thirteenth* of March) *The Renegade* was performed for Warde's benefit. It was a contemporary dramatisation of Dryden's *Don Sebastian* and *The Spanish Friar,* in which the big scene between them was the highlight of an otherwise dull play, and Conway had evidently drawn on Mrs. Piozzi's fund of knowledge in preparing for his part. A few days after the performance he sent another note across the square:

Mr. Conway has the honor of returning the volume of Dryden which Mrs. Piozzi was kind enough to send him, and takes leave to present his best thanks for the loan of the same. He has read Mr. Scott's criticism upon Don Sebastian, and the very able, though somewhat coarse, vindication of the Duke of Guise by Dryden, both of which have afforded him considerable entertainment: he perfectly agrees, however, with Mrs. Piozzi, respecting the *temperate* heat of the Northern Critic.

Mr. Conway had the gratification of seeing Mrs. Piozzi in her Box on Saturday evening, "the observed of all observers", and as usual most kindly attentive to the scene; which, as the Play had so little to *merit* it, demands more than the usual acknowledgements of himself and fellows—but "the less they deserve, the more merit is in Her bounty".

6 Princes Street
Tuesday Morning [16 March]

Her own comment on the evening had been: "Warde's benefit—Don Sebastian—admirable fine acting, fine speaking—fine poetry. Sebastian and Dorax excellent—The first best." A few days afterward, "wrote a Note of Criticism to Conway" and received "a sweet Note about the Dryden from him."

The prospect of losing Conway so soon filled Mrs. Piozzi—and Mrs. Stratton—with alarm, and both stepped up their efforts to entertain him. Mrs. Stratton had a party ("a very pleasant Day and Dinner—*very* pleasant indeed—Conway"—his name in microscopic letters), and Mrs. Piozzi was planning to have a party for Warde and Conway as soon as their engagements permitted. She was eager to introduce them both to Fellowes.

Bath
21 March 1819

I can now tell my Dear Sir James Fellowes that Mrs. Stratton's Party went off delightfully. I wish mine may be as gay & brilliant next Fryday 26th when my very best Dependence will be on you, my ever best Friend: we must sit down tho' as near to 5 o'clock as possible, because of Sir Walter James, who hates to dine later, and who has beg'd himself in with a Condescendance I little expected. You and he will find Warde most of a Scholar, Conway the Man of high Polish, and best natural Abilities. If you don't like them it will vex me. . . . Apropos to Authors, Actors, etc, I have had an Offer since I wrote last, not of Marriage, as Ninion de l'Enclos boasted when touching Eighty, but of a better Thing, *Money*. [A Mr. George Watson Taylor had offered £200 for Reynolds's portrait of Arthur Murphy and her Cipriani Magdalen.] It will go a long Way to making up the £6000 which dear Piozzi left to his Relations in Italy—& which I always have promised Salusbury to make up for him in the 3 percent Consols—after which Transaction my Money is my own—there are £5000 in now, you know . . .

Conway accepted the invitation with his customary formality:

Mr. Conway acknowledges the honor of Mrs. Piozzi's kind invitation, which it will afford him infinite pleasure to accept. He is particularly desirous of re-perusing Mrs. Piozzi's 'Anecdotes' of the immortal Johnson, and trusts he shall be forgiven if he ventures to solicit the *loan* of them, for a few days, should they happen to occupy a place in her library.
6 Princes Street
18th March 1819

There was a heavy week ahead for the actors before the dinner party, and the *Gazette* reported final curtains ranging from 11:00 P.M. to 12:15 A.M. On Monday they claimed that *The Winter's Tale* was badly cast, and only Conway's Leontes emerged unscathed. "Mr. Warde as Florizel was tame and spiritless; he appears to act on the principle of *aut Caesar, aut nullius,* and unless playing the first character seems to think he is placed in a situation beneath the exercise of his talents. This is wrong: he may be assured that an actor sometimes evinces more genius, in rendering a secondary character prominent, than in giving full effect to a first-rate one." He pulled his socks up for Miss Tree's benefit the next night, when he "played admirably, and gave us entire satisfaction." By the Thursday, Conway's throat threatened to give out:

Mr. Conway returns sincere thanks to Mrs. Piozzi for her kind enquiries, and begs to acquaint her that his throat is still very much inflamed; it will not, however, prevent his *attempting* his duty at the theatre this evening, as the performances are for a benefit, but *fears* it may deprive him of the honor and pleasure of seeing Mrs. Piozzi tomorrow. He will send again to her in the course of tomorrow morning.

Thursday [25 March]

Mrs. Piozzi was relieved to find that her favourite's throat did survive the performance: "Mr. Conway beyond even himself—convulsed us all with terror. Town & Country too—pretty enough." He was still overwhelmed by her concern for his welfare, and maintained a respectful distance:

Mr. Conway is really at a loss to express in adequate terms his sense of Mrs. Piozzi's very kind and flattering attentions to him, but though he cannot *express,* he *feels* them more strongly, and begs to offer his sincere and heartfelt acknowledgements for the same. He is happy to inform Mrs. Piozzi that notwithstanding the exertions of the scene last evening, his throat has *not* become *worse,* owing chiefly to the frequent application of the Gargle she was good enough to prescribe [she claimed to know "as much about the Materia Medica as any Apothecary's Boy"], and he therefore hopes to have the honor of paying her his respects at five o'clock this evening.

6 Princes Street
March 26 1819

"He came & was charming & read Merry's Address to the Critics:[13] I had a very nice Two Table Party," wrote Mrs. Piozzi. Fearing, perhaps, that she had made too much of a fuss of Conway that evening, her letters to Fellowes assured him that he was her "ever best Friend," and she had commissioned Jagger (a local miniaturist) to do his portrait from an original by Pelligrini. She shared a little joke with her medical and financial consultant, about the price of government stock—"I have seen the Consols down at 53 & up at 94—72 is the right Place, a'n't it? as it has a healthy Pulse"—at which price she could buy another three hundred pounds toward Salusbury's legacy. She wanted Sir James to be assured of "the grateful & everlasting regard due to you ever since the first day of the year 1815 from H:L:P." She could not afford to lose such a staunch devotee.

Mrs. Piozzi was in a flutter, and got out of step in her diary that week, ending it with "Miss Wroughton begg'd a place in our Box for tonight— Warde's Meg Merrilees. Oh dear—I am got wrong somehow. This is Saturday, not Fryday. My Party was on Fryday." Miss Wroughton was known as the Queen of Bath, sometime leader of fashion, now in her sixties, and former patroness of the late Venanzio Rauzzini, singer and composer. It was said that the season could not begin until she arrived, and her concerts and card parties excelled all others. Mrs. Piozzi was often seen at her musical evenings, but Miss Wroughton was not one of Conway's supporters and signalled her preference for Warde by inviting herself into the Dimonds' box for his benefit, in which he forsook the title role in *Guy Mannering* for the female part Meg Merrilees.

The end of the theatrical season was now within sight. It was to be rounded off with the usual Easter visit of Charles Mayne Young; and with three tragedians to call on there was a rare opportunity to present *Julius Caesar*. Mrs. Piozzi told Fellowes that she would spend most of the week "at the theatre, where Shakespeare's most agreeable Characters are exhibited; Fauconbridge and Marc Antony, for which my Favourite Conway seems to have been born"—she saw both characters as pillars of the established order. The Birmingham contract was not yet signed, and Mrs. Piozzi still hoped that she could persuade the Dimonds to make Conway an offer that would induce him to stay in Bath for another season. However, the prospects were not good, and from then on she determined to make the most of his company, even if she had to share him with the Strattons.

The sight of this little old lady trotting alongside her tall young beau was a feature of Bath that April: day after day, if he was not at 8 Gay Street, they were both at 13 Camden Place, where he was more interested in the girls, especially Charlotte, and they in him. One day she "called to see Sir James' portrait again—it is really very fine. Mrs. Stratton and Girls called—in Agony about Conway. Bank 553£ and 300£ Consols bought," followed by another "Gray Monday—White because I enjoyed Conway's charming company in the Morning & went with him to Mrs. Strattons. Thousands of droppers-in."

Mrs. Piozzi was now determined that if she were to lose Conway after all, she would see to it that he did not forget her, and she began to annotate copies of her books for him, just as she had for Fellowes. She began with *Retrospection,*[14] in which she "presented to Mr. Conway's kind Acceptance a Summary Review of the most striking and particular Events which have befallen this Earth & its Inhabitants during the course of 1800 years. The Facts selected and compiled par son Amie Octogenaire Hester Lynch Piozzi, Bath April 11th 1819." He must have blushed with embarrassment to read her notes—one of them, opposite a reference to "Edward III's great-grandson, the once-wild Prince of Wales," read, "*so* designated by immortal Shakespeare—*so* represented by incomparable Conway," and another, opposite a reference to Venice, "now to be best known to Englishmen by Otway's truly pathetic Drama [*Venice Preserved*], commemorating the Discovery of a Plot destroyed by Female Influence, and bringing into dramatic action, each in their day, the various but unrivalled powers of Barry, Siddons and Conway"(!)

The Easter festival opened with *Pizarro,* in which Conway took the title role and Young played Rolla, as they used to at Covent Garden; *Julius Caesar* was billed for the Wednesday, when Warde would be the Brutus, and Young, as always, the Cassius, but when the day came, the Mark Antony sent word to Mrs. Piozzi in response to an invitation:

Many, many thanks dear Madam for your repeated kindnesses: my obligations to you are increased each day. An *unlucky* engagement obliges me to say No, when my *inclination* would for ever teach me to say Yes. The tragedy which was announced for this evening is postponed to Wednesday, so "great Julius" may stalk abroad another week, secure from harm—Ward-ed off from assassination by "the well-beloved Brutus".

Conway was convinced that Warde had reported sick in order to deprive him of a rare opportunity to show off one of his best parts: "Dear Conway, who begs my picture, feels indignant that he has been hinder'd from acting Mark Antony by Warde's feigned illness. Warde ill and Julius Caesar put off." But as she discovered later, Warde was "sick in earnest," and she made the most of Conway's free night by asking him to dinner with Mrs. Stratton and the girls. They had a "sweet Day & Night, till Two o'clock in the morning." The diary went on:

Friday 16 April . . . I walked out and met mon bel Ami—Saw him at Night in Don Giovanni; admirable is not praise enough: *Incomparable Conway* . . .

Saturday 17 April . . . In the evening Young as Henry IV, and Transcendant Conway in his Falconbridge.

Sunday 18 April Unwell early in the morning. Dear Conway came to Breakfast. We had much Chat, and I sent my letter to Mrs. Dimond . . .

Tuesday 19 April . . . At 3 came our Matchless Conway, & we drove to Sir Walter James's, who was very kind. Then to Dr. Whalley's[15] where we saw Siddon's Portrait. Then to No. 13 for Chat, then home for Dinner & Supper at *Mrs. Bourdois's* . . .[16]

Wednesday 21 April . . . Dinner Miss Willoughby & Evening Mark Anthony . . .

Thursday 22 April [Callers] all, *all* in Raptures with my dear Conway. I lost Mrs. Dimond most provokingly: she called when I was out, but we had a gay dinner & a sweet Evening till past 12 o'clock—he went home with the *Strattons.*

Friday 23 April I went to Mrs. Dimond, saw her & her Son, & canvassed for Conway in my flighty way; feel full of *Hope*. Sir Walter James called upon *him* & upon *me* with invitations. Dr. Whalley called with Praises. In the Evening Young's Lear and Conway's Don Giovanni.

Saturday 24 April . . . Dinner and delightful Evening Mrs. *Stratton's.* W.A.C. at Dinner & Tea".

Monday 26 April Conway came to Breakfast. We sate late to it, & had much Talk. But I fear all will end in parting. I went at Night to the Bishop of Meath's & to Dr. Whalley's—much Praise of *My Hero;* Mrs. Brownlow's the most valuable.

Mrs. Piozzi's battle was lost: *Don Giovanni* had brought Conway's engagement to an end, and after their long talk he went off to Birmingham to sign the contract, hoping for greater success there than in Bath, where his benefit had earned him only £160 to Warde's £264. Mrs. Piozzi evidently thought that Mrs. Dimond ought to have done more to retain Conway, and she wrote to Fellowes enclosing

some verses which I have written, expressive of the indignation I feel to see our theatrical managers here, sacrificing my favourite actor to Mr. Warde's illhumour. You remember Martial's epigram?

Rumpitur invidia quidam, carissime Juli
Quod me Roma legit, rumpitur invidia
Rumpitur invidia quod turba semper in omni
Monstramur digito, rumpitur invidia
Rumpitur invidia quod sum jucunus amicis
Quod conviva frequens, rumpitur invidia
Rumpitur invidia quod amamur, quodque probamur,
Rumpatur quisquis—rumpitur invidia

The word *swelling* is more elegant in English than *bursting,* ain't it. So I turned the whole as follows, alluding to their orations, for both of which see Shakespeare's Julius Caesar which they plaid so admirably.

Swelling with envy, Brutus now appears,
Because the town lends Antony their ears.

Swelling with envy views his pers'nal graces
When girls point handsome Conway as he passes.
Swelling with envy, see him in retreat
At gay thirteen perhaps;—or number eight.
Such as so swell, would sting too, if they durst,
But since they swell with envy—let them burst.

Mrs. Piozzi added that "No. 13 is Mrs Strattons in Camden Place." A week later (4 May) she wrote to Fellowes again, reporting that Conway had returned from Birmingham with a contract in his pocket, and that she now had Fellowes's portrait. "Kind Conway has procured for me a proof mezzotinto of his likeness in the character of Jaffier by Harlow:[17] he says yours by Pellegrini is alive with resemblance: what will Salusbury say when he first comes to dine at his aunt's house? who *he* considers a superannuated old goose, while she is flattered and fed with soft dedication all day long." Fellowes himself was innocent of any such charge, but could not be sure that Conway had not been taking advantage of her extraordinary infatuation. In fact, the young man was preoccupied with Charlotte and intended to spend most of his last few days in Bath wooing her. Mrs Piozzi would have to share him with the Strattons and his mother.

Mrs. Rudd

For Conway, one of the other attractions of his long engagement in Bath was that he could easily visit Clifton, where his mother, Mrs. Rudd, lived at No. 10 Sion Row, high above the Avon gorge, directly above Hot Wells House. She owned several other large houses nearby, in the elegant Princes Buildings, Gloucester Row, and Royal York Crescent, and was listed in the Bristol and Clifton guide as a lodging-house keeper. Conway had not yet declared his love for Charlotte, but was well aware that she would not relish the idea of a landlady as a mother-in-law, and perhaps felt that the time had come to reveal that his real father was Lord William Conway. If so, he would naturally consult his mother and seek her consent, and although it is not clear whether he had already confided in Mrs. Piozzi, her diary for the next few days shows that she was aware of the significance of his comings and goings to Clifton. On Tuesday, 4 May, she "wrote to Conway with the Turkish slippers. He went to Bristol." Wednesday, "Conway called—his Brow clouded," Thursday, "Conway came to Breakfast; his Brow cleared. His Heart once more gay, lively, lovely. We walked to Jaggers and Roches.[18] 20 callers. Sir Walter James to ask me and Conway for Tuesday next. I dined at Strattons, a delightful Day—no Man but *The* Man. I left them at midnight." Friday, "sweet talk about Conway, but he was run to Clifton." The next day he sent word that he was back.

View of Clifton showing Royal York Crescent, watercolour by James Baker Pyne, 1836.
Reproduced by permission of Bristol Museum and Art Gallery.

My dear Madam,

      I am this instant returned from *Clifton,* whither I proceeded last evening, after the hour of *Eight,* upon an affair of interest. The occasion of my Journey you will easily divine, and I shall have the pleasure of communicating to you its *result* at five o'clock, if you will allow me, at that hour, to make one at your elegant and hospitable Board.

I am ever, My dear Madam,
Your faithful, grateful Servant
William Augustus Conway

Saturday 2 o'clock

The outcome of his talks was evidently favourable, but Mrs. Piozzi did not need commit it to paper:

> *Saturday 8 May* Many people dropped in & I walked in my Garden. Dear Conway dined with me & after coffee & after reading the Regatta letter,[19] went to the play. I dress'd & went to Mrs. Strattons, where he came at Night, and we were all happy. I left them not till *one* o'clock in the morning.

The Monday afterward Conway escorted her to the Sydney Gardens. "I wrote my Letter for him & feel assured of his Affections." The next day they both dined with Sir Walter James, took supper at the Strattons, and "came home *very* late!!! Charming Conway ador'd by All. Farewell! & Adieu! are the true Synonymes. Addio Conway! Addio!" And next morning the diary casually recorded that "Mrs. Pennington, Miss Willoughby & Miss Williams all dropt in."

Mrs. Pennington! They had not met or communicated for fifteen years, and yet here she was on the doorstep of No. 8 like any casual caller. Perhaps Mrs. Piozzi was half expecting a visit from her. They had now lived a mere twelve miles apart for the past four or five years, sharing the same friends in both places, and it was almost inevitable that one day their paths would cross again. Mrs. Piozzi had no wish to speed that day, but Mrs. Pennington always felt that she had been banished unjustly, and hoped for a reconciliation, as did their mutual friends in Clifton and Bath. Through them she gathered news of Mrs. Piozzi's activities, and the gossip about her tall young beau, whose mother lived nearby, must have reached her ears. Perhaps she could contain her curiosity no longer. Mrs. Piozzi was well aware that Conway could hardly avoid passing near Dowry Square on his visits to Sion Row, but she had studiously avoided mentioning her name to him.

Whatever the reason for Mrs. Pennington's visit may have been, it was driven out of the diary by the intelligence that Margaret Williams imparted after she had gone. The ink is blurred in places, but the gist of the entry is "M:W: thinks they [   ] Miss Willoughby to say fine things against Conway & she hires People to come & clap Warde by giving them free

Admission Tickets. *Oh! my exhausted heart.*" It was all too much for an old lady. First the loss of Conway, then the unwelcome attentions of Mrs. Pennington, and now another traitress? Miss Willoughby? If there had been an organised claque in support of Warde, it is surprising that Mrs. Piozzi had never been aware of it; and it is incredible that Miss Willoughby could have been its ringleader. But there was even more grief that day, with "Charlotte half-drown'd in Tears. What shall I do with them all!—I dine with them next Monday." In fact, Conway did not leave until a day later, after calling to see how Mrs. Piozzi was and staying for supper. "He is gone away now in earnest." He had gone to London before taking up his Birmingham assignment, and Mrs. Piozzi had asked him to call on Mrs. Siddons with an invitation to her "eightieth" birthday party on 27 January 1820, to which she had asked people "from all parts of the world & some have promised from farthest Thule."

Almost as soon as Conway had left, Mrs. Piozzi expected word of his safe arrival by every post, and day after day she would sigh, "no letters, tho' I dreamed of such." To fill the void, she began two more projects for him, correcting and annotating her *Letters to and from the Late Samuel Johnson* and sitting for Jagger. "A Letter from dear *Siddons*[20] gave me much Pleasure & shew'd me Conway was alive on the 18th."

27 Upper Baker Street, Regent's Park, May 18 1819

You can never doubt, my dearest Mrs. Piozzi, of the happiness it must always give me to see any testimony of your continued kindness. I only wish I could oftener "take the opportunity". I saw Mr. Conway only for a few minutes, and those in company with many talkers, but long enough to satisfy me that you are as young and gay both in mind and person as in those never-to-be-forgotten days of felicity at dear, dear Streatham Park. Many and happy returns of that day, which I wish I could participate with Mr. Conway and Susan [Thrale?], but dare not promise myself such happiness. But wherever I may be I will rejoice. . . .

Your ever faithfully affectionate
S Siddons

Mrs. Siddons's letter only served to increase Mrs. Piozzi's impatience for news from the man himself: Sunday 23 May, "I fancy dear Conway writing to me today. I fancy so. *Night* packed up Conway's Books & Letter & sent to Birmingham by George Bell"; Monday, "It is very unkind of Conway not to write"; Tuesday, "Letter from Bessy's Husband said Conway had my Letter safe—and the Books, Dr. Johnson's Letters." In Conway's defence, if any were needed, he had been busy helping Alfred Bunn to prepare the company for the opening of the newly refurbished Theatre Royal in Birmingham. As the local *Gazette* reported, Bunn had begun his new career as a manager "under a liberal system of expenditure"; he also relied heavily on his more experienced colleague, who was welcomed back with the prediction that "we shall have frequent occasion to refer to the arrangements of Mr. Conway as stage manager, and we anticipate considerable satisfaction in doing so, from the full conviction that his acknowledged talents, assiduity, and gentlemanly deportment will qualify him for that prominent situation, and will ensure the most correct conduct of the stage."

He set the season rolling by reciting an inaugural address, followed by a performance of *The Rivals,* in which he appeared, out of his usual line of business, as Sir Lucius O'Trigger, and the *Gazette* gave Conway, Bunn, *and* the "superb central gas chandelier" a warm welcome. Only then did he find time to write the "letter from charming Conway," which she received on 27 May. The previous day a letter from George Bell assured her that "Conway had my Letter safe; and the Books . . . Dr. Johnson's Letters." He was suffering from a sore throat, but as Mrs. Piozzi reported to Sir James Fellowes, "my justly admired Conway drives all before him at Birmingham, after ill-usage enough here at Bath; and now I tell him he must beware the tryals of Prosperity."

She was also pleased to tell Fellowes that Hammersleys had advanced the money to buy the last few hundred Consols, and she had at last reached the goal of six thousand pounds, after which transaction her money was her own. The next day Mrs. Stratton and the young ladies went to see her sit for her portrait, which was "lovely, and though lovely very like indeed," and she wrote another letter to Conway.

7

The Correspondence

DISREGARDING any correspondence there may have been between them when Mrs. Piozzi first offered her patronage, and the notes that had passed between them in Bath, the reply that Conway had just written from Birmingham (probably dated 26 May 1819) signals the beginning of what was to be a rather one-sided correspondence. Mrs. Piozzi believed in replying promptly to letters, and she treasured those writers, who, like Mrs. Pennington of old, could keep up a weekly exchange, but she reluctantly accepted the more measured pace of a Fellowes, and even tolerated with good humour Mrs. Siddons's almost total aversion to writing. Correspondence with her daughters was little more than minimal: Lady Keith sent birthday congratulations once a year, and the other daughters a "quarterly Review." She was yet to discover that Conway belonged to the Siddons school: as he once told Charles Mathews's wife, Anne, "I am either by nature or habit so averse from letter writing that except when called upon by the necessities of business or the established usages of society I never think of putting pen to paper, and I can therefore readily make allowances for a similar disinclination in another."[1] His letters to other theatrical associates were written in the same formal style, and there is no reason to suppose that his longer letters to Mrs. Piozzi, which have disappeared, would be any different. She kept them all (probably fewer than thirty), tied up with ribbon, until she died.

After this first exchange, letters flowed from Mrs. Piozzi's pen in profusion, reaching a total, according to Mrs. Ellet, of about one hundred. That may have been an exaggeration, but from the evidence of Mrs. Piozzi's diaries, she wrote at least seventy-five to Conway. Mrs. Ellet placed this "whole mass of correspondence" in the hands of the *Athenaeum* in July 1861, and within the space of two or three weeks the editor declared that he was "in a position to tell the exact truth about this pretended passion of the aged lady for the young actor." In support of that contention, he quoted short extracts from about fifteen letters which were written between May 1819 and May 1820, but he reproduced them without concern for chronology and ignored all that came later. The seven letters which were published in 1843 (in their entirety as far as can be ascertained) as

Love-letters of Mrs Piozzi covered an even shorter period, from September 1819 to February 1820, and in piecing together the story that follows, it has been necessary to make recourse, with due caution, to both of these secondary sources where the relevant originals have not been located. For example, the letter that Mrs. Piozzi posted to Birmingham on 28 May has not been traced, but is undoubtedly one that the *Athenaeum* printed in extract, dating it only "May 1819." Mrs. Piozzi, replying to Conway's first letter from Birmingham, would undoubtedly have dated it fully, as always. Conway was already overwhelmed by her output:

> Apropos to Notes, as dear Mr. Conway says, when do you find Time to write so much, Mrs. Piozzi? But the Annotations to Wraxall[2] don't distress me with Fears of falling into improper Hands, as Johnson's Letters did—because of those old confidential Stories,[3] and as your Fancy in a happy Hour prompted you to court Acquaintance with Thrale's Wife more than with Piozzi's Widow, I shall leave marking and margining my 'Travels' till the last. May all of them but contribute to amuse you, and keep me alive in your Remembrance, a Place I can't give up. To keep you in *ours,* no need of such a Contrast as little Mr. Booth[4] exhibits, surely; the Triton of the Minnows; and Miss Willoughby talks of some new Man—nobody knows who. [There is no sign of rancour in her mention of Miss Willoughby.] And Miss Williams says that if you ever go to Chester by any Accident, she could be useful to you. You will want none of us; and in two Years it will be *Virtue* in you to name our names in Kindness. Farewell, then, and Adieu! To these Synonymes the Latin word *Vale* is univocal. Romans often at the end of their Letters say "Jubeo te bene valere" you may observe,—"I command thee well" or "keep well"; but *Vale* in the imperative mood, is neuter, and Frenchmen best translate it "Portez-vous bien". *Vales* to Servants has sprung from the Latin way or idiom; meaning a gracious farewell; little as the word was understood to have a classical meaning. Yes, says Juliet, but all this I did know before; yet *thus* and *thus* I do beguile the time—ay, and the thing I am, by seeming otherwise.

That extract of about three hundred words, equivalent to about a page of her handwriting, is fine as far as it goes, having been chosen, in the words of the *Athenaeum,* to show that "her letters, like her books, are thickly sown with classical and historical allusions, in which Mrs. Piozzi's unimpaired memory loved to revel." But the remaining pages of this letter may have been more relevant to our story than the passages quoted. Hardly pausing for breath, she began another letter the next day, which the *Athenaeum* did not quote, and which is now in the library of the Historical Society of Pennsylvania (HSP).[5] Chronologically, it is the first autograph letter from her to Conway to come to light, and is reproduced below, almost in its entirety, as an example of the light-hearted ease of her chat with Conway and the kaleidoscopic variety of her subjects. It consists of two sheets, written on both sides, leaving part of the last page to show, when folded and sealed, the name "William Augustus Conway Esqr" and his address, with a proud flourish. In her fingers, the quill was as expressive as a violinist's bow, controlling the *tempi*, phrasing, and colour of her melodies as she switched moods from grave to gay, from the bold assertion to the confidential aside. There are no quotation marks to impede the headlong flow of her dialogue and even in print, her ebullience shows through; in particular in her girlish excitement over a budding romance, which her diary had so far failed to reveal.

Clearly Conway had been spending a good deal of time with the Strattons, with or without Mrs. Piozzi's company, and had shown more than a passing interest in the girls, and they in him. Charlotte was over twenty-one, and being well provided for by her late father, was free to marry the man of her choice without seeking her grandmother's consent; but in his letter from Birmingham, Conway had evidently asked Mrs. Piozzi whether he should acquaint Mrs. Stratton with his intentions.

Sat: 29 May 1819

How hard does that dear Mrs. Piozzi work for me! shall be one Day your kind Exclamation. & so I do—correcting the Wraxall &c. The Strattons were well Thursday & as I told you, ready to devour me when your Letter was in my hand. I read the Passage *shall I write to her?* rather archly—while the kind Lady gathering her scatter'd Features together, cried out Oh Surely, surely, I shall be most happy to hear from him under his own hand. They laughed & cried (the Girls did) all in a Breath & beg'd to come & see me sit at Jagger's the next day—so they did, and agreed the Portrait would be very like. I touch'd Charlotte's Elbow, & how lean young Lasses grow when they are in Love, quoth I. Oh, but, said Mary, we are all fatter now since Yesterday that the Letter came. The next Morning was a Blank to me, the Evening past [*sic*] at Dr. Fisher's, Brother to the Bishop of Salisbury. Today: Sat 29. The young ones came, & with them Clara Eckersall & said their Visit was to see Mr. Conway's Picture because *she* was going out of Town directly. I shew'd them the little Shade. No, no, the Print, the Print you said he gave *you* Mrs. Piozzi. In at the Frame Makers was my Reply, with two or three more he is doing for me. Where does he live? Why in New King Street——so away they trip, resolving to have a look at it: but not before they had engaged me to dine with them on Wednesday 2nd: June.

Mrs. Hudson was here when they enter'd & said somewhat sharply—So I hear you are sitting for your Picture in Milsom Street—a Gentleman told me so: What Gentleman? nobody knows it but these Lasses, and I am sure of *them*—— Yes, quite sure, was their Answer—Well replied I— 'tis not the first Time I have sat, there is no Mystery in the Matter. But I *must* see it. Why Jagger will scarcely let me see it myself; and there is one at Roche's now, done when I was three Years younger————No No No, I must see *This,* with a Sneer. By all means was my cold Reply, & there the Visit ended—I told you she would be among the Spiters. Bessy went to divert Chagrin at the play & saw Zorinsky, of which I know nothing & think she knew less. The Report ran that Kean was in our Town here to see Booth's King Richard——I gave James[6] leave to go. The House was full, he said, but not much Applause. The Courier however—a more Political Paper, bears Testimony to *Your* Merit—Oh yes! my matchless Friend will soon fill the World

with his Fame. *Your* Theatre is the Talk of all London I am told, & *you* are ador'd—
not quite as you deserve, but as your own generous heart is contented to be; ever
possessing that desirable Power, in *life* as in the Theatre, of hitting the happy Point
between Loftiness and Pride, between Modesty and Obsequiousness, ever stopping short of that seducing Wrong to which all that is Right will run, if not held in
like a high-mettled Racer at the Starting Post.

Good night then, and in Practice of my own Precept,——I will empty my Head of
dear Mr. Conway, & recollecting that Tomorrow is Whitsunday—fill it with
thoughts of those superior Powers who I will request to watch over his everlasting
Happiness: not praying for myself alone, while *he* desires that in my Orisons, he
too should be remember'd.——Partial Friend! I know that he thinks well of me,
and *that* Consciousness is my Delight. Why should it not be so? Our best Resolu-
tions are better'd by the Suffrage of a Man of Merit in our Favour, & the Pleasure
of Approbation is heighten'd, when that Approbation flows from a richly furnish'd
Mind.

30th: Church sends my Spirits home, tranquillised as usual. . . .

Monday morning May 31: brings me the Birmingham Gazette. [the diary recorded
"the dear *dear* Gazette, Conway for ever, HUZZA!"] Oh thank you for it, thank
you a Thousand times. What would I give to see your Zanga this Evening? & hear
him say characteristically: A Lion preys not upon Carcasses—Ay, and the Change
succeeding—which no Actor ever saw, marked so as to do my Favourite Author
Justice. And how is the beautiful Throat?—beware—The clear and Varying Tones
of a Voice seconding every Fine Inflexion of the Soul? I used to make dear Piozzi
swallow a raw new-laid Egg early in the Morning—against the Treacle Posset he
rebelled—yet 'tis the best Thing to prevent or cure a Hoarseness—except Asses
Milk. Pray be careful. Now I have read your Name in this darling Paper, it does
seem as if the Space between us was swallow'd up—as Irish People tell of the
Devil's Escape from St. Patrick, when he was driven into a preternatural Gulph of
immense Breadth; and the Space closed up suddenly between. . . .

——& now if you believe I will write another Word (tho' I *do* pelt you with
Letters so) during the pleasant Month of May as it is called——I shall cry out
Mistake. On the last Day of it I meant to see how No. 13 went on, but met dear
Mrs. Stratton in the Street, your sweet interesting Epistle in her hand. We ran to
my House to read it, and express our true Admiration of the Writer, whose Style is
like himself—Nature in her Spring Dress—how can you express so much Kindness for your Autumnal, not to say *Wintry* friend! The Throat does not get well,
tho' & not quick as it did the last Time. Sir, I'm sorry— but do now without Joking,
take Care of it & I could not have borne to have it cover'd tonight in Zanga either,
but it should be incessantly gargled, & you should eat Salads for Supper & drink
weak Brandy and Water, not Wine. Poor Soul! how you are worried!—but keep
your Spirits up, assured of a *true* Heart in Camden Place and one devoted to your
Service in Gay Street. To convince Mrs. Stratton how dearly I tender, "yea keep a
hair of you for Memory"—I shewed her my Trinket & she burst into Tears of Joy,
but charged me to say Nothing of it to Charlotte. The Responsibility pleases—
flatters me. Oh! if the *Island's* Welfare depended on the Honour of Augustus
Conway; I should esteem it Safe. So here's the 1st of June arrived at last, and now 7
Times more must Cynthia fill her Silver Horn—and then in Frost and Snow and
Rain We all perhaps may meet again—H : L : Piozzi.

[In microscopic writing down one side of the paper] I expect Sir James Fellowes in Bath today—not in his Capacity of my Executor—but in Consequence of some Freemason Foolery. Tomorrow a comfortable Dinner at No 13. Sir James was the man who stopt the Progress of the Plague at Gibraltar. He dunn'd my dead-cold Heart all thro' the Year 1815 for a Return of Kindness wholly out of my Power. But he would be Something to me, he said, besides being my Physician: be, said I, my Executor & be careful of my literary Fame. He married in March 1816 & has Babies. I hope you will be good Friends long after the Demise of poor H : L : P.

For her next letter, which has already been referred to, we must depend on an infuriatingly short extract dated "Bath June 3rd 1819," reproduced by the *Athenaeum*. Here Mrs. Piozzi speaks of Conway, her late husband, and Sarah Siddons in the same breath:

I wonder how you really like Johnson's and my Letters! I wonder if you recollect asking me once if I should like to lead my Life over again: such a *happy* one, as you then thought it. Poor H:L:P.! a *happy* Life! Yet few have been more so, I believe; and the Moments which gave Comfort to three unequalled Creatures— he, and the Siddons, and yourself, will come smiling to my Heart whilst its last Pulse is beating. Of the three, *she* was the one most immediately benefited; and I am glad she has not forgotten me. Naughty Lady! how they whistled her away from me, after—but no matter—try again, you see. What are hearts made for? The cook would reply, to be *minced;* but my *last* [meaning latest] friend will defend it.

There is no record of any occasion when she gave Conway comfort on a par with her ministrations to the other two. Mrs. Siddons's supposed disaffection may have occurred after the breach with the Penningtons, and Mrs. Piozzi changed the subject abruptly when she realised that she was about to mention their name. The next day she wrote yet another missive, from which the *Athenaeum* quoted more extensively, but with only a passing reference to the Strattons:

Fryday June 4th

And now, whilst all the World is preparing in some Way to celebrate our old King's Birthday, my dear Friend is rehearsing Bassanio for this Evening, having first read his Letter from No. 13. It must ever be a Matter of Curiosity to me to think that so strange a Tale as Shakespeare founded his "Merchant of Venice" on should be familiarly related in three Kingdoms. I have read it in Gregorio's Life of Sextus Quintus, and again in Spanish, where Portia's contrivance is called a *milagio d'ingenio*—a miracle of ingenuity. We have it likewise in Percy's collection of old ballads; but, perhaps, for I have not the book, it may be told there as an Italian story. Have you a good Launcelot?

After more diversions in similar vein:

And now, if you do feel rejoyced that the last Morsel of Paper will soon be covered, it will vex me. So it will if you fancy I require Answers to all this *congerie* of Sense and Nonsense. Indeed, I am not *exigeante;* all I wish, all I *beg,* at least, are the three Words I used to teize Salusbury for when he was at Oxford; *safe—well* and *happy;* but let me have those magical Words sent soon. Or how else shall I be a *funny little Thing?* as page 56 of the 2nd Volume calls me. The history of that last Appellation is as follows: Some Arrival was announced, a man with a new name, so I began imitating him before he appeared, and made him describe all the Friends he found at Streatham Park in a letter he was to write to his Friends in the Evening. Ay, added Johnson, and there was the gay Mistress of the House, who I expected to see a fine Lady; but soon found she was a funny little Thing.

Sir James Fellowes, still in Bath, teased Mrs. Piozzi over her concern for her new friend and his affair of the heart. On 8 June he "came to breakfast—charged me with promoting dear Conway's Happiness. I owned the Charge & wish for the Power. Dinner at the Strattons. Romeo & Juliet.[7] Rec'd a Letter and Confession of Love to Charlotte from our Invulnerable Truant," and the next day "I mediated a long letter with Encouragement—but not Advice, to my amiable and elegant friend." An extract from that letter, which appeared in the *Athenaeum* article confirms Mrs. Piozzi's reluctance to be drawn on the question of Charlotte's suitability, and reveals that she had already suggested some other "scheme of happiness" for him:

Your friendship is my boast, and your felicity my truest wish; my unfeigned approval follows your every step. But how can I advise in such a case? I *dare* not! Oh, but too well does dear Mr. Conway know that I think no fortune good enough—no applause loud enough for his talents and merits; well does he know, too, that I felt ready to promote a more splendid scheme of happiness than this, although my heart knew that its completion would have estranged us from each other. But to decide against one's self is a trick played by delicate minds perpetually; and Johnson always warned me to beware of it. "Scrupulous tempers always make few people good," said he, "and many people miserable".

Her letter continued in a less introspective mood:

This moment and not before—Wednesday, June 9th—blows Sir James Fellowes hither—And how, says he is Conway? *He* is your favourite! Ay replied I. We went to the play last night—the dear Strattons and myself, for the first time since he left us. Stratton, Stratton! Oh that's the pretty girl that has a likeness of Catalini[8] and is in love with Conway. Mercy on me, my dear Sir James! Why do you say such strange things? Nay—nay; I never saw her nor him but one day, you know; one Spanish proverb though, comes in one's head of course: Love and a cough can never lie hid. He has, replied I, a return of that vile sore throat—Merely an affection of the membrane, was the answer, caused by perpetual irritation. You and Miss Stratton will hear his voice ne'er the worse for it—Thank God for that, was my reply.

The Jilting

Two days later the Strattons dined with her, and she learned that "Charlotte seems resolved to jilt poor Conway after all. I feel quite shocked by her Behaviour.—4 weeks today since he left us, & now—jilted. Mondo! I wonder how they dar'd use us so!!! . ." Her indignation spilled over into her commonplace book:

Strattons pretended passionate love for Conway—I thought them in earnest—so amiable a Man so incomparable his Talents, but tho' they talked of no one else for four weeks—it provoked me to write this Epigram in Consequence of their well-feigned attachment. They dined here yesterday, and said *all was over* because the Girl's Friends would not agree to the Connection.

> I mentioned the old Spanish Proverb you know,
> From the Man with one Book and one Story defend us.
> *We* vote for the Muse that can fly high and low
> And now talk of Garrick and now of Gassendus
> But Number Thirteen is in no better plight
> How quickly reduced to the same Situation!
> Of Conway alone can we talk, read or write
> His talents, his Graces, his sweet Conversation.
> And we're living at last like King Midas of old
> who starved because all that he touched turned to Gold.

It was left to Mrs. Piozzi to break the news to Conway, and as she waited anxiously for his reaction, "the best Dropper In was dear Conway's seal. Very handsome. Imperator Augustus. No Letter & my Nerves are all in a Tremble—fluttering me to Death." But the letter that arrived the following day turned out to be "very kind indeed & very wise. I went in Consequence of it to Camden Place, and was well received & hasted home to answer it. Poor Fellow! He has been cruelly treated *by us all*. I have got his portrait too—how fine it is.[9] He gave it to me himself. I shew'd it to Mrs. Stratton." It was to remain in Mrs. Piozzi's possession, and give her much comfort, for the rest of her life.

8
"Fev'rish for Want of Rest"

CONWAY'S "kind and wise" letter had been written at the theatre, under difficulties. His sore throat had prevented him from acting for a week after his appearance in *The Merchant of Venice,* but he was busy at the theatre day and night supervising performances and rehearsing J. H. Payne's tragedy *Brutus,* or *The Fall of Tarquin,* in which he was to play Lucius Brutus. Mrs. Piozzi, still seething at his ill-treatment by the theatre management, and now by Charlotte, began another letter. She had almost completed annotating Wraxall's *Historical Memoirs,* and as soon as her miniature was finished, she would send it to Birmingham with a boxful of treats for the comfort of body, mind, and spirit.

> begun 15 June
> Tuesday

Could I have sate down to *this* Desk as my dear incomparable Friend did to that of the Prompter—with a Score of People round me I might have written as just and as affecting an Account of my Feelings as he has done of his.

> But *You* whom Nature taught the Art
> To pierce, to tear—to cleave the heart

Superieur en tout as the King of France said to Jarnac when he gave his Life & Sword to his Enemy—write as You think and act,—tousjours Noble—Semper Augustus!

Not a Tear did I shed—not a Morsel did I swallow, not an Hour's uninterrupted Sleep did I enjoy till that Modèle des Lettres blest my Eyes this Morning. *Such* a Letter! But the best Praise is Obedience, and I went directly to No. 13. *They behaved quite right* & I found my Reward on my Return. Your dear Resemblance. It really does look like a figure animated by *such* a Soul. I am delighted with it.

As for *me* & my Portrait—The little Michaelmas Daisy beat by a Hundred Storms, still holds her head up; & salutes the towering Tulip with true and disinterested Friendship.[1] Bessy will tell you *half* of what I have suffer'd. She did not see me in the Night, changing from Book to Book—no Book would do till

> Fev'rish for Want of Rest I rose & walked
> And by the Moonlight to the Window went:
> There, thinking to exclude him from my Thoughts

> I cast my Eyes o'er all the Neighb'ring Plains
> And to myself sigh'd e'er I was aware.
> So, restless, roves my Friend

Dryden

She was still fretful as she penned the next few lines, anxious for news of Conway's talk with William Dimond, who had driven over to Birmingham to discuss business, and who may have been the man she referred to as "M. Ci-devant." As ever, she was oversensitive about friends and enemies, and was aware that her championing of Conway had set tongues wagging, but her plan to attend his benefit under the cloak of a visit to London was devious in more ways than one:

> Your Interview with Dimond—too, how ended it? do you come hither in November as usual? or only to my Fête in January? 'Tis 20 years till *then* & Bessy's Manner of pacifying me was always Why Madam! You will not live to see Mr. Conway again if you go on *so.*
>
> Well then, was my Reply—go and see him yourself:—and bring word how he looks; what he says, what hopes of his Return—& tell him *truly* that I will come to him in Autumn to his Benefit, and go thro' Birmingham to London—Thence to Adbury on my Way Home;—no need for People to stare, & make a Wonder of *that* I suppose.
>
> So far my Dialogue with Bessy. To you alone I confide my Intention of silencing *Monsieur Cydevant;* but you must tell me the when, the where & the how—in due Time.
>
> Miss Williams is your active friend; and the Strattons! now bound in Duty as once in Fondness—you will I am sure do ten Times more than ever—'Twas odd enough to see how much they love, & *fear me.* Oh I was *very* angry, *very* like a Welshwoman: nor would I ever have spoken to them again, had it not been *Your* Wish.

Mrs. Piozzi went on to quote Homer's "A generous friend no cold medium knows, / Burns with one love, with one resentment glows, / *One* should our interests and our passions be; / My friend must hate the man that injures me."—"& finely said it is, when Christianity had no Place to soften Anger into sweet Forgiveness." Her mood changed as she reported that Miss O'Neill was back in Bath, and "pleases in Comedy very much indeed"; and after offering more theatrical diversions, listed the presents she was collecting for him:

> The Miniature very fine indeed. I have not yet seen the setting; Jagger will not suffer the Jeweller to touch it; he will do it himself he says, but the Glass & the Hair and the Words are not come home yet. I like your Seal excessively; Hamlet[2] has cut it on a Blood Stone. . . . The Pastiles will make the Moths Sick; and leave a pleasant Scent upon the Clothes they preserve—The Lozenges & the Honey will I hope make the Throat well.

She compared Conway's fate with Piozzi's:

You have been a luckless Wight my admirable Friend, but Amends will be done one Day, even in *this* World I know; I feel it will. Dear Piozzi consider'd himself as cruelly treated—& so he was by his own Friends as the World perversely calls our Relations; who shut their door in *his* Face, because his Love of Music led him to face the Public Eye and Ear. He was brought up to the Church; but, Ah! Gabriele, said his Uncle, thou wilt not get nearer the Altar than the Organ loft. His disinclination to celibacy, however, kept him from the black Gown.

After covering over six pages of anecdotes "to amuse your hours of Leisure," Mrs. Piozzi put the letter aside for another day. She recorded in her diary that the "truly dear Mangins" called, and were so eager to listen to her recollections of the Johnson days that she revealed the existence of *Thraliana.* Mangin was so fascinated that she rewarded him with a glimpse of the *outside* of the volumes. He could only speculate as to the contents,[3] for much as Mrs. Piozzi respected Mangin and admired his erudition, she had preferred to entrust its secrets, and the rest of her literary remains, to Fellowes.

She added another five pages to her long letter while she waited impatiently for the miniature to be delivered, and at the end of the week wrote a short note to go by post.

Sat: 19 June 1819

If my dear my admirable Friend had not written me that wonderfully beautiful Letter which he finished at the Prompter's Desk last Monday, I wonder what I should have done by now?

Never did anyone fret as I have done—reflecting on the silly Part I was induced to play by Baby Ladies, when at four Times their Age. That Letter, however, the very best written I ever did receive, consoles me when I read it & gives me power to extract Compensation from *Your* incomparable Conduct, teaching me too—Oh how kindly—to forget as soon as possible—my own.

Mrs. Stratton, my fellow Dupe, has suffer'd severely in her Health I know, & this Town is full of Typhus Fever now. I will be gone when you have got the long expected Box, but Riviere's People[4] make the delay, & Jagger, when the Setting comes, will not permit them to touch it: he says they cut his Pictures to fit their Glass—he will do it himself. It is the *first* Portrait of H:L:P. I ever did present to anyone out of my own family:[5] and you express yourself so sweetly about it, I wish 'twas at its Place of Destination. . . .

Mrs. Bourdois & her Sisters & your old Friend go to the Play tonight, *The Point of Honour.* I know nothing of it: but think it should have been Yours exclusively. The best Joke going is that Mr. Vallobra hangs about Miss Brook, but that there is no Weeping Willow*by*. . . .[6]

I feel so cross & impatient, that it comes into my head just now to send Bessy with the Box in her hand, when we have it to send. She will be Pandora, all Gift— Lozenges for the cough—Books for the Shelf—Grand Donations truly! but not like Pandora's Box, all Evils, save only Hope at the Bottom, & that not for Prometheus, who stole Fire from Heaven—Dear Mr. Conway came *honestly* by *his*

& may he long delight & illuminate our Island with his Talents. So prays his truly obliged and ever faithfully attached friend

H : L : Piozzi

This letter is very dear at Nine Pence: [it consisted of just one sheet and a wrapper] one from You to confirm the Report of Your being engaged here for the early Season would be worth Nine Pounds.

Having posted that note, Mrs. Piozzi returned to her serialised epistle:

Here comes poor penitent Mrs. Stratton lamenting of her silly young Grand-daughter for which She herself has suffer'd most severely,—and here She brings me her Letter to read before she sends it & begs *my* Pardon again for the Disquiet she has caused to Mr. Conway & to *me:* who She considers in the Light of his injured *Mother.* And indeed my dearest Friend, no *Parent* could feel more than I have done, & still continue to do on your Acct.—let me hear thro' Bessy, that your dear noble Mind is put to rest; & left free to exercise those glorious Talents which have been given by God for useful purposes, and which it is is my hope you will so cultivate that *all* may be constrained to *admire* You as *I* do; altho' to love you so is quite Impossible, as no one knows your Worth—& your Inestimable Value as it is known by your truly & tenderly attached H:L:Piozzi.

Little Angelo is quite well; Mrs. Stratton brought him a Horse today, as a Peace Offering to *me* I believe; and She charged me to tell you that the Worked Collars are *her* particular Present & that She shall not feel quite easy till you have written to her & sent the Measure for the Cuffs. She & I went into the Dining Parlour, and looked at your beautiful Portrait. . . .

I hope poor Bessy will get Safe out & home: & with good Acct. of your Health & sweet Expectation of Your Return. Miss Penruddick told the Strattons that W[illoughby], not D[imond] was in fault about your Reappearance on these Deserted Boards, and now I feel inclined to believe it. . . .

[Sunday] Just come from Church: the Bishop of Meath preached a *full hour,* yet was no one weary. . . . You will find him in the Marginal Notes upon your Wraxall 2d Vol Page 354. You did find his Wife & Daughters [the O'Biernes] here that happy Day when you got Miss Willoughby to bring you—one Morning in last December I believe *12th,* since when we have been Acquaintance—& since the next Month *Friends.* 15 Characters only have you exhibited upon the Stage however *in my Sight:* so Justice will own my Eyes have not had their Share— and they may lose the Powers of vision they possess perhaps, before You come again. . . .

But here's a brighter ray of Pleasure long desired. We have got home the mounting of your Miniature; it is heavier than I hoped for, & *larger;* but *large* in every Sense of the Word is the gallant Heart you kindly destine it to cover; and Jagger did not like to paint a tiny thing, altho' he saw a tiny Thing enough to sit to him so many Days. . . .

Miss O'Neill laughed last Night at her own Foolery and Grumio's in Catherine and Petruchio—& the Taylor & the Gown: the House was in a Roar. I have seen Siddons in the same Character—but after Woodward and Mrs. Pritchard all seemed flat. . . . The Point of Honour is an Affecting Drama, it took me by Surprize & kept me *so* hot & *so* relaxed. Miss O'Neill is like "ditto repeated" in the Articles of an Apothecary's Bill—an unvaried Sameness runs throughout all she does, everybody tells how much she likes Mr Warde & I am sure it must be true; They are congenial Souls no doubt. . . .

So now Dear Mr. Conway will have had enough of Mrs. Piozzi & her Writings—Print & Manuscript; I will not plague you again, God knows when. Soyez sage, as you said to me, and Farewell, Adieu! Jubeo te bene Valere; and never forget the Friend made by your Talents & Virtues: but whenever you think on *them*—think on the disinterested Esteem & Value they have purchased for you—continue your own bright Career to Fortune & to Fame & prefer the Love of Virtue to every thing this World can give, remembering only the bright Track which leads, the Father that points to everlasting Happiness. Accept this Sermon from a Second Mother, who is most truly & faithfully your attach'd Friend H:L:P

[Monday] Just come home from Archdeacon Thomas; have heard that Miss O'Neill & Mssrs. Warde and Green sup with Miss Willoughby tonight; Good Night!

Little Angelo knew my Picture, & cried out Mamma.

At last the box and letter were ready, and Bessy was packed off in the chaise at six o'clock the following morning with instructions to urge Conway to meet her mistress somewhere convenient, as soon as he could get away from the theatre for a day or two. Later that morning there was a letter from Conway and a copy of the *Birmingham Gazette* which reported that *Brutus,* or *The Fall of Tarquin,* had opened on 18 June, to an overflowing house, when "the principal weight of the tragedy fell on Mr. Conway," whose acting, in some parts, was "never excelled in any histrionic attempt whatever." Even the long delay between the third and fourth acts caused by problems with the machinery redounded to Conway's credit, when his apology in front of the curtain was received with "the utmost good humour." Mrs. Piozzi was impelled once more toward her desk (HSP):

Longest Day
of A.D. 1819

& did I actually know my own Heart so ill as to protest that I would write no more for weeks or months to come? It was a senseless Confidence indeed—unlike that which I repose in *Your* stronger & fresher Mind. The charming Letter I receive this Moment claims earlier & grateful Thanks. The News it contains enchants me. November brings you here, not gloomy but chearful November:—brings the Brutus I would give Worlds to witness, *in vain,* yet who shall detain my Fancy from following the noble Figure exhibiting that almost superhuman Dignity with which I *see* him go thro' the Scene that tumbles Tarquin from his Base?

do I *not* see him? & did I not hear?—"& yet I kiss'd her first" spoken with happy Archness, quickly quench'd by the Assumption of a dull Simplicity?

I never saw the Play in my Life, nor ever read it till I received the Birmingham Gazette 3 hours ago, & now I *feel* the Part was made for you.

Other Performers might touch their hearers' hearts in the last Scene—few could miss doing so; but as Doctor Johnson said of Clarissa,[7] by the Merit of fine Discrimination will be found in earlier Volumes; for, added he
Give me a Death bed, & a Christian beauty I'll be as pathetic as the best among you.[8]

And so you want more Books, more Manuscript Stuff too, scarcely legible sometimes: the Paper is so bad. Pens have no more to do with Writing than a Voice with Singing. Did you get my long Letter sewed up in blue Paper 14 Pages long? or did you & Bessy—forgetful of it Contents—fling it away? I should have written on the outside for fear of Chances, & Mrs. Stratton's Letter to *me,* which I never sent, deserved your Perusal—Poor Soul! She has been really vexed and disappointed— *We* certainly had hoped much from the Connexion, of Comfort to ourselves in Your Society—& to whom the breaking up of all was owing, I remain Ignorant as Fancy.

No Matter—Your Horoscope was ill read by all of us; only your Sibyl saw it pointed at good Fortune; the Accomplishment is at Hand—London Managements, Thunders of Applause, Brutus & Conway for ever! and in short Time your Mode of Tryal will be changed.—did I not say once, it would be *Virtue* in you to remember Bath in a very *very* few Years. Oh Then, Then, soyez sage Dear Friend; Prosperity is perilous; be firm: you will have prouder Foes to trample on than Youthful Disappointments. . . .

Wednesday 23d.

I begin to feel anxious for Bessy's return now. Her Dear little Boy unwell; & my Man James is ill—all since this Morning Breakfast Time—& here comes Miss Hudson to ask me for Friday to meet Warde, Willoughby & Co.—*The whole Firm of them.* I declined the honour, but left a Loop-hole if Curiosity should prove stronger than Dislike when my Mind's more at Ease. Mr. Young is said to quit his Profession this Year—Your Name was not mentioned, the Apothecary's Visit to Angelo prevented further Talk with the Ladies. I never saw the Baby sick before.

8 o'clock

But here comes faithful comfortable Bessy—will not even caress her *now* soft-sleeping Infant till she has express'd her Admiration of my kindest, dearest Friend, & told me how in earnest he does love *me,* and likes my Picture here. She confirms all that my heart is hoping for—Fame, Fortune waiting on your Call. . . .

Bessy had I believe unfeigned Delight in imbuing your Mind with hers & Miss Williams's Suspicions of the *Willow Tree* [Willoughby]. They think *she* set those Unitarian Teachers to terrify the wretched Victim of her Spite—& possibly it *may* be so; but it was deep Manoeuvring. She says you seemed generously unwilling to think my Servants knew the Business.

The next few lines are incomplete, the page having been torn at the seal.
Mrs. Piozzi recalled the insulting behaviour of Charlotte and her friends,

after such Protestations of pure Love to the Man for whom I felt Attachment as
a Friend, Affection as a Parent, Admiration as a human Being not unaccustom'd
to Talents, but hopeless of seeing such displayed during my Temporal Existence.
  Oh how they will repent their own capricious Folly! and Mrs. Stratton said so
loudly while looking at your Portrait in the Parlour.

Thursday 24th

A good Night has restored us all: Angelo drags his Cart again & is merry. Bessy
has made me more than happy by describing Your kind manner of accepting
Your Play things: & she gives hope that I may see you next Saturday Sennight. Is
there so much Felicity in Store? and shall we not be grateful? Do not despise the
Pastils, but light the narrow End of one or two or three, put separately under
your Clothes as they lie on Chairs, each in a Penny Saucer—or they will burn
the Boards. They are the nicest Things for the Purpose after all, & 'tis only fear
of Expence keeps them from being common. Burning Cascarilla Bark on Coals
is a good Substitute & the Scent wholesome tho' not offensive. The smoke of
the Pastils however has my Preference.[9]
  Adieu! my Dear, all my accomplish'd Friend! may Guardian Angels ever
watch over your Steps; & keep you 40 Years in fair Remembrance of that best
Ornament of my now *only* Mansion, No. 8 Gay Street Bath, a Place I will not stir
from till I hear whether you can come for a Day's Chat without great Inconvenience, tho' [continued in microscopic writing] I will meet you at the Gloucester
Hotel Clifton[10] if you like that better & think it will save Time—only say *when* to
H:L:P. If we eat our Cupboard Dinner here comfortably, I can take you to
Bristol at Night.

Morng. 7 o'clock

Conway replied to say that in ten days' time he would be able to get away
from Birmingham for the weekend, that he would take the night coach to
Bath after the curtain fell on *Brutus* on the Friday, and that he would
accept Mrs. Piozzi's kind offer to drive him as far as Clifton on his return
journey. That arrangement would allow her to meet his mother, an opportunity which she was clearly angling for. In the meantime he would be able
to digest her long letter and leaf through the two volumes of Wraxall's
Historical Memoirs of his Time, which Bessy had delivered.
  Nathaniel William Wraxall had waited thirty years before writing his
recollections of the events and personalities of a short but significant
period in British history. He had spent many years abroad, playing an
active part in foreign affairs, before entering Parliament in the general
election of 1780, which had seen the demise of Henry Thrale as MP for
Southwark. He paid generous tribute to Mrs. Thrale, as she then was, for

her works on Samuel Johnson, and described her as better informed, more cultivated, and wittier than Mrs. Montagu. Mrs. Piozzi had presented Sir James Fellowes with a copy of the memoirs soon after they were published in 1815, adding her own gloss to the views expressed by "my friend Wraxall," and returning his compliment by agreeing with most of his assessments of their contemporaries.

Perhaps the main reason for annotating a copy for Conway was that Wraxall was well acquainted with the Seymour-Conway family (see Appendix) and especially those who were prominent in public life. He wrote at length about the achievements of General Henry Seymour Conway, a Whig MP for forty years who had bitterly opposed the government over the war with America, and to a lesser extent about the general's elder brother, Francis Seymour Conway, the earl of Hertford, Lord Chamberlain of the household of George III. The earl's eldest son and heir was Francis Ingram Seymour-Conway, known by the courtesy title Lord Beauchamp, and one of the wealthiest men in England, whose person was "elegantly formed, his manners noble yet ingratiating." The earl's fifth son, Lord Hugh Seymour, was a naval captain, and "like all his six brothers he exceeded in height the ordinary proportion of mankind, and he possessed great personal advantages, sustained by most elegant manners."[11] "How like dear Mr. Conway, toujours noble, semper Augustus," Mrs. Piozzi might have written in the margin,[12] knowing, or at least believing, that his father was one of those brothers.

She had begun her annotations in joyous mood, ready to celebrate Conway's impending betrothal, but before she had finished, Charlotte had rejected him, and it was perhaps this turn of events which prompted Mrs. Piozzi to suggest an early conference, to discuss that other "scheme of happiness" she had hinted at. But when he arrived in Bath shortly after noon on the Saturday (3 July) for "Coffee and Consultation," he found Mrs. Piozzi in some distress: "he comforted me about Lysons & offer'd his best Assistance." Samuel Lysons, who had just died, once showed her a corner of his library where he kept a collection of press cuttings and other material that had been written about her. Ever sensitive about her reputation, she jumped to the conclusion that the collection was mischievous, and John Kemble, who was present at the time, confirmed that Lysons took a sadistic delight in collecting scurrilous material about famous people. She was afraid of the damage it might do if made public, but after Conway offered to buy the collection if it ever went on sale, they were able to devote the rest of the day to *his* future. On the Sunday "Conway came at 12 for breakfast. Poor Soul! How he is fagg'd and fatigued. We put his Seal and Name to his Portrait & carried him to his Mother at 6 o'-clock—whence he ran to Birmingham in the Mail all night."

Lord Hugh Seymour, elder brother of Lord William Conway, engraved by S. W. Reynolds, 1802, after Hoppner. *Reproduced by courtesy of the Trustees of the British Museum.*

Lord George Seymour, younger brother of Lord William Conway, engraved by E. Fisher, 1771, after Reynolds. *Reproduced by courtesy of the Trustees of the British Museum.*

Next day, Mrs. Piozzi dined with the Lutwyches in Marlborough Build-ings, and was surprised to find Mrs. Pennington there too, but all she could muster for her diary was "Met Pennington. Talked much Talk." She did not tell her former friend that only the previous day she had driven past Dowry Square twice, nor that in two days' time she would pass by that way again. Having contrived an introduction to Conway's mother, she was anxious to see her again for a longer conversation, and the last thing she wanted to do was to get involved with Mrs. Pennington.

9

Weston-super-Mare

ON Wednesday, 7 July, Mrs. Piozzi "went to Clifton. Saw Mrs Rhudde [she had not yet seen the name in writing]—asked her to Supper, talked of dear Conway for 3 hours." She was on her way to Weston-super-Mare, to get away from Bath society, and where, free from interruptions, she could think about the man who had unaccountably become the centre of her world. She could have reached the Bristol Channel, thirty miles from Bath, comfortably in three hours, but the road took her close enough to Clifton to justify an overnight stay at the Gloucester Hotel, where she could entertain Mrs. Rudd.

Mrs. Rudd may not have been ready to reveal her secret on such short acquaintance, but the two ladies struck up such an easy relationship that it would not be long before Mrs. Piozzi heard the full story. Unfortunately, the only hard evidence that is available today about Conway's birth, around which one could weave a web of speculation, is that Susannah Belcher married William Rudd in the church of Saint Mary, Marylebone, on 10 November 1788, and their son, William Augustus, was baptised there on 18 May 1789. He must have been about four months old then, if, as Mrs. Piozzi believed, his birthday was close to hers, and Susannah must have been heavily pregnant on her wedding day; so either William Rudd thought that the child was his (in which case why so late at the altar?) or Susannah had confessed that he was not, and he was willing to marry her for the sake of appearances. The only other clue which may be of some significance is that their son was born in fashionable Henrietta Street, home of the nobility and gentry.

Lord William Conway was then a twenty-nine-year-old bachelor, and if he *were* the father, there was no impediment to marrying Susannah, except for difference in rank. William Rudd seems to have disappeared from the scene quite early, for William Augustus grew up without knowing a father, legal or natural. It is not known how soon he was told the truth or when he adopted the name Conway. No trace has been found of his childhood and youth in Barbados, but he was apparently supported there by friends of his mother's family.[1] It appears that Mrs. Rudd had made no claim on Lord

William or his family, but she had obviously made herself independent, having a business of her own in Clifton.

The morning after her evening with Mrs. Rudd, Mrs. Piozzi "climbed the Crags at Clifton in good Health and Spirits," and called on Mrs. Lambart,[2] a very old friend of hers (and of Mrs. Pennington's), who recommended her to try Fry's Hotel at Weston, whence they set off later in the day, arriving, "a Man, 3 Maids & Self & Baby" at four o'clock. Her expenses at Clifton, including "horses on," came to £5 12s, and she settled on £10 5s. a week for board and lodging for the whole "family": far too much for what turned out to be a very seedy hotel. Next morning she unpacked her books and began reading and writing letters. Later she sampled the bathing ("4 Shillings a Time," she complained), began to write "The Abridgment," and looked for cheaper lodgings.

The first letters flowed in from her friends, but the one she wished for most did not appear, and one she least expected came from Mrs. Pennington.[3]

College Square [Bristol] 14 July 1819

When I had the happiness of meeting you at Mrs. Lutwyches dearest Madam! I did not understand you were so soon coming into this neighbourhood, or should have requested, as I do now most earnestly, that you would not pass us by on your return. We may not be got back in our own house at the Hot Wells, but can give you a boiled chicken in our present quarters at Dr. Randolph's while your horses are changing or refreshing; and we *may* be returned to our former dwelling, where a comfortable bed and every accommodation it can afford will be at your service, and most delighted I should be once more to chat over with You, uninterruptedly former times, occurrences and connexions:—the longest night that Schearazede [*sic*] ever passed with the Sultan would appear short to me, compared with an Evening so spent! but I should be cautious in betraying you into the smell of Paint, which might be particularly obnoxious after the pure Breezes you have been inhaling;—and therefore, perhaps, must not expect this gratification in its full extent, unless your stay at Weston is extended beyond what you may probably be disposed to make it, as I fear you do not find its accommodations very satisfactory, but I trust that you will, at least give us a kind look in *College Green* as you pass on your return to Bath.

Mrs. Piozzi ought to have realised that Mrs. Lambart would have told Mrs. Pennington of her visit to Clifton en route to Weston, but the persistent Penelope was too intent on healing the breach to take offence at being so studiously ignored. For five years after their quarrel in 1804 she had tried to conciliate Mrs. Piozzi, but her letters had been ignored. At last, it seems, she had succeeded, for Mrs. Piozzi recorded in her diary; "I am glad we have shaken hands," and wrote to Mrs. Pennington for the first time in fifteen years. Her reply has not been traced, but it was, according to Mrs. Pennington,[4] "a kind letter from dear, dear Mrs Piozzi in the Spirit of former Times, so delightful that it filled my Heart with Joy, & my Eyes with Tears of Pleasure.—who but you, dearest Madam, can touch upon & give Interest to every passing Subject in a single Page!"

Mrs. Piozzi continued to enjoy the bathing, but remarked on page 355 of the first volume of the travel book that she was annotating that "in Italy it was considered very vulgar & indecent for *Ladies* to dip in the sea. Mr. Piozzi could not reconcile himself to it for a long Time after we came home." She had now added Mrs. Rudd to her long list of correspondents, and hoped thereby to keep in touch with her son; but he did not write to his mother, either. Day after day, the diary deplored his silence: "A long Letter from Miss Williams did not mend matters: hers is not the Letter I am wishing for." Her patience was running out by "the 15th day since I saw him, so it was, the day he went to Town. . . . What can be come to the Man that he never writes?" Three days later, after moving out of the hotel into a cottage, she made up her mind that "if no letter before Monday I will send James. My heart half broke about Conway. What can be the matter?" On the Sunday, still only three weeks since she had last seen Conway, she wrote to Mangin, complaining in passing that she "never can learn what is become of my friend and Favourite Conway", and repeated her fears about Lysons's library collection.

When Monday brought no news, James was packed off to Birmingham, glad of the outing, and no doubt amused at his mistress's obsession with the handsome actor. He returned three days later, saying that "poor Dear Conway" had been very ill, and had promised to write. The *Birmingham Gazette* too reported that in *Evadne* he was "labouring under the effects of a severe indisposition," but in spite of a slight fever, he continued to perform. The promised letter never came, however, and Mrs. Piozzi pressed on with the journey book, which was completed on 9 August; three days later, James was dispatched once more to Birmingham, with a fine, freshly caught salmon, the volumes, and a letter "full of gentle reproaches." The next day she dined off salmon herself and "felt as if dining with Conway." James returned after *four* days on the loose this time, "with a letter from poor dear Conway. Very ill he has been, and will come here and be nursed in Two Months. Paid Fortnum and Mason 8£–7s. for his food."

The *Gazette* noted that Mr. Conway, appearing in the musical *Guy Mannering* that night, "is always anxious to contribute, in whatever way it may be required of him." He was also heavily engaged in rehearsals for *Conrad,* which left him little time to study the journey book, its manuscript additions, and "The Abridgment." Four years earlier, in a similar autobiography, she told Fellowes that before he arrived in Bath "there existed not a human creature who cared one atom for poor H:L:P"; and now it was Conway who had really made life worth living. On page 134 of volume 1 she noted that

When Piozzi was dead & Salusbury married & I could find no old friends at Streatham Park—I threw all up and ran to Bath *to die;* disregarding every thing and every body—till Mr. Conway's Pierre [in June 1818] waked me from my stupor to admiration of his astonishing talents.

On page 72 of the second volume, she referred again to the time when she left Wales

meaning to live at Streatham Park, and if not so, to go and die at Bath, which I was trying to effectuate, when dear Conway's Talents and offered Friendship shewed me there was something yet worth living for.

She compared her annotations with those of Tetrarch, who

never meant for our Inspection what he wrote down in his own Virgil, and in that lies the Charm. Whatever is professedly decorated for our Admiration is received as a Debt, and dear Mr. Conway in the Characters even of Prince Hal or Faulconbridge is not remembered by me with the Delight or Triumph of Imagination. I beheld him handing his Mother up the Hill at Clifton, radiant with Beauty and glowing with grateful Affection, and now he is ill & writes neither to her nor me.

She now explained the deep impression his Comus had made earlier that year:

I should like to know if dearest Mr. Conway recollects the Coldness with which I heard him repeat these enchanting Verses. It was *not* Coldness—I dared not trust my Eyes, my Hands, or my Heart with Liberty to express these Feelings at the Recital of Lines I used to read Day & Night when no Words of my own would express the Passion of my Soul which Piozzi's Voice excited & called forth. When in the Summer's Gloom at Streatham Park he used to sing to me under the Trees at Evening how sweetly did his Notes—how cruelly did they float upon the Wind—so that ten Years after I could not sit Comus out, it was as if *new* to me; Your Manner, your Voice affected me so strongly. The tender Tones shook my very Recollection! and next Time you acted it I pretended Engagement after the Play and—ran. I was but lately waked from my Torpor succeeding the Torture of losing Piozzi! 10 years Torpor.

On page 171 of volume 2 her text quoted "Sis tu felicio Augusto melior Trajano," which was translated in a footnote, "May thou be happier than Augustus—better than Trajano!" and her marginal note read, "Ah me! the foolish anagram comes in to my head." A copy of the foolish anagram, which she had evidently shown Conway already, is to be found in her hand on a card in Broadley's extraillustrated edition of Knapp's Piozzi-Pennington letters in Princeton University Library.[5]

Picking out anagrams I find your name
Returns me only this
hoW ILL I AM?
Or if the second word we trust to
Read Sis felicior Augusto
*N*orth *E*ast *W*est *S*outh, I send my muse
But C no WAY to get good news

Toward the end of her "Abridgment," Mrs. Piozzi admitted that she "loved spoiling people, and hated anyone she could not spoil. Am I not trying now to spoil dear Mr. Conway?" Her old friend Charles Shephard had said the same about her affection for Salusbury:

"Mrs. Piozzi cannot exist without somone upon whom she could energize her Affections; [Salusbury's] Uncle is gone, and she is much obliged to [him] for being ready at hand to pet and spoil; her Children will not suffer her to love them, and what will she do when this Fellow throws her off, as he soon will?" Shepherd was right enough. I sunk into a Stupor . . . [until] your Talents roused, your offered Friendship opened my Heart to Enjoyment. Oh! never say here-after that the Obligations are on your Side. Without you, Dullness, Darkness and Stagnation of every Faculty would have enveloped and extinguished all the Powers of hapless H:L:P.

Her confessions must have surprised and embarrassed her reader, but he had little time to reflect before another letter arrived. This one is now in the Pierpont Morgan Library (PML) in New York, where there is a collection of ten more:

Weston super Mare
Wednesday 18 August 1819

I would not teize you for the World, dearest and kindest Friend! My heart grieves to recollect how I *have* tiezed you: but pray impute it to the true Cause,—restless, unsatisfied Anxiety: You will feel *something* of it yourself forty years hence for a favourite Son or Daughter. Meanwhile let us not cease to thank God—who chas-tises the Children of his Choice,—that our Tide of Sorrow is turned at last. I knew there were more Billows to break upon our heads when we parted; but my Confidence in your Strength was too high, my Reliance on God's Mercy too weak; & my Spirits all *up* (in our Welsh Phrase) among the topmost Boughs. They have paid for it since, but "against Ill-fortune Men are ever Merry, While heaviness foreruns the good Event", as says our Master Shakespear.

James brought me a very much improved Acct. of your Appearance, I mean *en Robe de Chambre,* for on the Stage our incomparable Conway will make us believe what he will, sick or well. How lucky it was that we could catch a Fish the only cool Morning we could have sent it! I eat [*sic*] Salmon myself that Day—Fryday 13th: that it might seem as if we dined together.

Oh I shall be quite well presently. I have no real Ailment; but I wish you could see Bessy—so like a Hen with young Ducks when I go into the Water, and 'tis my only Amusement. . . .

What a hot Summer 'tis? good for everybody & everything but you, and would have been fatal to any other Mortal engaged in such a Profession—fatal to the Profession too—for who would go to a Theatre in an inland County Town through such a Vertical Sun to see less than Conway. . . . Would it were all over and you safe at Weston!

After her usual interlude of amusing anecdotes, Mrs. Piozzi concluded

I shall leave this open because perhaps Yours written on Sunday may come tonight. 'Tis the oddest Post in the World—a Walking Post between here & Bristol—till he stands still & turns to a Wooden Post from mere fatigue and Inanition. So Good Night! Tuesday Night and may God bless & preserve my excellent, my all-accomplish'd Friend even from himself & his own Apprehensions. Come now—be well persuaded as I am of your Advance towards Recovery, and be careful while in this State of Irritability, not to let any Cares come near you—least of all Thoughts of my Displeasure about your not writing. Write *when* you can & *how* you can. My whole Desire is to do you good in some Way. May it be in my Power!—either to assist or to amuse you. Fix'd Air must be good for you, I think, Cyder or Soda water [usually prescribed to alleviate the effects of fever]—all my old Hock is gone & I am so sorry! . . . The dear elastic noble Mind will cast off every Cloud & soon shine out unchanged & with redoubled Brilliancy—unalterable as is the honest true & tender heart of H:L:P. James never got home till Monday evening.

There was now another letter from Mrs. Pennington, saying that she had been unwell ever since their meeting at the Lutwyches, and Mrs. Piozzi's holiday had given her the idea that sea air might do her good. Weston was becoming too popular, she thought, but it was conveniently close, and perhaps it would be possible to take over Mrs. Piozzi's cottage when she left? Mrs. Piozzi replied by return that she had no plans to leave Weston for quite awhile (not revealing that she was expecting Conway to join her), which prompted Mrs. Pennington to suggest that some other accommodation might become vacant while Mrs. Piozzi was still there. Could Mrs. Piozzi's servants look out for a cottage that might become available? Letters now passed between Bristol and Weston as fast as the walking postman could carry them, and the diary wryly noted "fresh instructions from Mrs. Pennington." Eventually a cottage was found in Sea View Place, owned by a Bristol tradesman, and Mrs. Pennington reported that "I think I may say as the stage coaches advertise, 'that God willing' we shall see Weston on the 14, or 15th at farthest."

Meantime Mrs. Piozzi heard that "Conway is alive and acting Conrad"—evidently with some vigour: the *Birmingham Gazette* wrote that the part afforded him with "several opportunities for excellent declamation," and her next letter, dated 21 August and reproduced at length in the *Athenaeum,* was curious about the plot:

The dear Newspapers came to hand whilst I was writing. Oh, thank you, thank you for it 1000 times! And which of the Conrads known to historic Truth is dramatized, I wonder! The elder was proclaimed King of the Romans about the year 1220 or 30; but would absolutely be *Emperor* in spite of the Pope; to annoy those Italian Dominions he drove into the Peninsula, and committed famous Cruelties at Naples, Capua, &c., after having behaved beautifully the early Part of his Life; and so they compared him to Nero. He was poysoned by his brother Manfred, but left a son whom the Italians called Conradino—the little Conrad; who had a great Soul, however; set an Army on Foot to recover some of his Father's Conquests, possessed by Charles of Anjou, who defeated him and hs martial Cousin Frederick at Lago Furino—and as they crossed a River to escape, caught both the Fugitives; and hapless Conrad lost his short Life on the Scaffold at Naples when only eighteen years old. He was a Youth of quite consummate Beauty; which was the Reason our King William the Third used to laugh when German Friends and Flatterers compared them. . . .

But, as Dr. Johnson said to Mr. Thrale. Oh, sir, stop my Mistress! If once she begins naming her favourite Heroes round, we are undone! I hate historic talk, and when Charles Fox said something to me about Cataline's[6] conspiracy I thought about Tom Thumb. Poor Dr. Collier loved it no better—he used to say, Leave thy historians to moulder on the shelf. And yet their adoring Pupil distracts her latest found Friend with it in the year 1819—and all out of her own Head, as the Children say, for ne'er a Book I have. Send me the Tragedy if 'tis good for anything, and you can do it without Inconvenience. Once again, I wonder who wrote it! Who acted it last Night you have told me; and it was very kindly done; and I am now more easy about your Health and more careful about my own—that I may the longer enjoy the Comfort of being considered as dear Mr. Conway's admiring and faithful Friend, H:L:P.

Mrs. Piozzi's speculations about the Plot of *Conrad the Usurper* were wide of the mark. Its author, identified only as the author of *Tancred*,[7] had set it in Sweden at the time of the Crusades, because, as he wrote in a preface, it involved "the fate of crowned heads," and he thought it expedient "to choose a country whose history was little known at that period." He acknowledged that but for Mr. Conway's "unremitting kindness" in reading the play, it might never have been performed, and "all that zeal and talent could effect he accomplished for its welfare."

Two days after that letter, Mrs. Piozzi "waked with Spontaneous Diarrhoea," and was so ill that she thought she was about to die. She packed up her favourite alarm watch ("Viner's best," which she paid forty pounds for) with a farewell note in case she did not survive (PML):

Weston super Mare
August 28 1819

Having been vouchsafed a Sort of Warning that my Temporal Existence is at length coming rapidly to a Close,—I write these lines to my best loved, my latest found Friend, whose Talents and Kindness have so contributed to Sweeten the last

Eight Months of it. They accompany an Excellent Gold repeating Watch destined as my *last* Present.

> Down Time's rapid Stream to eternity's Ocean
> Here see the swift Moments each other pursue;
> Nor take without feeling some Tender Emotion
> *My* Time's old Accountant,—transmitted to *You*
>
> *Your* Monitress still, in this low-voic'd Repeater
> A useful Memento recorded may be;
> If wishing once more in the next Life to meet her
> You scorn not the Precepts of poor H : L : P.

If you should be able—by any Accident to benefit Poor Bessy & her dear little Boy—remember how much I loved them, and Adieu but surely not for ever!

Mrs. Piozzi's fears were unfounded, as her next letter, known only because it was printed in 1843 as the first of her "love letters," revealed. It may not justify that description, but there can be no doubt of its authenticity.

Weston-super-Mare
1 September 1819

Three Sundays have now elapsed since James brought me dearest Mr. Conway's Promise to write the very next Day—and were it not for the Newspaper which came on Tuesday the 24th of August—sending me to rest comfortable, tho' sick enough and under the Influence of Laudanum—I should relapse into my former State of agonising Apprehension on your Account—but that little darling Autograph round the Paper was written so steady, and so completely in the old Way— whenever I look at it my Spirits revive, and Hope *(true Pulse of Life)* ceases to Intermit for a While at least—and bids me assured we shall soon meet again. I really was very ill three or four days—so was Bessy and the other servants.

Food poisoning was the likely cause of their sickness, and now that they had recovered, Mrs. Piozzi put all thoughts of death behind her, as she continued:

We are now removing to a Palace [No. 2 Sea View Place]—a Weston Palazzino where we propose receiving Mr. Conway, and the Weeks are within Count now. Mrs. Stratton writes affectionately, asking after your Health and Engagements, of which I know no more than little Angelo, but the Bath People say we are *sure of you.* . . .

Cowper the Poet says, in reply to a Friend who begs Pardon for writing so seldom, "Why, sir, I infer nothing from the Silence of a correspondent but that he wishes me to be silent too". I do not, you see, infer *that;* I keep pelting you with Letters which tell you nothing you knew not long ago! Unless it comes into my Head to give Information of old Doctor Whalley's Wife running away from him. . . .

Good night! and God bless my dearest and most valued Friend! for whose perfect Recovery and long continued Happiness I will pray till the Post comes in; yes, and until Life goes out from poor H:L:P.

I would keep up my Spirits as you wish me—and your Spirits too. *But how can I?* Send a Newspaper at least. Oh! for a Breath of Intelligence, however short, respecting Health and Engagements.

She had in fact just been given some news, but by an unwelcome hand, as she told Miss Williams. "Miss Willoughby has written to me quite out of her own head, for I never called on her for Correspondence, & at the Top of the long Letter these Words. I hear our favourite Mr. Conway is engaged for the Winter. . . . My Answer was Cold, short & Dull—that I was glad Conway was engaged at the Theatre, & no Wonder if he came slowly, who was so loaded with Laurels." All she could get out of Conway herself was that he was "fatigued to Death; and in very low Spirits, though in high favour with the thronged Audiences at Birmingham." She could not afford to send James to Birmingham again, "and nothing else will make him write," so she packed up a salmon and some wine and sent it by carrier. On the same day (7 September) her diary cried out, "He writes, he writes, he *has* written, poor Soul—from a Couch of Agony." It is not clear whether he had suffered a relapse after the fever he had fought for some weeks, or whether this was a new illness, but it was serious enough for Alfred Bunn to send for James Warde to take over the leading roles, and for Mrs. Piozzi to offer to send him money (she was still holding the proceeds of his Bath benefit).

Now, having survived the sickness which had threatened her "temporal existence," she feared that her *accidental* death might deprive Conway of the gold watch and his own money, and packed both up in a small box with a slip of paper (PML) on which she wrote in a bold, deliberate hand

Monday 13 Septr 1819
Weston Super Mare

My Dearest Friend—I am going on the Sea—a Party of Pleasure; but lest the Vessel should upset, and I should be lost, I leave *your* Money—50£—and *your* Watch—a Gold Repeater—safe in this Box; which if Bessy fails to deliver by any Accident, dear Mr. Conway must claim from the Executors of his truly attached Hester Lynch Piozzi.

In the event, the sailing trip was cancelled, and Conway would have to wait some time for his watch. Two days later the Penningtons and a companion, Miss Wren, arrived in Weston.

10

"No more examining the Postman's Hand"

THE day after the Penningtons arrived, Mrs. Piozzi, perhaps showing off a little, bathed in a heavy swell, was dashed by a wave, and felt her finger go dead afterwards—"the first time I ever had that sensation. Perhaps Palsy, perhaps Death is coming. I shall be a loss to Conway and Angelo. I wrote to Birmingham." It was time to introduce Mrs. Pennington to Conway, and to explain why her name had not been mentioned before. She did not go into detail, but it seems that when they were wintering in Bath in 1803, Gabriel Piozzi quarrelled with Mrs. Pennington, and on their return to Brynbella, Mrs. Piozzi's letters grew cooler, less frequent, and trivial. Eventually Mrs. Pennington protested that she would not be talked to of "the cat, the dog, and the times and the weather," and Mrs. Piozzi retorted that "cat and dog" was a fair description of "you quarrelling disciples, and I will not, like Grumio, talk to *you* of how bad my master was when your letter came to *him*. . . . Farewell then, and be merry, and believe me with every good wish, your ancient jig-maker, H : L : P." That had been her last word for fifteen years, but it did not take long for the ice to melt when they next met, judging by her letter to Conway.

Weston super Mare
18 Septr 1819

My dearest Friend
        will like a Letter dated on Doctor Johnson's Birthday, so I begin it now, though it will not go till Monday when I send Bessy to Bath on Twenty little Errands & charge her to send You these Books which I have just received from Upham, & not quite cut open; yet could not help my old Trick of making Mr. Deformed in the Margin
        but I want to tell you of Mrs. Pennington

She is the Lady who once lived much with me, chiefly on Acct of Cecila Mostyn then Thrale, to whom I thought—& thought wisely—She would be a very proper & Advantageous *Companion*. After her own Marriage, however, and Cecy's, She disobliged dear Mr. Piozzi by a hasty expression, and we met no more till a few

Weeks ago, just 16 Years—during which Time she has continued her Connection with Doctor Whalley, and with *Mrs. Siddons,* as far as Connection can be kept without Correspondence.

Last Night we talked freely, and this was Part of what She said when I express'd my Wonder that Sid's only remaining Daughter,—Maria died in this Lady's House & Arms—was not yet married; "Why Doctor Whalley you know is that Child's Godfather, & one Day when the Mother was from home he pass'd an hour in confidential Chat with *her,* with *Cecy* Siddons: and asked—as you do me—why she was not yet married? Dear Sir was the Reply, with whom should I ever be married? No young Men of *my own* Rank in Life are admitted to *my Sight:* and the Quality Beaux my Mother wishes as Visitants come more on *her* Acct: than mine: whom they despise Connexion with of Course:—their Friends would not endure the Daughter of an Actress in their Family—a Feeling She cannot understand, because She sees them so polite to *her*—Oh Sir! assure Yourself *I shall never be married".*

The Commerce Table was now called for, and the Conversation changed. Your name was never mentioned of Course, but I hasten'd to my Desk that every Word might be recorded.

From Mrs. Pennington she had "heard Cecy Siddons' views on Marriage—think them favourable for my Conway." Cecilia was now twenty-five, and perhaps it was going through Mrs. Piozzi's mind that being both an actor and a "quality beau," Conway might have exactly the right qualifications to suit both mother and daughter. It was not long before his name was brought into the conversation:

This Mrs. Pennington is the Lady who, going to see Miss O'Neill play Juliet,[1] had her Attention all attracted away by the Romeo who she pronounced Inimitable—to me at Mrs. Lutwyche's—and I fancied her Acquaintance with my Admiration of your Talents—but No: & when I said, why, Conway is the handsomest Man in England, I dare say he is, was her Reply: but so much was I astonished & delighted with his *acting* I should not know his *Person* again was I to see him, except upon the Stage. How different this from Mr. Mangin's Speech! Who said Oh Conway's Beauty sets Criticism at Defiance; one cannot think otherwise then well of what is done by so graceful a Person. . . .

Our Talk here is not good—too much about one another; but Mrs. Pennington likes a fine Sunset or a bright Rainbow as well as I do. We have a Gentleman here who they say writes Hunt's Speeches for him, and at Bristol has declaimed publickly in his Praise: he is the Son to the exemplary and Orthodox, the learned & pious, the Venerable Sir Abraham Elton! whose heart he is breaking—but you may observe upon the *Coins* how every Son & Successor regularly sets his Face the contrary Way from his Father.

I wish you had a son tho'—nevertheless;—You promised me to keep my Portrait for him, and I think you will never part with the *Repeater* till *he* takes it with him to the University. What an Immeasurable Length of Time *that* seems to my Friend as he reads this! but to me who have lived four Returns of the 20th Year what is it? *Un beau Reve . . .*

Mrs. Piozzi passed on the news to Miss Williams that Conway was on the mend after an attack of typhus and had turned down a "fine offer from Drury Lane, preferring us & Bath," that the Penningtons had arrived, and now

> all Bath and Bristol is in Weston . . . those who come hither for Privacy mistake the Spot. Everybody is watching Everybody, even while they bathe. Ladies take their Book or Work & sit upon the Crags to see each other wash their Faces with a Care & Curiosity to me quite wonderful. Yesterday was Lady Keith's birthday: and I did not find the Ocean wide enough to wash away the Remembrance of her Wit and Beauty—though so long lost to me—from the Mind of her much-despised mother, driven to seek other favourites from other Spheres of Life. . . . Today is Doctor Johnson's Birthday: and how chearfully did we use to keep the Whole Week at poor Streatham Park!! . . .

> Love to the good natured Mrs. Dimond, who like yourself was kind when Kindness was valuable; . . . Sir James is too happy now ever to write to Dear Miss Williams's truly faithful H : L : P.

She had been rather tactless, when mentioning Sam Lysons's "literary gleanings," to add that "dear Conway's kind offer of buying them instantly for me, should they be set for sale, would have won my heart if he had not gained it before; but I hope the danger is over now." Fellowes was well aware of Conway's place in Mrs. Piozzi's affections, and so, by this time, was Mrs. Pennington. She told her friend Maria Brown that she had spent some hours every day with Mrs. Piozzi, "and our evenings always together, in the most perfect harmony. We seem entirely to have regained our former footing, and to revert to past times, persons, and anecdotes of mutual pleasure. She has sought no other,indeed sedulously avoided all other society since we have been here, and is happy and cheerful when with us, as I ever saw her. . . . It is not however with *me* exactly the same thing. I *was Prima Donna,* now I feel that many new friends and new connexions, with new interests and novel attractions, occupy the ground that *I* exclusively possessed; and I can only expect, in future, to be one of this larger group."

The next event on Mrs. Piozzi's horizon was Conway's benefit, scheduled for 15 October, and Alfred Bunn was surprised to get a request from her for a ticket. "Mrs Piozzi," she replied, "considers herself as deeply indebted to Mr. Bunn for his obliging Communication. She certainly means Ticket of Admission—tho' distant; as it will afford her an opportunity of proving the sincere esteem she feels for Mr. Conway's Merit added to the truest Admiration of his Talents." Later in the day, "Rec'd to my Astonishment a chearful letter from *London*—more pious than chearful, but full of hope." She replied "with a *Promise,*" perhaps that she would travel to Birmingham for his benefit. The newspapers, however, doubted whether he would be fit enough to appear. The *Birmingham Gazette* regretted to announce "the departure of Mr. Conway, whose alarming and increasing indisposition has induced his medical attendants to advise him to proceed to London for further professional aid. We hope this gentleman will be enabled to return prior to the close of the season, but should that unfortunately not prove to be the case, we feel assured that his interests will not be allowed to suffer." The *Courier* of 28 September carried the same news, and added that he was under the care of Mr. Astley Cooper, the king's surgeon.

Mrs. Piozzi "wrote to London again in low spirits," (HSP) and instructed her London wine merchant to deliver some wine to Gerrard Street, where Conway and his mother were staying.

Weston super Mare
1 Octr. 1819

If heaviness *indeed* foreruns the good event, dear Mr. Conway is getting well apace: I never felt my heart weigh half as much—tho' infinitely more uneasy, & *with cause*. You are now where your best friends must wish, & full of those sentiments *I* have always pray'd to God that you might be inspired with. You have the best medical advice which I suppose *Europe* affords; and you are *not* alone & desolate, as my distracted imagination had depicted you—dying at an inn upon the road.—Much as my hapless friend has endured, the agony, consequent on such a fancy, has been spared him; and a very little more of it *must have killed me*. . . .

No letter since Sunday night—here's Fryday come. How shall I bear another day or two?

I will run to study

Dearest Mr. Conway has sometimes in his partial Way asked me how I came to *know* this and that. It was because whenever Affliction seized upon my Mind, two Cities of Refuge alone presented themselves—Prayer and Study. When I have wearied Heaven & my Heart with the *first* I always used to run with the Strength received—to the *Second*—and so I will tonight. What is there else to hope for?

When Bessy went to Bath for Books. I made her bring me Parkhurst's Lexicon, the Hebrew Lexicon—such studies *force* Attention. Those which *induce* it merely, will do when the Spirits are calm. Let me have a sweet encouraging Letter tonight. I will read Shakespeare tomorrow.

Sat: Morning 2d Octr.

No Letter, no Sleep, no Shakespeare—Well! like the skinned Eels—I am used to it. I expected some Account of my dearest Friend for *5 long Weeks* since I lived here—& then for *4 Weeks in Succession* after James brought me a Promise that you would write. Yet notwithstanding *that;* and notwithstanding the horrible Intelligence which last Thursday 23d brought me, & notwithstanding the Courier's cruel Paragraph which I read here last Thursday 30th, and which nearly demolished me—I rose this Morning with hope in my heart.

Did you never observe that let one have

pass'd the Night in what Anguish of *Mind* you *will;* a chearful rising Sun relieves Fatigue, and with a Burst of Tears washes *some* Weight from the Soul. I feel that Sensation now!

If Bessy could leave her Baby, *but she can't;* or if she would let me go without her, *but she won't*—and if it was not a mad manner of spending the Money which may be made more useful *to us,* you should see me at No. 41 [Gerrard Street]. & if you grow worse instead of better,—I *will* come.

I'll not forsake the Ship, and haste to Shore
When the Winds whistle and the Surges roar—

so if you *want* me *call* me; or *will James be useful*? By the Time you can answer this Letter, we shall be able to spare him. In order to strengthen my Spirits I rushed into the Sea last Monday, but the Waves were too strong, & I was too awkward—not what I was 40 Summers ago—and as I came out a large Billow flung me down and bruised me—but to be a little frightened *did me good:* and changed for an Hour or Two the Course of my Ideas.

Mrs. Stratton has written me the sweetest Letter in the world. You must get well & keep well for everybody's Sake—particularly for *hers* who will be true to her deserved Vows of unalienable Friendship while she can write H:L:Piozzi.

You should tell me the *last* Letter from Weston came safe: it was dated Weston Wednsday 29th & these walking Posts are *so* dangerous! The Men get robbed & lie drunk in Ditches. Here shines the *4th full moon* since I took my dearest Mr. Conway to Clifton. How happy then! How wretched ever since!! Oh what have we both endured!

This Moment brings your dear dear Letter—No Thanks are due—your Letter was miss-sent somewhere. ["Dear excellent Creature," said the diary, "Alive, Alive, Safe, tho' far from well"] These Posts are dreadful. . . . Give my Love to Mrs. Rudd—how I rejoyce she is with you! Make her write for you & don't put yourself to unnecessary Pain—let her just say it seems Safe.

Mrs. Piozzi's relief on hearing from Conway was short-lived. She was certain that he was not telling her the truth about his condition—"I will send *James*. I cannot bear this suspense," and next day, "James went at 9 o'clock: took a Cheddar Cheese & a Pint of Tokay & a Panic striken short Letter." James was only halfway to London when Mrs. Piozzi wrote again to Conway. The letter was reproduced in 1843 as "Love Letter II," and, like "Letter I," is indisputably authentic and unadulterated. In fact, she mentioned it in her diary, saying that she had asked "whether his mother had received her letter, and a little Preaching. Poor Man!"—and told him that she had heard from Mrs. Stratton, who was very much concerned for him.

Thurs 7 October 1819

I write—unlike my dearest Friend—a brief Communication; not to beg letters—
the last [five days ago!] half-broke my heart—but to tell you that having directed
mine to Mrs. Rudd 41 Gerrard Street I fear it will not be received safely. My Fear
arises from *this*. I wrote to fine Mr. Divie Robinson, Villiers street, in the Strand,
and bade him when he sent my Stock of Wine to Bath, put 1/2 a dozen Bottles of
the very same in a Basket and deliver to Mrs. Rudd, 41 Gerrard Street, Soho. His
Clerk now writes me Word she cannot be found—does not live there &c. So
perhaps the Postman may say so too. Jalds does not know the People—nor I
either—but they are Grand folks, Friends to Sir James Fellowes: I have written to
the Clerk again today, and suppose you will get your little petty Present of six
Bottles at least; but I am uneasy for my *Letter,* which you and your Mama went
halves in. The Date, Wednesday 6 October—make them ask for it. I wish my
beloved Friend to keep his Spirits up, but have enough to do on his own dear
Account to keep up my own. Yet shall not the one alleviating Drop of Comfort, as
you kindly call my Letters, ever fail.

Mrs. Stratton saw the "horrid paragraph" in the *Courier*—she writes with all
possible Tenderness and, I really do believe, True Concern. Mr. Bunn's elegant
Expressions of friendship pleased me too. How will you get your things from
Birmingham to Bath? For Bath at last will be your Home and mine: would we were
there! I grieve that the changes in Shuttleworth's Arrangements[2] will chace you
from your old Haunts—but don't go too far off your old and honoured Mistress.
The Stories of Yesterday and Today are *terrific;* was I happy, I should call them
magnificent—so do our private Feelings operate on Views of Nature and Language. Your being shut out by ill Health from Fortune and fame is very affecting
indeed. . . . Suffer nothing that you are not *obliged* to suffer, however; we shall get
through the Dusky Night, and enjoy a bright Morning after all. Your Youth &
Strength are in full Perfection, but 'tis on God's Favour I depend for your Recovery.
Whose Gifts are indeed those of Youth & Strength? Body & Soul? His only.

And wicked as the World is, I hope it is not necessary for the Warning of Others
that *your* incomparable Talents should be shown in a State of Subjugation. My
Heart assures me 'tis a momentary Chastisement; for what at last is one year out of
70—the regular Life of a Common Man? Oh, there is much for you to do—much to
enjoy: and many a Day of Care for Others now unthought on.

How did I ever dream—in 1791—that fretted as I was about my own Affairs; a
Baby just born—or not born,[3] should in the year 1819 take up the whole Attention
of H:L:P.—and Sir John Salusbury not yet in the World which I thought every
Hour crumbling about me. . . . Here I am, however, praying most fervently for
your Restoration to all that makes Life desirable, and giving God thanks for the
Power he lends me, of affording Solace to the finest Soul that was ever inclosed in
Human Clay—such Clay! But we must be contented to bear our Cross. . . . Let us
take Things as God sends them, and be thankful—
Dear Hope

a cordial innocent as strong
Man's Heart at once inspirits- and serenes.

She sweetens Pains & Sorrows into Joy, and sends *me* smiling (thro' my Tears) to rest. Good night—God send his Angel to watch over you, and grant us yet a happy Meeting by 20 October—H:L:P.

Bath is the place where you must seek your final Re-instatement *as you say*. Bath was the place where you sought and found a Friend.

James's visit spurred Conway to reply immediately, assuring her that all was well, and she responded likewise (HSP).

9 Octr: Saturday 1819

Now then at *last* after four or five Months Changes of Agony does H:L:P, like your Astley Cooper pronounce herself *satisfied*. The *great Affair* is in the state we wish it, certainly; or you would not speak of a carriage as Indulgence: I can now with Admiration unmixed with Terror reflect upon the dreadful *Past* & like Mariner in Lucretius cry *suave mare magno* &c

'Tis safe 'tis pleasant to behold from Shore
The tossing Waves and hear the Tempest roar

Till your last Letter came, *Hope* rather than Confidence sustained my Spirits. I will not burn that Letter till you bid me—There's not a Word in it from whence any possible Consequence could be drawn, but that you are better, and do not want James. He is a Blockhead I fear, & if he has broke my only Pint of *Imperial Tokay* in his Journey—I shall just hang him. It made me so happy that I had it for you.— Now, Dearest Friend forbear fretting about your professional Duties. It *is* hard & cruel to lose that Applause your Talents *so deserve,* and I am jealous for their Reputation as *You* can be; but nothing else shall be lost. Manager *Amethyst* will do all that Manager *Diamond* would have done, till after our Birthdays [close enough to be shared] are over. "Then to the Elements, be free & Fare thee well".

I hope Bath Waters to bathe in will be approved; if not, go with Mama to Clifton: live quiet & drink asses Milk. Wherever you are sent, my Friendship will follow; & perhaps you won't wish a *Town* to be convalescent in, for 20 reasons. . . .

Live long and happily, & love my Letters; I wonder when you will be sick of them: but I shall release you soon. That my Portrait's strong Resemblance struck Mrs. Rudd rejoyces me. That too delicate Trinket inclosing your fine hair has vexed my Heart. One day I saw the Platt badly displaced ('twas when your health was at its worst) and in my female foolish Mind a Thousand silly superstitions crowded. It shall be laid by for the *Wife* we talk of, and I will court your Mother to get me a genuine Bit, which She and I will put into a Plain Chrystal Locket, that I can wear as you do Miss Jagger, about my neck by a Black Ribbon.[4]

She signed off her work for the day with a prayer from "his highly honour'd Mistress & Manager for Three Months H:L:P," and continued after church the next day:

Sunday 10 Oct: My first Wedding Day, when I was married at St. Anne's near you [just across Shaftesbury Avenue] I made impromptu Verses to the Psalm

Tunes & sang them unknown to anyone. Ever kind! ever considerate Mr. Conway. . . .

James will get home tomorrow, and we shall get away next Thursday sennight from Weston super Mare. . . . The sun shines bright & my Heart fancies You in Hyde Park now . . . blessing in Spirit the Power you enjoy of tasting the fresh air after so long Illness. . . . I drink to the health of the two Cs *now;* Conway convalescent

The "very tolerable Acct." that James brought back on her wedding anniversary made her "too happy . . . much happier than I was the real Day 1763." Two days later, the Penningtons left Weston, having been in Mrs. Piozzi's company every day for nearly four weeks, trying to understand her strange infatuation with this young man and sharing her anxiety for news about his progress. Mrs. Piozzi declined their pressing invitations to call at Dowry Square on *her* way home, two weeks later; she had been away from Bath long enough, and wanted to get home as soon as possible. After they had gone, she wrote again to Conway.[5]

Weston-super-Mare Oct.
14 Thursday 1819

I partly think that this will be the last letter that my dearest Mr. Conway will be plagued with from this out-of-the-way Place which his Illness has render'd hateful to poor H:L:P., nor can her present Comforts yield her Compensation for what She & her truly inestimable Friend have suffer'd since it was fixed on for her Residence. James's Report was in no wise worse—but *better* than I hoped for, except for the green Shade over those all-expressing Eyes . . . faintly described by Lady Randolph when Mrs. Siddons speaks Hume's Sentiments—warming the cold Declamation by her Energy. I had no Notion *they* had suffer'd *seriously;* Weston would have driven them distracted: the Glare of our Sands is such that Bessy quite complains of it,—mine love a strong Light,—so do those of your Likeness.

A Birmingham playbill announced that "this present Friday, October 15 is appointed for the benefit of Mr. Conway. . . . Mr. Bunn ventures to hope that the unavoidable absence of Mr. Conway, through severe and dangerous disposition, will not be considered as diminishing his claim to that support which might be anticipated from his arduous professional exertions." The play was to be *Brutus,* and the title role was to be filled by J. P. Warde, a thoughtful tribute from his supposed archrival, which failed to get a mention in Mrs. Piozzi's diary, though she did record that she had sent Bunn ten pounds for a ticket. The same day, she "tried to secure watch for Conway by writing his dear Name in it."

Mrs. Pennington reported their safe return, thanking Mrs. Piozzi for "the hours you rendered so interesting, amusing, & instructive at Weston-super-Mare," and complaining that the holiday had unfortunately not done her health any good. Mrs. Piozzi marked *her* return home with a fond letter to Conway (PML).

No. 8. Gay Street Bath,
Fryday 21st . . . no, 22nd October 1819

No more examining the Postman's Hand,
Nor fond Initials traced upon the Sand,
Nor Empty Projects idly plann'd
At Weston super Mare;
But Resignation, Hope and Joy
By turns possess, by Turns employ
L'Amie Octogenaire

No Landscape boasts such beauteous Dawn of Day
No Sea so red with Titan's parting Ray
As Weston super Mare.
But here at Bath Th'Autumnal Daisy blows,
And flourishes the Winter Rose,
With Friendship's Flowers the Year to close,
Consoling Pain and Care

When will you come home dear Mr. Conway? When will your Medical Adviser trust you to Female Management and Governance?—a Horse for your Doctor,[6] an Ass for your Apothecary; an old Woman for Your Companion when you prefer that to Reading; and a large Poke Bonnet to Gilt Leather and Marbled Leaves.

I got home yesterday very safe, & little dear Angelo was as glad to see himself in the Old Place as I was. . . . Miss Williams, was my first Visitant, said she was sorry to bring bad News—which she would not *send*. It was a great Pity—so it was, but poor Mr. Conway's leg was cut off Two Days ago in London—and now, thought I, 'twas no Folly to send James—for this Nonsense, nonsensical as it is, would have lost me a Whole Night's Sleep had I not known its Falsehood.

I have written for the Salusburys for the 20th of Decr. & he has offer'd me some Pheasants, very prettily; if the Weather is cold enough, you shall have some in London, but I hope you will come and eat them at Bath. Write to me dearest Friend, and say how Matters go. *I* say, when asked, that you hurt yourself in the Mad Scene from Conrade, and that the Cold & Fever which follow'd made a Deposit, bringing on a temporary Lameness, which Astley Cooper has now removed; and you are now getting well under his Directions. It is not all True? . . .

—but here come Interrupters, & the Post goes out at noon here, not at Night—and tomorrow there's no Post at all, & Your Watch is striking four: and I will just say how truly—not how much I am Your faithfully attached Friend H:L:Piozzi

11

"22 Weeks since we parted"

ONE of the first callers at No. 8 was Mrs. Dimond, in a great state: she had heard that *both* Conway's legs had been cut off! Mrs. Piozzi dashed off a letter to Mr. Astley Cooper to pass on the gossip, and received a "pretty note" from him in reply. There was "Good news from Conway *too*. He has had *such* offers." She took another step toward ensuring that he would eventually get her gold repeater by having his name and hers engraved inside it, though she did not intend to part with it in her lifetime. Even one night "without my pretty Watch" was too much. Conway's next engagement in Bath and the gala for her "eightieth" birthday were the next treats in store, while the resumption of correspondence with Mrs. Pennington added a new dimension to life. Letters flowed between them almost by return of post, on every topic of common interest, from their own ailments and the welfare of Conway to the state of the nation. "I fear your poor friend Conway will appear too soon on the stage—but what can a professional man do? he may as well die as starve, and the anxiety attending on the suspension of his powers, is often as fatal as the too early exertion." Mrs. Piozzi agreed that "Conway will sure enough come to the case you assign for him:—work, and die nobly, or starve, and pine away."

Diplomatic relations were resumed with the Strattons, who were "all low about Conway," but Charlotte's name had not appeared in Mrs. Piozzi's diary or her letters for months. She continued to fret about Conway's silence, and soon after her return to Bath she made an unannounced call on Mrs. Pennington, ostensibly to inquire after her health, but in reality to see Mrs. Rudd, perhaps to discuss matters too delicate to be written about.

It seems to have been during his recent convalescence that Conway first tried to approach his father, doubtless with his mother's approval, in an attempt to secure recognition of their relationship. He realised that if Charlotte had been deterred by the lowly status of the acting profession, any other young lady of quality might be equally unwilling to share its nomadic life and fluctuating fortunes. But if his natural father were to acknowledge him, even at this late date, and make some provision for him, those obstacles might be removed. And Mrs. Rudd, however proud she was of her son's celebrity, would concede that it had brought him no prosperity so far, and that his chosen profession would always be precarious. On those grounds alone, she may have agreed to a course that she had denied herself for thirty years.

There is no record of what influence, if any, Mrs. Piozzi exerted over Conway, or indeed what she thought about his intentions, although in principle she would rather see him succeed in his profession than as an appendage to the aristocracy; the price of recognition might be retirement from the stage. Her diaries and surviving letters reveal little about the history of his endeavours, and it was not until after her death that Conway himself left an account of his successive approaches to the Hertford family in a letter to his friend William Jerdan.[1] He recalled that after writing to Lord William to no avail, he tracked him down to an inn at Ringwood in the New Forest, on a date unspecified, where he prevailed on the landlord to place a note in his hands, asking for an audience. "Instead of granting it, however, he referred me in general terms to his family."

Life had moved on a generation since the period of Wraxall's memoirs, and the head of the family was now the former Lord Beauchamp, aged seventy-six, who had long since succeeded his father both as marquess of Hertford and as Lord Chamberlain of England (virtually the head of the Royal Household). Two of the six brothers had died, survived by Lords Henry, Robert, William, and George. Their nephew, Lord Castlereagh, was Leader of the House of Commons,[2] and the family was one of the wealthiest and most influential in the land. They were generous in supporting their many offspring, legitimate or otherwise, in or out of wedlock, and in fact one illegitimate boy, Richard Wallace, the twelve-month-old grandson of the second marquess, would eventually inherit most of his wealth but not his titles. On the other hand, the family would have no difficulty in seeing off any false claimant to membership, and there can be no doubt therefore that our Conway, who was nothing if not honourable, was sure of his ground in pursuing the matter further.

A direct approach was out of the question: convention demanded that someone of suitable rank, known personally to the marquess, should convey his request for an interview. Fortunately, Conway had friends in the dowager duchess of Roxburghe and her second husband, the Honourable John Tollemache, and was a frequent guest of theirs at 32 Portman Square that autumn; they agreed to pass on a letter from Conway to Lord Hertford.

Mrs. Piozzi heard from Conway on 16 November that he would be returning to Bath in less than a fortnight, but he was still not well, having caught cold "changing his Bed & Lodgings at Midnight." Shortly afterward, Miss Willoughby came to tea and said how "she longed to see Conway's *dear* face. Sure Miss Willoughby is Falsehood personified; we all

know she hates him." (She called again two days later to borrow money—
"a likely matter!") The next two weeks passed slowly for Mrs. Piozzi, who
was unwell, and impatient for news from Conway.

Thursday 25 Nov. 1819

What can be the Matter Dear Sir? What can be?—after promising me a Long
Letter & saying return the Envelope &c. What *can* be the Matter? After such a
long Illness one trembles for Fear of a Relapse; or Cough brought on by Cold.
Have you provided a Warm Travelling Dress for this dreadful Weather? I shall not
enjoy a quiet Moment till your Arrival. . . .

Bessy believes you on the Road, and says truly that if *I* could have gone to London
I should have wrapped you up in an Eider Down. One of your last to *me* says how
you wish to get out of Town. God only knows how much & how sincerely *I* wish it.
Write to me,—or come. Attamen ipsevens. My Mind is enfeebled by Sickness and
Starvation, and though I have lasted through the five Months, I feel the five Days
very sharply; & often assure myself that Age & Death will be swifter than your
Post Chaise: for certainly no Man in his sober Mind would venture a *Stage Coach*
such Weather after such Illness. . . .

Do not *you* by any Accident or Omission hurry out of the World at last L'Amie
Octogenaire—I really am unwell, and a Letter would do me *so* much Good. Shall I
have one tomorrow? Did Cooper give you kind Encouragement on Parting? You
will make me love that Man at last, whether I will or no. . . .

Once more Adieu! Shall I ever see You or Your handwriting *again* I wonder! as you
said to the Fellow here when packing up last July. Shall we die in our Beds after all
this d'you think? Was my lost Letter ever found?

Mrs. Pennington had been overwhelmed by Mrs. Piozzi's solicitude in
driving twelve miles just to see how she was, not realising that her visit
was probably a cloak to divert attention from her visit to Mrs. Rudd:

Hot Wells 3rd December 1819

I am anxious, dear friend, to hear that you cease to feel any effect from the cold
caught on your kind flight to Dowry Square. The remembrance is still sweet and
cheering & the effect was rather extraordinary, for it actually banished from my
mind all thoughts of the spilling of blood. . . . Dr. Dickson, the gentleman you
found with me, tho' not professionally, when you so agreeably surprised me, I
believed thought me a little out of my mind. I hear he has spoken of it since to a
Lady of my Acquaintance, & said "he scarcely ever witnessed an expression of
such pure Joy." He might well marvel if he supposed such a rapturous reception
was given to a mere Morning Visitor, but when *you* are in question I never can
command my Feelings. . . .
    In addition to my other 'hills', to use Mr. Kemble's mode of pronunciation, I
have got such a Lumbago that I cannot stir without screaming out. . . .
    Is poor Mr. Conway recovered well enough to appear? The papers speak so

highly of Mr. Macready, that it almost excites a wish in me, who have nearly lost sight of every gratification in that line, to judge for myself. If his Coriolanus delights and surprises after Kemble, it must be excellent, for nature gave *him* a Roman cast in body and mind.

Mrs. Piozzi replied that she had "little thought to bestow on Dramatick Exhibitions; but Mr Mangin, who is a classical scholar, and has leisure to amuse himself with those who provide pastime for the rich and idle, said, when Conway acted Coriolanus here he had never seen the Roman toga worn so gracefully.[3] He has not yet left London. Macready was a fine promising actor when I saw him last, three or four years ago." The same day she sent "a cold Note to poor Worthless Willoughby."

At last Conway returned to Bath, and when they met, the occasion was almost too much for Mrs. Piozzi:

> *Sunday 5 December No church—too sick*—but Conway came, just 22 weeks since we parted—I had feared many times our meeting was put off—but, God be praised we *have* met and dined together, neither dead, tho' often both in danger. I choked with my first glass of wine—very frightfully.

He had taken lodgings at 5 Kingsmead Terrace, to the south of the theatre, a little farther away from Gay Street than his previous lodgings in Princes Street, and was once more a daily visitor at No. 8. Mrs. Piozzi confessed to Mrs. Pennington that "I do not think Conway's all-expressing countenance showed him contented with the looks of his Patroness yesterday, when he dropped in with the other morning callers," and Mrs. Pennington feared that "if I am to lose you just as I have regained you it will quite break my Heart. . . . I am afraid your contention with those rough Billows at Weston has been too much for your Frame—perhaps you are not what you were, tho' still a Wonder, 20 Summers ago." Mrs. Stratton paid her respects at No. 8 and "renewed her just Panegyrics on our Incomparable," hoping that Charlotte would change her mind. Conway called again and "we chatted till his tongue was sore, and my throat."

Bath 10 Dec. 1819

Well now, dearest Mrs Pennington, I have got a complaint I *can* talk of or write about—a sore throat! I fancy it is caused by relaxation,—talking about you to Conway. . . . You are a very dear Creature, but am I wrong in thinking it very ridiculous to proclaim the Distress of Mrs. Piozzi's Peristaltics to Town and Country?

—and how will my Gala get forward if I do nothing but write funny letters to Mrs. Pennington, instead of calling names over to fill up the cards with, or sit and chat with dear Conway concerning past sorrows and future prospects. He says he is come to act Master *Slender:* and thin he is most certainly: but so young-looking, *never.* I hope we shall make a full house to witness his first performance in Coriolanus next Monday. Can't you come over anyhow without serious risque? It would be a pity to miss such an exhibition, and your retentive memory has Kemble's mode of acting it well impress'd. Mine reflects back only one scene, I think, and *he* [Conway] never saw Emperor John in *his* short life.[4]

The Salusburys come next Tuesday sennight, and where shall I get them lodgings? I am all in a *fuss.* . . .

Conway's Acct. of Carlile's Tryal[5] froze me with horror, & the night he supped with his Patroness The Duchess of Roxborough, there was much Conversation that you would like to hear, but that I should *not* like for you to read repeated after hearing Talk only—under the Hands of Dearest Mrs. Pennington's ever obliged

H:L:Piozzi

Did I tell you that Conway has refused *for us,* Engagements in London, Edinburgh & Dublin?—*Proofs in hand*

This was the first time that the duchess's name had appeared in their correspondence, and the absence of preamble suggests that Mrs. Piozzi had already revealed Conway's aristocratic connections to Mrs. Pennington, who was now more eager than ever to meet him. Before he left London, Conway had probably received, through the duchess, Lord Hertford's reply to his appeal for recognition, which was that "the Marquess acknowledged that he had always *understood* me to belong to his family, but added that unless Lord William became *himself* my advocate he did not feel called upon to render me assistance."[6] This suggests that the story of his younger brother's dalliance was known to the rest of the family, and while Conway would now have to consider how to bring his father to book, the marquess's acknowledgment might stand him in good stead with Charlotte, who was the real reason for his preferring Bath to London, Edinburgh, or Dublin.

Mrs. Piozzi was about to enter her second year as his (theatrical) patroness, and this time she was ready to do battle with any opposition and to ensure that his engagement was profitable. She set the scene with a party in his honour.

> *Sunday 12 December 1819* Dreadful Weather, but I had our Dinner Party. OUR ANNIVERSARY as I call it. Conway, Gifford, Strattons, Burneys & 15 more in the Evening. Sharpe bought her Guitar & sung.

The engagement opened with *Coriolanus* ("ever & ever more incomparable Conway"), and he, "kind Angel," called at Gay Street afterward, "but I was gone to my Room and never saw him." The theatre was now in full swing; Conway was a daily visitor, seeking Mrs. Piozzi's advice on the roles he was to play and discussing the performances afterward. Droppers-in innumerable sang his praises, and Miss Willoughby came to "kowtow." Within a few weeks, Mrs. Piozzi would celebrate her "eightieth" birthday, and preparations for the gala began to compete with her theatrical interests. "My Ball and Supper begin to plague me," she told Mrs. Pennington, "but somehow I hope that they may be of use to *him* whose Welfare is really near the Heart of yours faithfully."

Hot Wells Sunday 12 Decemr. 1819

What a delicious Letter you have sent me Dearest Friend!—so full of kindness and good Humour! I am glad I know what *is* wrong with you—of the "Peristaltics" I hear a good deal at Home, & the Case is bad enough, & little pleasure, or propriety as you very justly say in talking of . . . even to one's Physician.—But the Douce take you for tantalizing me with the information that your Conway plays Coriolanus *tomorrow* night, for my dear tyrant of a husband will not let me stir this weather. . . . However I trust he may again appear in the character when we come over to your Gala. . . . I recalled that "Emperor John" impressed me strongly in the chiding scene—but then what a Volumnia [Siddons] he had to give it effect.

Mrs. Piozzi offered another date.

Bath Fryday night 17 Dec, 1819

On Wednesday Conway acts Iachimo to Warde's Posthumus. They neither of 'em every performed the characters, and it will be a Pleasure. Worthy Mrs. Pennington—how will you manage? Better make Business subservient to Enjoyment, and *come*. The Coriolanus electrified us all and my amiable Friend gets Admirers and Invitations every day . . . who will attend when Benefit time comes on, and will, I hope, compensate him in some Measure for his past Sufferings, and reward the partiality he has shewn to Bath, in preferring our boards to those of Edinburgh, London or Dublin. . . .

I suppose the Salusburys will just come time enough for my Foolery, which plagues me to death already.

Mrs. Pennington accepted eagerly, though she would rather see Conway as Posthumus than as the "Rascal" Iachimo, and asked to be remembered to Mrs. Stratton, "who always cordially wished to see us as, thank God, we are, once more firmly united." In the event, however, Mrs. Pennington caught a cold and could not make the journey.

I do not regret not seeing our friend (for he is yours, and must be mine) in Iachimo. One hates Iachimo and Iago so much that the better they are played, the worse one likes them. Pierre is a good, bold, open-faced villain, and I have not the same objection to him, but I wish to see Conway in the tender or the grand. Has he never performed Hamlet? . . . I feel your friend and I shall not meet as strangers; the connecting bond is so pure and disinterested between us, it must produce the effect of mutual esteem; but for Heaven's sake do not let him see all the nonsense I venture to submit to your indulgent and impartial eye.

What said the people at Covent Garden for your Pearl of price? Miss O'Neill is married, or to be immediately.[7] . . . what does Mr. Conway say of the lady in her own character?

Mrs. Piozzi commented that "Mrs. Stratton bore true Witness to your Impatience of our Separation; and indeed when the fine Statue we disagreed about has been pulled down a dozen years!!! Of Miss O'Neill the *Pearl* of her Profession I know Nothing but that she is a Roman Catholic. Mr. Warde censured her Conduct towards the Managers very loudly— almost bitterly—at a Dinner Party [for Conway] two days ago—I heard him. But I am no Judge whether or no she deserves such Disapprobation."

The next day was Christmas Eve, which Mrs. Piozzi spent with Conway, to dinner and afterward to *Messiah,* and Christmas Day was, of course, for "Church and unfeigned Thanksgiving for such Mercies to me and to my Friend." Mrs. Pennington looked forward eagerly to her friend's first visit to Dowry Square in over sixteen years, and to meeting Conway for the first time:

Hot Wells Xmas Day 1819

May nothing interfere with the Promised Pleasure!—Next Week will have a beautiful, early Moon,—I trust the *Friends* will avail themselves of it, & not quit with daylight. Meanwhile how do you think Miss Wren & your P.S.P. are amusing themselves?—why truly Reading over Volumes of your dear Letters, which I *can* revert to now, and oh! how proud I feel of the Praises and Kindness they express, feeling, as I do, that the beloved Writer is still the same. Mrs. Stratton is a Kind-Hearted lady, but indeed dearest Mrs. Piozzi we never had any disagreement on the Subject of that ever-Esteemed Statue you allude too, nor on any other Subject, only some misunderstanding. . . .

If you wish to come straight [to Dowry Square], without going first up to Clifton, you should direct your Driver to turn off at the Bridge, and bring you by the Side of the new Docks;[8] it will give you some pretty Scenery, and save you going through all that rough, & ugly City; it is the direct Road to the Hot Wells.

You were right to correct my phrase respecting the Pearl of the *Theatre.* I simply meant an allusion to the very high Price that Lady sets on the exertion of her Talents.

It was the pantomime season, and Kean had been released from Drury Lane for a two-week engagement—a treat for Bath, but not without its problems for the management. Kean and Conway had never appeared on the same stage before, and were unlikely to. Apart from their differing styles, the difference in height between them would have turned tragedy into farce. Mrs. Piozzi did not attend the opening night when Kean appeared in *Richard III*, as she needed to make an early start for Clifton the following morning, and that evening Conway was free while Kean played Sir Giles Overreach in *A New Way to Pay Old Debts*. Conway arrived at No. 8 for breakfast, and in heavy snow drove with Mrs. Piozzi to Clifton, up that treacherous hill to see his mother, for a long talk about Charlotte and Conway's next appeal to the Hertfords; and back down the hill for a long-awaited introduction to the Penningtons.

The next day Mrs. Piozzi received "a sweet letter from Conway which I tied up with other favourites" and sent him a note in reply, which in 1843 was raised to the dignity of "Love Letter III."

Wednesday 29 Dec. 1819

Accept a real Christmas pye—it will be such a nice thing for you when, coming late home, there is no time for a better supper; but Bessy begs you will not try to eat the *Crust;* it will keep for weeks, this weather.

The Fleece should be a Golden one, had I the magic Powers of Medea; but I think I was Baby enough to be ashamed last Night of owning I had not Three Pounds in the House except your money, laid by for my Benefit Ticket, which shall be replaced before that day comes—because the Manager's Box resembles Prospero's Bough, in Virgil, where *Uno avulco non deficit alter.*

Farewell! our Happy Days are marked most Classically in white you see. What a delightful one was yesterday for your really *obliged* as faithful H:L:P.

Send back the waistcoats if they don't suit; and we will change them for unmade up stuff. No letters returned from No. 13.

The Penningtons had been delighted to receive their callers:

Hot Wells, Wednesday [29 December 1819]

How are the dear snow-covered travellers? . . . It was an hour of true intellectual enjoyment, and *real* happiness. Of your friend, and *mine,* since so kindly permitted to use the, to me, always *sacred* distinction, I can only say he appears worthy of all the esteem and regard he has been so fortunate to obtain in your opinion. If that fine ingenuous countenance, conciliating voice, and gentle, elegant demeanour deceive me, I will never trust those tokens again. There is a certain *something* in his appearance that interests me more strongly in his happiness than I ever felt on so short an acquaintance; and I long for an opportunity of discussing with you, dear friend, those points that are most immediately connected with this object.

So sensitive as he appears & so attractive as he is, *Love,* I conclude, will be the polar star of his destiny & he will hasten, or be hastened, by the aid of well-meaning friends into the haven of matrimony; but let him beware & keep in mind *that* is a result in all probability to be tried but once, and if it fails, what a bankrupt in happiness it would leave. Oh let him not hastily take this important step, but rather wait until the exercise of his own fine talents, *unshackled* has raised him an independence of fame & fortune that may give him a *right* to challenge what at present might be yielded as a favour.

Mrs. Pennington hoped to visit Bath and go to the theatre before the Gala, and if Mrs. Piozzi were unable to accommodate her, perhaps Bessy could find a "roost."

Sent Thursday
Morn:—your Letter recd.
late on Wensday Night

My dear Mrs. Pennington

is a kind & generous Friend, but her *Anxiety* was superfluous. We got Home without an Atom of anything resembling Alarm, or *Cause* for it; and found the Way short—I speak for myself—it was shorten'd by talking of You. Conway does certainly merit all our Care, and all our Admiration; may he be as happy and deserving! But you who are seldom wrong are right in all your Surmises.

The *Roost* is the Difficulty. I never could accommodate even *Salusbury* when he was a single Man: & 'tis now a Pleasure to me that I could *not,* because he will feel that it is not Angelo who excludes him—tho' he and his Mother occupy the only Closet resembling a Room which my House exhibits. Some Hope, however, is held out by Bessy of a Bed at a private House over the Way, when anything is done worth your Attention and this fine Mr. Kean is out of Sight.

A Cold has broken out round our Friend's Mouth, he writes me Word—so that he will *mimp* in tomorrow's—meaning today's Chevalier de Morange.[9] You would have thought him touch'd by Ovid's Wand had you seen him in *that* Character after the Romeo—nothing else intervening, but he did not wish you should.

How good Mr. Pennington was to us! and all Your friends: and how far from cold it was going home with that Eider Down Bag that covered us so. I wonder where such Things are to be had!
. . . the Salusburys will not come this fortnight, the *Ladies* God knows when . . .

In the morning Mrs. Piozzi invited Mrs. Stratton and Conway to Gay Street, recording in her diary that "they had their own Talk quite out in my Room—uninterrupted," and Conway was presumably encouraged to re-open his suit with Charlotte.

That evening Mrs. Piozzi saw Kean's Hamlet and Conway's Morange. Conway's contribution to Kean's engagement was to take the lead in the supporting items on the bill, leaving Warde to play second leads to Kean.

When it came to *Othello* the following night, New Year's Eve, Warde declared that Iago was quite out of his line and refused to go on. And as Kean and Conway were agreed that a six-foot Iago to a five-foot Othello would not do, either, the inferior Rowbotham was pressed into service, allowing Conway to see the old year out at 8 Gay Street, "with Dinner & Songs & Refreshments: and everything went off well—Felloweses, Pinelles, Williams, Wickens, Conway, Gifford, Hudson, & many more to the evening party."

Mrs. Pennington rounded off the year with a word of caution to both her oldest and her newest friend: to the first, an undisguised hint to remember her age, and to the second, a repeated warning not to be hasty in choosing a wife.

Friday the last of 1819

Remember me kindly to dear Conway, towards whom I feel disposed to indulge more kindness than I ever thought to entertain again on so slight an acquaintance. I hope *personal* knowledge has not injured the impression your partial friendship sought to create on my part. On his, the materials, all in prime keeping, are too excellent and admirable to admit any doubt on the subject. But we are, alas! something fallen into "the sear and yellow leaf", and cannot cope with summer blossoms. If, however not downright *scarecrows* to the young, "the beautiful and brave," we may at least be useful land-marks and monitors, if they will permit us.

Pray tell him from me, that in the experience of more years than I think it necessary at this moment to enumerate [she was 67], I never knew a man or woman completely ruined until they were married. Observe, I do not say nor *always* then, and I heartily wish him the best luck in the world in that fearful and doubtful lottery. But I entreat him, by the friendship you have united us in, that he will not be hasty in chusing his ticket, and that he will endeavour, as coolly and dispassionately as possible, to examine the *number* before he makes his election. . . .

I have a notion the Salusburys will not look with a kind eye on dear Conway, little Angelo, or even your happy, restored, and faithful friend—therefore I want to luxuriate with you a little before their arrival. "The Ladies" I know will not trouble their pretty heads about any of us.

12
The Gala

MRS. Piozzi's first letter of the new year to Mrs. Pennington began

Bath 2d. Jan: 1820

No proof more perfect can be given or received, dear Mrs. Pennington, of our hearts being well united once again, than your sudden, as surprising, expression of favour in our common friend's *happiness*. I have studied nothing else since I knew him: yet I must confess his power of raising such *real interest* is a singular one, and your oraculous determination concerning what passes in the minds of the absent Thrales and Salusburys is no less absorbing.

Mrs. Pennington could not forget that their friendship had been broken once before, almost irreparably, by a word out of place between her and Gabriel Piozzi, and had recognised when she was at Weston-super-Mare that the price of reconciliation would be to share Mrs. Piozzi's passion for her new favourite. Now that she had met him, she had fallen for his charms herself. Sir James Fellowes was less susceptible, but accepted Mrs. Piozzi's devotion to the actor with good-humoured tolerance:

> I passed yesterday at Mrs. Lutwyche's, and missed the Comus my heart was set upon, but Sir James Fellowes dropt in while I was writing this letter, and said it was *inimitable*. Ay, replied I, the Scholar's correctness, levigated by the wit's elegant hilarity. The answer was that Conway should have a patent for acting, and I should have one for praising him.

"Mr Kean and his fine sword" were seen at No. 8 a day or two later, when he would have heard at first hand Mrs. Piozzi's enthusiasm for Conway, which was the gossip of the Green Room and of the Pump Room. There can be little doubt that Kean was the source of the garbled story that appeared in James Winston's diary shortly after his return to Drury Lane, to the effect that Conway's real name was "Rugg" and that he was about to marry Mrs. Piozzi, who was "upwards of eighty and whose income exceeded £7000 a year." In fact, Conway was still hoping to marry Charlotte, and had just called on Mrs. Piozzi for a "confidential chat; sorrowful."

Evidently his talk with Mrs. Stratton had cut no ice, and indeed Charlotte then seemed to raise a new objection: Conway's father may have been a nobleman, but his mother was a mere boardinghouse keeper.

After he had left, Mrs. Piozzi wrote him a letter which she later regretted, and immediately penned another—"two different letters of *bear* and *forbear*," as she called them in her diary. The first of these has not been located, but the second is in the Beinecke Library at Yale.[1] It reads:

5 Jan. 1820

I could not sleep last Night for Hatred of my last Letter, & hatred of myself for writing it. How could I say—*Bear it:* when my whole heart revolts against the Idea of your *bearing any* Pain, mental or bodily. Oh! if I had not engaged in this expensive Gala, you should have defied them all—but 'tis too late now, and the Gala was meant to mend the Benefit, which will be a *splendid Triumph*—I am sure it will; as well as a Solid Profit of 250£; or 300£—Madness only would give it up;— & Mrs. Rudd will be of my Mind. Foolish H:L:P! here have I been trying by all Arts, all Expences to increase her Consequence—that She might be of use to *You* and now You are suffering for *her;* for H:L:P.—what a world it is!

I was at a Party last night [at the Mangins]—says a Lady to me Suddenly. Is Mrs. Stratton going to marry her Daughter to Mr. Conway? *Why?* why do you ask? replied I. Because she introduced all her Friends to him the other evening;—So did *I*, was my answer; and I'm sure I have no Daughter to give him: Oh yes *one* I have; and she is exactly 20 Years older than himself.—A Laugh ended the Conversation.

Your Health and your Heart, your Soul your Purse, incessant subjects of my Thought, Objects of my Care; are however going on well; and Johnson said he could not endure Distresses of Sentiment in a hard Winter when so many poor Creatures were starving. I will therefore try to suppress my Fears lest these Fools should make you withdraw a Particle of that Regard for *me* which I am so Solicitous to obtain, so earnest to deserve;—& without which, Life would now be a complete Blank to me.

People however naturally *do* love those they are plagued about; and if God lends me Life for a Year or Two;—*Every Compensation Possible* shall be made for what you now suffer on Account of your poor H:L:P.

I am jealous of Mrs. Rudd's good Will too; & she will feel disagreeable Feelings toward anything or anybody that causes You discomfort.—How did you get to her? How did you get home?

Conway had evidently been to consult his mother, and returned in time for the theatre that night. Mrs. Piozzi "went to the play—Incomparable Conway. He play'd Fitzjames in The Lady of the Lake," which followed Kean's Orestes in *The Distress'd Mother*. The next day she heard from Dowry Square:

Hot Wells Wedy. 5th Jan. 1820

Friday, Dearest Friend, I hope to be with you,—Saturday there is usually something good at the Theatre and the Evening of my arrival I shall be glad to have *snug,* for I am still but a poor Creature & should hardly be up to the enjoyment even of our Friend's exerted Talents after a cold ride to Bath. Sorely against my Will I was at a party at a Clifton Ball last night, it was for our Friend Mr. Roberts, dear Pennington's successor, & an act of Duty;—but chilled with the Cold & half frighted to death by the slipping and sliding of the horses on that odious hill. I am completely *done up* today, but intend to rally by Friday.—Leave the roost to Bessy—at any rate York House and the Castle and Elephant are never-failing resources. . . .

Conway's Comus must have been perfection, and you were unlucky not to see it. His classic taste, his fine proportions and youthful graces make him the very character—in appearance only, however, thank God! Remember me kindly to him—I really do feel a solicitude for his happiness that I can in no way account for, but that it seems connected with yours, for I find myself ever more entirely and truly, dearest friend, your affectionately devoted P S Pennington."

She arrived in time for the last night of Kean's engagement, in which, according to the *Bath Journal,* he had displayed "skill and genius we never saw equalled, and though by some he may be considered too small to give full effect in all parts, yet he is formed with much neatness, and possesses the air and elegance of a gentleman to a greater degree than any actor we know of (Mr. Conway not excepted)." Kean's life of debauchery *offstage* would have appalled Conway's admirers.

Mrs. Pennington remained in Bath for a week, seeing Conway onstage and off, meeting the Strattons on several occasions, and sizing up Charlotte. At Conway's request, Mrs. Piozzi had a private talk with the young lady, and thought there was still hope, but Mrs. Pennington was less sanguine, as she reported after Conway escorted her back to Clifton.

Hot Wells Monday 17th Jany. 1820

We had as pleasant a ride as it was possible to have on a road that carried me 12 miles from *you.* So interesting was our Conversation that we felt no cold, and were surprised when we reached the end of our little journey. You may easily guess our subjects;—but I am sorry to say that in the discussion of certain points, I cannot find reason to think our dear and amiable Friend so near the goal as your ardent and benevolent spirit is disposed to believe.

In fact, she thought the goal not worth striving after. The fair lady was, in her opinion, too timid and diffident, creating obstacles that a bolder spirit would ignore.

Such only, in my opinion, can deserve the man who gains, every hour that I see more of him, such an increasing interest in my regard, that my anxiety for his happiness is become painful. My Husband is highly taken with his fine manners and intelligent conversation. He says he has seen no such man since the prime days of his friend, Governor Tryon,[2] who was reckoned the handsomest man and finest gentleman of his time. Oh! no Lady need fear she can lose consequence by the side of such a man, who will always cast a Lustre about whatever profession he may follow. . . .

I am on very ill terms with myself respecting the silly speech I made about your pretty *Silver Tea Pot*. You have shown me you cannot *leave* it to me, and I *will not* deprive you of the use of it. That would be foolish indeed; for *I* want no Remembrancer of you, and *have many;* besides I do verily believe I am not likely ever to receive it on the terms I *asked* it. Sincerely and fervently do I pray and believe you have many more years before you, than I have any right, from constitution and the present state of my feelings, to reckon upon. And it would be worse than absurd to rob you of an article of daily use, to throw it into the hands of other people. All I *can* consent to therefore is that you continue to use it, dear Friend. Long may you do so, and should the most fatal Deprivation I can now ever feel (but one), desire Betsey to deposit *that* with dear Conway's watch, and I will drink my tea from it for the rest of my life, and mingle tears with the fragrant libation.

Mrs. Piozzi overlooked her friend's indiscretion over the teapot but chided her for sending Conway home "ready to cry." Mrs. Pennington was unrepentant.

I am sorry I sent him back "melancholy", she wrote on 21 January,— "gentlemanly" he must always be. My pathetic Powers were only exerted to induce him "to stand prepared for Endurance of an Evil, 'tis but too possible may be hanging over him" & which, I fear from his sanguine Temper & want of due Preparation will fall most heavily upon him. *Entre nous,* I cannot persuade myself the girl has the spirit or stamina to set her above, and carry through those disadvantages which others (called the world) would see and condemn in such a connexion. If she insists on his giving up his profession, he is shorn of half his beams; more especially as her fortune will not supply that independent respectability which would be some compensation for the loss of the *éclat* he cannot fail of deriving from the exertion of his talents. If she cannot make up her mind to take him *as he is,* I verily think she does not deserve him. . . .

It was entering deeply into this question that left so serious an impression on our Friend's mind. I am not *very* sorry it did so, as the Effect may be salutary. . . . He has the power of exciting an Interest I have not often felt for any one & as I believe him most deserving of Happiness & most unhappily susceptible of misery, my Solicitude for him in this case has more apprehension than Hope.

Sir John and Lady Salusbury had arrived in Bath for the birthday celebrations, which were now less than a week away, and another round of entertaining began. Conway had a busy week on stage, and Mrs. Piozzi was able to catch him for only a moment's confidential chat at a party.

He must be diligent today (she told Mrs. Pennington), for he is to act Mark Antony tomorrow, and you will not see him, which will mortify us both, but he had no Notice until this Morning. He dined here Yesterday & I think made fresh Conquests. The dear Strattons & a genteel Mr. Fuller from Egypt were of our Evening Party & Lady Salusbury seemed amused, tho' Sharpe did not bring her Guitar. Indeed everybody seemed earnest in Talk & the Time passed without making more Entertainment necessary. . . . Mr. Burrell and Dorset Fellowes[3] proposed Mr. Conway at some quality Club—I forgot the Name of it—and his Admission was carried by Acclamation.

As to the supper ball, Mrs. Piozzi was "sick of the Foolery before it begins." There were "foreign visitants & domestic too, near innumerable. Dinner Miss Willoughby. Evening Play. Incomparable Conway! Mark Antony the character, Cassius Mr. Yates good." The fête demanded her full attentions, dealing with a flood of letters, receiving many callers, and keeping the Salusburys amused. Her last, brief note to Mrs. Pennington before the event confirmed their prediction that Sir John would not share their admiration of Conway.

Monday [24 January]

My Dearest Mrs. Pennington

must stay over Saturday: Our Chevalier comes out in a new Character[4] & seems to like it. His Mark Antony transcended all I ever saw of scenic Perfection, *dramatic* rather—The tender Pathos with which he said "Oh pardon me thou bleeding Piece of Earth" was beyond all Praise; and *Lady* Salusbury also liked it—Sir John seems to consider Conway as much inferior to Warde in Beauty, Voice and Action: and the Chevalier's bright Eyes, seeing how Opinion goes, drop when he enters the Room. They have dined but once together indeed, but both can see into a Millstone as far as most Men. We meet at Bourdois's and Burney's tomorrow, and he acts Morange on Wednesday. He will be introduced to Masonic Honours on Thursday & *then* give You whom he justly adores, the Meeting at my Concert. If he does not dance with the proper Partner, it will vex you & me both; but he *will*.

Meanwhile here's a Flood to fright one; he and all the People at the Bottom of our Town are in real Danger. He especially, whose late Illness has left Pains in the Legs &c. I have not seen him since he played in Julius Caesar, and want some Chat with him cruelly.

A last-minute letter from Mrs. Pennington announced that she would have to attend the party on her own.

Every Tribute to the dear Chevalier delights me—you know I never give my Heart by *halves*. You have the *largest part* of it between ye.—May he be, in *all* things, as fortunate as you & I wish him. He need not desire more.—I am perfectly *up* to the preference given to Warde's *Talents* and *Beauty*. I *foretold* it. He, *our favourite* is so *very Superior* that he is more likely to excite Envy, than Admiration, from his own sex. In this instance it is indeed "Hyperion to a Satyr"! God bless him & shape his fortunes to his deserts—all will then be well.

If I stay over Saturday—(which must depend on the state of dear Pennington's health)—I *must* stay over Sunday; for the only public conveyance I ever trust myself in does not go on that day, & you shall not send me again in such a magnificent style to set all the neighbours staring. . . .

I hate all *new* characters & *new* plays; but too plainly perceive it will never be my good luck to see our favourite in any that are worthy of him. My heart was in the theatre all Saturday evening. "Mark Antony" would have been such a treat indeed! I trust he will not have that odious "Ethiope" for his benefit—I positively will not see him in it. . . .

Take care, dear friend, this letter does not lie about, or pass into any one's hands but yours, & the dear Chevalier, for reasons good and cogent, & believe me ever, affectionately as I am,

Your truly devoted
P S Pennington

It was "Eveng. at home. Early go to bed" for Mrs. Piozzi on 26 January, and her birthday next day began with "Plagues all Morning for Cards & Refusals and Requests and Visitants"—and the evening "Foolery: Well conducted tho', and very much admired."

The *Gazette* reported (on a black-bordered page, in mourning for George III, who died two days after the fête) that Mrs. Piozzi had given tickets to over six hundred guests. They arrived at the Kingston Assembly Rooms between 9:00 and 10:00 P.M. for the concert, which was "most scientifically conducted by Miss Sharpe, in the vocal, and Mr. Loder in the instrumental department. . . . At 12 the Supper Rooms were thrown open, and exhibited a scene which, if not calculated to feast the reason . . . was substantial as well as elegant, and displayed not only the liberality of the mistress of the feast, but the skill of the provider, Mr. Tully. . . . The dancing commenced at two, when Mrs. Piozzi led off with Sir J. Salusbury, and proved to the company that infirmity was yet far distant. Quadrilles and country dances were kept up with spirit till 5 o'clock, when the company separated with great good-humour, and hastened to their respective homes to dream of scenes and impressions that will not quickly vanish from the memories of the lovers of gaiety, as well as the admirers of science and of literary recollections."

13

"Une petite Traitresse"

THE least sociable person present at the ball must have been the man who was meant to be its principal beneficiary. He was unwell and miserable, and not at all in the party spirit. He was ignored by Charlotte, who had already told him that his suit was hopeless, and he had not called on Mrs. Piozzi for several days for fear that the news might spoil her great occasion. In fact, she narrowly avoided hearing about Charlotte's rejection from Mrs. Stratton, who had tried to buttonhole her during the course of the evening.

Mrs. Piozzi was up and at breakfast five hours after the party ended, and looking forward to a second performance that evening for the servants—while Conway took to his bed and refused to see callers. Mrs. Piozzi sent him a note ("Love Letter IV"):

29 Jan. 1820

Half-dead Bessy, more concerned at what I feel for *you* than what she feels for herself, brings this Note. Mrs. Pennington left me in real Affliction; and if she found no Billet at the Elephant and Castle directed to her from Kings Mead, will carry home a half-broken Heart. Let my Maid see you, for Mercy's Sake.

Lord Ma'am said she, why if Mr. Conway was at Birmingham *you would send me;* and now he is Three Streets off, GO I WILL—if I die upon the Road, rather than see you swallowing down Agony, and saying nothing but *how well you are* to everybody, when I know you are wretched beyond telling.

On the outside she had written, "Instead of Bessy, James goes.—please let him see you and speak to you." If James did not gain admission, Mrs. Pennington did, at the second attempt, and sent her report to Mrs. Piozzi after returning to Clifton.

Hot Wells Sunday
30th Jany. 1820

. . . As the old lady used to say at Commerce, "always per*se*vere" when I feel I am right; finding no answer to my "affectionate Enquiries", you dearest Friend will not be surprised to hear I determined to call again. Our Chevalier was come down into his little Parlour; I was admitted & found the sweet Fellow like the "mobled" Hecuba—hooded up in Handkerchiefs and Bandages without end, but relieved and better. He assured me that the loss of Blood, which was profuse, had allayed the Fever raging in his Veins, his *Mind* had become more composed—& that he had reflected on all the sage Counsel we had dosed him with, & would *try* to be worthy of our Friendship, happen what may. I had only a few minutes to stay with him & could not say half I wished; besides he was in momentary expectation of Mr. Hicks,[1] & I did not wish to be *catched* Tête a Tête, even at sixty odd, not willing, at any rate, to bring such a Reflection on his Taste.

He was more than satisfied with your reasons for *not* accompanying me, & most grateful for all your kind attentions. I have no doubt that had you done so it would by some means have reached Sir J—

It was a great satisfaction to me to see him & to ascertain his state before my return,—and it is very fortunate for him that the theatres will now be closed in consequence of our venerable Monarch's death. . . . When dear Conway gets well enough to move without the hazard of taking cold, the wisest thing he *could* do would be to take advantage of this Interregnum, and the benefit of Clifton air for a few days.

My ride home was not as pleasant, indeed a striking contrast to my last return, but I had a genteel man & woman in the carriage & got safe.

I send no compliments because you will not, of course, communicate the contents of this foolish letter—which says I am yours, & dear Conway's faithful & devoted P.S.P.

Mrs. Piozzi thanked her friend for her solicitude:

Sunday 30 Jan: 1820

My dearest Mrs. Pennington's sweet Silver Tongue has done our Noble-blooded, noble-minded Friend more *good* than all my *written* Wisdom. He promises me now explicitly (& Conway will keep his word) that he will in all Things take your Advice. Kind, charming Lady! is his Expression, she has bound me to her with Ribs of Steel. He is however bad in health still, & the King's Death will throw him out of Employment when he recovers. Well! we must get him a glorious Benefit when the Time comes. . . .

Take Care of my restored Friend Mrs. Pennington,—for *my* Sake, and his,—who I shall Leave a Legacy to you when Sudden—I hope not quite unprepared-for Death Seizes Your H: L: P.

Bessy's increasing Illness grieves me—Doctor Gibbes tries to save her from Consumption. . . . She is now cover'd with Blisters; after which come Leeches and James's Powder: with orders to eat nothing at all, but Milk.

Two days later, returning from an evening at the Dorset Felloweses', Mrs. Piozzi found a pitiful letter from Conway and sat down at midnight to reply. (It was reproduced as "Love Letter V," but the original has not come to light.)

Midnight of 2d. Early Morning of 3 Feb.
I would not hurry for the World. Take your time, and do it your way; or rather suffer Nature to do it—that has done so much for you; more, I *do* think, than for any Mortal Man. See what a scar the Surgeon, however skilful, would have made on that beautiful neck, while Nature's preparation, thro' previous Agony made suppurating ease come on unfelt, and the Wound heals almost without a Cicatrix— does it not? So will it be with the Mind—my own hasty Folly—and my "Violent Love outran the Pauser Reason". Whilst I am advising my beloved patient, how- ever, to *turn* the torrent of his Fancy toward the past occurrences of human Life, the dear pathetic letter now in my bosom forced me on the same method this afternoon, when my heart really sunk at the thought of such coarse conduct—la Grossièreté de la conduit de Mademoiselle par égard à votre famille (supérieure a la sienne de deux côtés)[2]—je sçais ce que je dis; me fait frémer. Nor could I conceive how you could wish for a *Remembrance*—they did well to deny it—no honour could result to them from recollection of such behaviour. We shall meet at Mrs. Eckersall's this evening, for 'tis now two o'clock, and I solemnly promise to command—as you bid me—both tongue and eye. Who I wonder was that Tall Man I met at my last Party! his Aspect shocked and haunted me like a Spectre—so apparently Majestic in Misfortune. The Master of the House was pointing *me* out to him—as if to win his Attention, but no Look, no Smile ensued. He was not *like* you except his lofty Carriage—yet I kept *on* thinking—so will my Conway stand when I next see him. It was an odd feel; and your Distress presented itself so forcibly to my Imagination at the Moment, that my Mind instinctively understood *all was indeed over.*

That nothing should strike my fancy at the Dorset Fellowes, I played Loo, and lost my money. He called on you, he says, and Mrs. Eckersall made kind Enquiries— very *kind*. Her own son has been to Kings Mead Terrace too. Everyone loves you—Bessy cries, but begs me not to lose *my* Life between my Scorn of your Tormentors, and Tenderness for your Health. I was unwell *today*—meaning Tues- day—and poor Fellie[3] was too sick to make one even of their own Family Party.

Morning Thursday 3d. Feb. I have had some Sleep; and am now on my Knees giving God Thanks for the Power he has lent to you to resolve against Sinful Dissipation. Oh spare the Soul which He thus deigns to preserve; Oh keep that Person pure, which his good Spirit will one day inhabit—throwing Radiance round. Accept my best Acknowledgement for having promised me so sweetly that you would try to rise superior to all low Desires.

Nor doubt those pious Wishes to obtain
Since but to *wish* more Virtue is to gain.

We see Pleasure often represented as a beautiful Lake covered with Flowers—but the Gratification of mere Appetite, amongst coarse Females, is a Pitfall covered with Weeds. Such grovelling Dispositions are well wondered at by Rousseau, who says, "Ils sont très contents ces Messieurs la quand ils peuvent cueillir d'une Bouche affamié les tendres Baisers de l'Amour". Shun all such mad Companions, dearest Conway. They are *Erect* in Stature, prone in Appetite; Patrons of Pleasure, posting into Pain. Keep your fine Intellects clear, and use them rightly; Improve the talents committed to your trust; and love your anxious trembling, tender parent; your *more* than Mother, as you kindly call your affectionate H:L:P.

Later that morning, in reply to an impatient letter from Dowry Square, Mrs. Piozzi reminded her friend that

> You have seen our Chevalier since I did; he keeps very close, and Bessy, whom I sent to comfort him in his Illness, brings me no good Accounts. She is bad enough herself, poor Girl, but pities him; I wish they were both at Clifton under your Care. Salusbury looks so *stern* when Dr. Gibbes comes to see her, I feel indignant—but Things will not go your way or mine—or dear Conway's.
>
> Miss Williams, unhappy as she is herself, still thinks of me & of those I love. She says Mr. Hicks commands Miss Wroughton, who hates Conway; wishing perhaps that no one should be handsome out of Katherine Place.—This Recess, shocking as the Cause may be, is fortunate for our Chevalier; and I hope he will shine out and dazzle all Beholders at his Benefit. Don't you remember Siddons saying she never acted so well as once when her heart was heavy concerning the loss of a Child?

That evening there was "Music and Flattery and the Camden house People at Eckershall's in the Evening. I came home early and wrote all night—shocked and robbed of Sleep by Wonder and Indignation at the astonishing Conduct of the Strattons." That letter has not been located, but it appeared as "Letter VI" of the so-called love letters.

Thursday Night 3rd Feb: 1820

I came away as early as I could ('tis but 11 o'clock), so I will go to bed that Bessy may believe me asleep, and try to rest herself, poor Thing. Now, however, I rise to say how the Evening at Ecksall's passed off.

Mrs. Stratton and her eldest Granddaughter came early so I returned their Salutation much as usual—only refusing hands I could not touch—and talked with Mr. Fuller about ancient Thebes—its hundred Gates &c. The young Lady's airy Manner—such as you describe rightly—contrasting with your own cruel Situation—quite shocked me. No crying, no cast down Looks, no Whimpering, as last Year—changeful as the Weather or Wind, she seems at perfect Ease. Mrs. Stratton *not* so. Waddling up to me in the course of the Night said she wanted to talk to me. Impossible was the Reply. My Life is spent in such a Crowd of late—but on a particular Subject, Mrs. Piozzi—Lord, Ma'am, who can talk on particular Subjects in an Assembly Room—and the King ill besides. So there it ended and for *me* there it *shall* end. You and your Favourite have changed Characters.

'Tis not a Year and a Quarter[4] since dear Conway, accepting my Portrait sent to Birmingham, said to the Bringer: Oh, if your Lady but retains *her* Friendship; oh! if I can but keep *her* Patronage, I care not for the Rest. And now, when that Friendship follows you through Sickness and Sorrow; now that her Patronage is daily rising in Importance, upon a Lock of Hair given by *one petite Traitresse* hangs all the Happiness of my once high-spirited and high-blooded Friend! Let it not so be. Exalt thy love-dejected heart,[5] and rise superior to such narrow Minds. Do not, however, fancy that she will be punished in the way you mentioned. No, no, she will wither on the thorny Stem, dropping the faded and ungathered Leaves:—a China Rose of no good Scent or Flavour, false in apparent Sweetness, deceitful when depended on—unlike the Flower produced in colder Climates, which is sought for in old Age, preserved even after Death, a lasting and an elegant Perfume, a Medicine too for those whose shattered Nerves require *astringent Remedies*. And now, dear Sir, let me request of you to love yourself—and to reflect on the Necessity of not dwelling on any particular Subject too long or too intensely. It is really very dangerous to the Health of Body and Soul. Besides that, our Time here is but short: a mere Preface to the great Book of Eternity;—and 'tis scarce worthy of a reasonable Being not to keep the End of human Existence so far in View, that we may tend to it either directly or obliquely. This is Preaching—but remember how the sermon is written, at three, four, and five o'clock by an octogenary Pen, a Heart (as Mrs. Lee says) twenty-six years old; and as H:L:P. feels it to be, all your own. Suffer your dear noble Self to be in some Measure benefited by the Talents that are left her; your Health to be restored by soothing Consolation *while I remain here,* and am able to bestow them. All is not lost yet. You have a Friend, and that Friend is Piozzi.

I must go to Bed. That Booby James waked my poor, perhaps unrefreshed Correspondent yesterday. I was extremely sorry, and now beg your Pardon for helping to torment him whom I would die to serve—and desire to *live* only that I *may* serve. There was much talk at Dorset Fellowes's about the true *Falernian* Wine, of which accept a Bottle: 'tis a Rarity; I likewise send a Partridge. Miss Williams was right. Miss Wroughton asked kindly for you last Night, and said Mr. Hicks would cure you, &c &c. The Courtneys all enquired for my Conway—all who seek Favour from me, ask for you. All *but* William Augustus Conway.

Two days later they met for the first time since the Gala, when "poor dear Conway called in the morning, & half-destroyed me by the Tale he told," but Mrs. Pennington was still in the dark:

Hot Wells 5 Feb.

Your letter, dearest friend, nearly paralysed me. Poor Bessy ill!—dear Conway no better!—everybody sick or dying! I am absolutely ill with terror and solicitude! . . . Thank God the accounts of the King [George IV] are more favourable. The first impressions I had of perfect manly grace, and princely dignity, were drawn from the fine form and gracious manners of our present Sovereign. Early impressions are always the most lasting. Never have I seen, but in our favourite, dear Conway, anything to compare with him, nor ever shall I see his equal again.

I do not wonder that you should feel indignant at young Sir John's "stern looks". I pray you not to pay the least regard to them. It is strange indeed that you may not call in the aid of a friendly physician to a faithful Domestic, without incurring the *Reproof* of *Eyes!* Every Body was pleased with the *respectful* & affectionate attention at the Ball,—but *I* was a little surprised at something in the Domestic Carriage that assumed a different Sort of Air—We can allow Influence—but not a gleam of Authority. I charge you, dearest Friend, to guard sedulously against allowing the *slightest* degree of that Spirit to reappear; *check* it, as well know how, in every Instance, as you value your Independence.

I was surprised at some hints dropped at the chagrin he felt on the subject of your *increased* acquaintance; and could not help telling him, tho' in perfect good humour, that *my* claims in that line were prior to his own. I was sorry I did not recollect to observe to him, that it was a maxim of Dr. Johnson's, whose wisdom no one could question, that we should renew, and keep our acquaintance and our friends in *repair,* as we did our wardrobes, *because they would wear out.*

I have written dear Conway a parcel of nothings. . . . If "Mr. Hicks *commands* Miss Wroughton", surely our favourite will gain some influence over Mr. Hicks, and if he could win *her* over it would be a host gained at his benefit. Can our Chevalier *any* way make his court to this Dame of celebrity and Queen of fashion? But alas he has chosen another patroness & I fear she bears no rival or partner in her favours.

Mrs. Piozzi's reply (6 February) was by our own admission also "a heap of wise nothings," saying little about Conway except that "Bessy is safe, dearest Mrs. Pennington, by dint of bleeding, starving, blistering, Bessy is safe, poor little Angelo's mother, and our noble-minded, tender-hearted friend is better too. . . . Dear Conway called on me yesterday for the first time—our confidential talk lighted up such varying expression in his face, I knew not whether he looked ill or no." The next day she "sent little Pet to see great Pet. They are both beautiful Creatures. Conway drank Tea with my Lady [Salusbury] and myself. She *likes* but her Husband *hates* him."

Conway was well enough to take advantage of the theatre recess and set off to London at five o'clock the following morning, after writing a reply to Mrs. Pennington's letter, and leaving his patroness to talk to Mrs. Dimond about his benefit. His news came as no surprise to Mrs. Pennington, who said so at length in her next letter to Mrs. Piozzi, on 9 February.

From the time she made his quitting his profession a condition, I was sure the feeling in his favour was not *sterling,* nor would stand the test of opposition;— and what would be gained by such a sacrifice? She would have shorn him of his beams, she would have eclipsed his glory & not with her turgid relations done away the reproach of having married an actor, but retained it without the emoluments or éclat that must result from the fair & untrammelled exertion of his talents.

No one admires dear Conway more than myself in his *own* character, which I think would do honor to any situation;—indeed I have had few opportunities of even approving him in any other—but without fortune, or Ministerial interest there are so few avenues for a man's success out of the Line he has started in, and that his talents point to, that I saw innumerable difficulties & obstacles in the path, even had *he* made the sacrifice, & had she been firm, & generous, & tender enough to have yielded to his wishes. . . .

I fear he will contract a hatred of Bath, and I shall see little more of him for the rest of my life: and what a silly thing I have done to interest myself thus deeply in his concerns. The most astonishing thing of all is the power he possesses of creating so strong and pure an interest in his favour, especially with me, who have long since ceased to feel the influence of that sort of enthusiasm. In very few instances have I *ever* experienced the attachment I feel to him! It seems as if *that* girl alone was exempt from the power of the magic he bears about him. . . .

He says, poor fellow! that "not one word of sympathy or tenderness, from the only hand that could have rendered it effectual, has softened this blow"!! Perhaps this may also prove for the best. . . .

I wish I was near to you, dearest friend, at this time, for I can think of nothing but our dear afflicted chevalier, of whose affairs, of course, I do not allow myself to talk, & therefore appear abstracted & unsocial. I did not get an Hour's sleep last night—so much had his sorrows engrossed me. . . .

Sir Walter & Lady James are at Clifton for a few days change of air. They pass some hours of each day with us, & shew us *so much* kindness I must think it sincere—for why should the poor be flattered? I am trying to improve our chevalier's interest in that quarter.

Mrs. Piozzi agreed with her friend's predictions:

Thursday Evening 10 Feb. 1820

My dear Mrs. Pennington's Prognostics are always wise, lucky, and fulfilled; and I doubt not but we shall lose our accomplished Chevalier,—after this Season,—for ever. Let us get him a good Benefit first, and send him down the Wind with fav'ring Gales. I will leave, in the vulgar Phrase, no Stone unturned to serve him. Meanwhile, he is in London, escaping our wise Letters of good Advice; of which, if he is now weary, he will on a future day be proud. . . .

Yesterday at Dinner Salusbury broke one of his fine Teeth. Today it was drawn, and they are gone to Shropshire. So runs the World away. Jealous of Aunt's Favour, and glad to carry little Wifey far from that widely spreading Influence which, as you saw, throws an attractive Halo round us all: which *she* feels among the rest; for who can 'scape? Sir John's Chagrin won't kill him; and says he will perhaps come again—*by himself*—but he will find enough to do at Home.

Our Benefit will probably take place towards the end of this Month. Conway comes back to open the Theatre with a swarthy Face on the 18th, in a new Play written by Mr. Dimond—St. Clara's Eve. . . .

I hope you will begin next Month with *me* under St. Taffy's Influence: and if you invite me early in the Spring when our tall Beau is gone, or going, I will come to Clifton, and escape Visitors. My Door never rests here, and when once out of Town, they may knock in vain. But till the Theatre is shut, or the great Light of it extinguished, the Halo hangs around me, and I shall be neither willing, nor *able* to stir. The Less indeed, because persuaded that his Return hither (unless either the Gentleman or the Lady is married) is very unlikely, and would perhaps be Imprudent. I mean his professional Return, as now, in the Character of principal Performer.

Adieu, Dear Mrs. Pennington, continue to him your Regard; do not willingly lose Sight of him; your Value is by him duly appreciated, and I depend on living long in both your Memories.

14

"Adieu pour jamais"

MRS. Piozzi was not entirely dismayed by the thought that Conway might never return to Bath after the present season; she might not remain long there herself, having concocted a plan to sublet 8 Gay Street and to live more cheaply in Penzance, at least until she paid off Tully's bill of over six hundred pounds; but before exiling herself in the farthest corner of the kingdom, she would rent one of Mrs. Rudd's houses in Clifton for a few weeks. By strengthening her ties with his mother, she might hope to keep in touch with him. Meanwhile "a letter from darling Conway [from 3 Macclesfield Street, Soho] consoled me for many uneasy reflections. *He* is wretched still, but I think mending in body and mind: I answered his letter."

Sunday Morning 11 Feb:—no, no, 13[1]

Reading your dear loved Letter over and over again—I feel quite flatter'd that you wish to hear from me, & seem to think the *Separation* long. You have been so harassed with sententious Foppery I feared lest Distance might be deemed a release.

Meanwhile that you keep your Mind engaged by public and political Events delights my Heart. They were never more worthy of Attention: & among them all, *I* seem most interested in the Fate of our intrepid Discoverers. They have realized all our Conjectures, & solved all our Geographical Problems, & have ascertained the free Passage under the Pole, and effected what so many brave Fellows have perished in attempting.

No great Benefit will indeed accrue to us, save Honour and Glory; we shall get easier to America, whither 'tis no Matter how seldom we go; so that the *Cui bono* Men as I call them,—those who consider Money as the Sole Sovereign Goodwill say in every Language, what *Use* can be made of the Voyage?

—but 'tis a pleasant Thing for Loyal Hearts to hear of a new Reign beginning with so magnificent a Disclosure of National Spirit and Greatness.

I brought the Frank home with me last Night from Dr. Fellowes's where the Party was so dull—Miss Willoughby fell fast asleep,—the best Thing one can do, when there are just People enough in the Room to exclude Confidence, and not enow to ferment into Conversation. Cards were produced, however, and then I came home to pray for Blessings on my dear, my latest-found Friend: which shall be reiterated in Church this Morning—I think I may walk there and back, the Weather is so fine.

You will read this at breakfast, Monday—Valentine's Day & you will send me six Lines just to say that the *Ivory* is faultless & without a Crack in it. That you will travel all Night on Tuesday, go to Rehearsal instead of to Bed on Wednesday, & eat your Red Herring with *me,* remembering that 'tis Ash Wednesday, & being contented with Maigre in the Society of her who is yours while H:L:P.

I carry your letter with me, & put it in the Post myself. The World says you and Mr. Bunn are connected in the Birmingham Theatre & that Warwickshire is to be your future home—of course. I should be glad on *one* account. You would be near a true and faithful Friend,[2] a *feeling* one if I judge rightly:—In case of harm happening to poor No. 8.

Mrs. Pennington took it for granted that Mrs. Piozzi intended to stay with *her* when she visited Clifton, and her next letter was devoted almost entirely to Conway and the unworthy Charlotte, who had told him that she "could not support the idea of being sunk in her Rank of Life & be looked down upon and to his future prospects." But, as Sir Walter James now realised (if he did not know already), Conway had aristocratic connections.

Hot Wells 13th Feby. 1820

Blessings on You my beloved Friend for your charming Letters. They are the delight of my Eyes & the Joy of my Heart. I seem to live only for them. Now I feel I have my restored Friend securely my own again, for the promises to come "to Clifton early in the Spring", which I chuse to translate the *Hot Wells,* where no form of Invitation can be wanting. . . .

I am relieved to find from the chearful Style of your Letter, that no worse Intelligence has arrived from our dear Chevalier. If it pleases God to restore his Health pure & perfect . . . all will be well in Time—except with us—who shall, as you say, too probably "lose him for ever". . . .

You know that I am not lightly attached, nor at all changeable,—and if I ever lose the strong Interest he alone in these *cooler* Days seems to have had the power of inspiring, it must be when *I* become *Torpid,* or *he* proves unworthy. . . .

I wrote to you Sir Walter James was here. . . . I hope he will not be absent at our dear Chevalier's Benefit. I had a long Chat with him (Sir Walter) on the Subject, & he seems well and *kindly* disposed;—but said to me "It is a most extraordinary Thing I can never see *that* young Man without almost fancying my old College Friend *William Conway* stands before me".[3] I replied—"There is nothing very extraordinary in that, for if I am rightly informed, tho I do not undertake to answer for the *particular* Circumstances of the Case, there is a near Connexion between them"—"Ah! I see it all now" said he, *"Conway must be his son!"* He then declared *any* thing he could do to serve him he would.

He said of his acting that he was the best Pierre he ever saw . . . that he would advise him by all means to keep clear of the London Theatres for two, or three years, and then burst on them a finished Actor. He said it was remarkable that they never received an actor as such, whatever his merits, so young, or so young-looking as Conway, until more matured by experience & knowledge of the business, & instanced Mrs. Siddons's failure in early Life, Mr. Young's &c. It was some years before Kemble made his way. . . .

What a Pity under these Circumstances that our Fav'rite should be driven from Bath, which is an Elegant School & where an Actor can always have the advantage of being seen *nearly,* & his Talents appreciated by an enlightened Audience.

As Mrs. Pennington spread on to a sixth page, she confessed her envy of her friend's "concentrated Style—conveying so much matter in so few words," and regretted that Mrs. Piozzi would have to pay "two Groats instead of one" to receive her ramblings. Mrs. Piozzi responded with unusual brevity, giving nothing away about Conway's business in London, but according to her diary, he had returned "blooming" and gone straight to the theatre for rehearsals. The opening night, after the recess, began with a rendering of "God Save the King, in Verse and Chorus, by the WHOLE VOCAL COMPANY," which Mrs. Piozzi found "Very solemn." *St. Clara's Eve,* or *The Conquest of Taranto* was the main item on the bill, a historical play with music by William Dimond, in which Conway, as Aben-Hamet, Admiral of the Saracen Fleet, was, of course, "transcendant." In Mrs. Pennington's next letter she offered a word of advice to his patroness from her own experience in the entertainment business:

Hot Wells 18th Feby. 1820

I begin now to get very anxious on the subject of *our Benefit.* I know by experience that only general and simultaneous impulse will fill a theatre or a ballroom. The pit and galleries are prime objects, a showy play is the best attraction there. The boxes there can be no doubt about, and Bessy must exert all her influence with your tradespeople, not only to take tickets for the other parts of the house, but to dispose of as many as they can. Not a word however about these sordid matters to our high-minded friend.

The days leading up to the benefit were almost as important for Mrs. Piozzi as those before her own fête a month earlier; she wrote letters to drum up support, ordering tickets by the score, and acted as Conway's treasurer. He gave her a deed box in which to keep unsold tickets and the proceeds, and they solemnly counted the money in Miss Williams's presence. Meanwhile, Miss Wroughton was planning to hold a musical evening on Conway's benefit night, and Mrs. Pennington thought that Conway ought to try to get the "Queen of Bath" on his side. "I wish he would, in his sweet manner, move Hicks to conciliate Miss Wroughton. . . . It really may be worth while to make this effort, though I know any effort of the kind is unpleasant to such a mind." She was also concerned about the Strattons. "If they absent themselves, known as they have been as dear Conway's staunch and particular friends, surely it will excite remark? And yet, how can they be there? At any rate, if they are, I trust it will be in a situation not to meet *his* eyes; I should dread the consequences, at least I know I shall feel for him in every nerve."

A note from Mrs. Piozzi, which became the seventh and last of the printed "love letters," showed that the door was closed on the Charlotte affair.[4]

Late o'Monday night 28 Feb: 1820

I was happy to see my dear friend's handwriting as soon as I came back home—and the tickets. You see by the enclosed how they will insist on coming to what they call *my* Places. My Welch Friends, however, have more Wit. I must certainly have another box secured in my name if you have no objection. Mr. and Mrs. Lutwyche gave me 2 banknotes for 2 tickets—and they must have front seats in the next loge to where I sit myself.

Mrs. Stratton and I have had our talk, the result is to me a proof that your happiness has on this occasion been Heaven's peculiar care. Her last words to me when we were interrupted were If you do love Mr. Conway, dearest Madam, teach him to despise her. Tell him so yourself, said I—after the 11th of March, but let us not shake his shattered nerves till then,—my own can scarcely bear the Conversation, for tho' I thought [Charlotte] false and unfeeling, my belief could not stretch itself to what you inform me now; nor will my mind be less easy till he is assured of her unworthiness either by your hand or tongue. Est il possible? is all my Wit could suggest in Answer to her Story.

. . . There were no proposals of marriage made—she will fade like the china rose as I said she would—and so let her. Come in the morning—You will sleep better tonight—than Mrs. Stratton will who has endured *such* insults; or her whose indignation swallows every other Sense—except that of her affectionate and all-subduing Admiration of *you*. H:L:P.

Our canvass goes on triumphantly. Let us think of Nothing else. The young lady is happy in her emancipation, it seems. Pray let us be happy too.

Mrs. Pennington arrived in time for Mrs. Piozzi's "Taffy's Day" party on the first of March and stayed at No. 8 Gay Street for three weeks, which brought their correspondence to a temporary halt, and Mrs. Piozzi took her own advice and thought of nothing but the benefit; seeing people, ordering more tickets, "counting my money for Conway all day & he came this morning & other 100 people. They crazed my head and I lost a £1 note. Miss Willoughby canvassed Conway thro' me to act Col. Briton for Warde's benefit." On the day, there were "people all morning about the benefit, and at night the benefit itself, very fine, very brilliant, & I *think* very productive. Clara's Eve and Frank Poppleton." The *Bath Journal* reported that "the performance was honoured by as brilliant an audience as any our theatre has this season boasted of. . . . The Moorish hero of the

Conquest of Taranto exhibited in him all that rage for revenge . . . for which that character is remarkable. . . . In the new farce of *Too Late for Dinner* Mr. Conway sustained a principal character, for the purpose, we should suppose, of exhibiting the versatility of his talent . . . in fact it delayed us until it was Too Late for Supper."

A few days later Mrs. Pennington fell ill and was taken home by Mrs. Piozzi, but not before they had seen Conway's last appearance as Fitz-james in *The Lady of the Lake:* " 'Addio'. Oh what a darling Look," and he had talked over his plans for the future, the most immediate of which was another approach to the Hertford family. Mrs. Piozzi realised that his "darling look" might have been the last impression he left with her, for "my heart fears I shall see him no more *on the Stage.*"

Begun Thursday Night 24 Mar: 1820

Dearest Mrs. Pennington will be glad to know that four horses and three able-bodied men brought my little person safe home at 9 o'clock last night. Had I died . . . I should not have seen our tall Beau for 5 minutes after breakfast;—*a morning call.* He looked in high health and good spirits, said your eloquent praises had produced others—he does indeed deserve all praises in every situation—in all situations of life—and his adoring mother says he was from infancy the best boy on earth. We had no time to talk of plans, present or future—he will go to London next week, whether to return again I know not.

Mrs. Pennington replied:

Hot Wells: Sunday
26th March 1820

I was indeed glad to get your letter dearest friend, for tho' I entertained no fears for your personal safety, I was anxious lest the evening air should increase the choaking, and in great dread of dear Bessy's everlasting displeasure for suffering you to depart at half past five o'clock without anything to sustain you on the way . . . but I was sick at heart & could only feel regret at parting from you . . . & the rest of the party lost all useful recollections in the pleasure of listening to you & looking at you. They declared that they would have gone without dinner for a week to have prolonged the gratification. Maria [Browne] is a paintress, & a really good amateur artist. She says "She cannot take her attention away from your forehead and eyes: the unfurrowed smoothness of the one, & the lucid, sweet, & bright lustre of those blue orbs giving a youthful expression that might pass for 20!"

It is *this* that Jagger has hit off so happily, [she had seen Conway wearing the miniature of Mrs. Piozzi] & that Roche could not touch. I *must* have a copy of that picture some day or other, if I sell my silver spoons, for my tea pot I will never part with.—but mind, I am not begging, nor mining; I will never have it from *your* purse until Hammersley has the proper quantum of cash in hand. . . .

My new friend Mr. Gifford was so obliging to send me the Bath Chronicle of Wednesday last. We had agreed to the paragraph in the short conference we held in the theatre on Monday night. I *thought* it would be a good one. [A letter in the *Chronicle* from "a constant reader" asserted that Mr. Conway's benefit was a bumper, and the brilliant patronage he received sufficiently testified how justly and how highly his talents are appreciated.] Oh! if dear Conway had remained in Bath, we would, between us, have worked the opposition party to an oil; not a beauty, or point of acting, should have passed unnoticed;—however I think he has given them a tolerable touch of his art, from Coriolanus to Prince Hal;—and from Colonel Briton to my dear whimsical friend Frank Poppleton, squat on his hams before Mother Egan! Never shall I forget the moment, or my delight at tracing the elegance of the *gentleman* preserved through a situation so ludicrous! . . . what a comfort it is that a being who thus commands our admiration, esteem & affection should be altogether so deserving of it!

Say all that is kind for me to *the* friend we both best love & who is worthy of our regards. The best wishes I can form for anyone will follow him where ever he goes from the warm heart of

My dearest Mrs. Piozzi's every faithfully devoted & affect.

P S Pennington

Mrs. Piozzi to Mrs. Pennington:

28 March 1820

. . . It vexes me you ever saw Miss Jagger—alias Madam HAGger. 'Twas my own overweaning vanity threw it in your way, & pride of the wearer's partiality. The loss of *his* company and talents will be a great privation to me, but on *his* account my heart feels no fears. Conway's virtues are not, I trust, what Johnson would call ambulatory, meaning dependent upon climate and company. He will come home to *you* I hope, in seven years' time, two or three little children at his side, his own incomparable soul unsullied, his merits unmolested, his beauty unimpair'd. . . .

Those who converse with the great expect our King to be crowned on his birthday, the 12th of August. My dividends will be come in by then, and Salusbury may have his promised £100 to see the Coronation. I hate being worse than my word. Our friend Fellie may not perhaps find *her Grandees* so scrupulous. But she has had many assurances of the Herb-woman's place in the Procession, which I have heard was worth £400 or £500 o'year for life.

It was Holy Week; Mrs. Piozzi went to church every day, and tried to see Conway as much as possible before he left Bath. On the Wednesday, "Conway never came till dinner—then went away la café dans la bouche"; and on the Thursday, "Mrs. Stratton called—to ease her heart. Miss Fellie to give her true love to Conway—and to tea he came himself. Adieu pour jamais! Dieu te benefice!"

Once again, she was upset about the theatre management, though the reasons are not known. It was on the Tuesday after Easter that she "saw Mrs. Dimond and William, 20 fools—very indignant in my mind about the theatrical people—they have used Conway and me most cruelly," and she reported to Sir James Fellowes, whom she seems to have neglected to late, that "the fête was a long-promised foolery, and can never happen again, and did exactly what I meant it should, it procured me the power of making Conway's benefit equal to that of Warde's. He has left our town and stage now, and I shall trouble my head no more with theatrical affairs." Mrs. Pennington shed a tear, too:

I presume our tall Beau has ere this left Bath; his society must be a real loss to all, who like ourselves know how to appreciate its value;—but it is a great privilege, and what seldom occurs in life's dull round intimately to have known a being of such various excellence. A boon never bestowed on me before, and never do I expect to encounter its like again. If we are destined to meet again I shall rejoice to see him, and may it be prosperous and happy;—if otherwise nowhere will he find truer sympathy than in the heart of your PSP. . . .

I hope our friend Fellie will get her promised post in the Grand Procession . . . but I very much doubt in these retrenching times, that the pension for life will follow. Dear Maria is coming to me again for a few days on Saturday, and then a long farewell. Without you or this sweet friend I feel a lost thing.—This is a wretched, lifeless scrawl;—excuse it from a poor, tremulous invalid.

15

"Longing for Clifton"

MRS. Piozzi consoled Mrs. Pennington in her "sad loss of Maria Brown," and agreed that she too had a sad loss in Conway, whose "steady resolution not to write is such a bad trick. [She had already marked off "*One* week past *tonight*" in her diary.] Siddons has the same, you know; and Dr. Johnson used to complain, I remember, of David Garrick." But Conway had little news to impart, except that he had been asked, at short notice, to play Hamlet at Drury Lane, after Charles Kemble and Macready had both declined because of sickness. Conway turned down the request, too; having established himself in Hatchett's Hotel, Piccadilly, ready to lay seige to the Hertford family, he thought it was not the right time to be seen on the stage. In fact, he had no plans to appear in public until later in the year, when he would join forces once more with Alfred Bunn at the new Birmingham Theatre Royal (the old one had been destroyed by a fire after a Twelfth Night party). However, he kept in touch with theatrical friends in London, and was to spend a good deal of time with Charles Mathews and family at Ivy Cottage in Highgate, while Mathews was appearing at the Lyceum and enjoying a respite from touring.

It might be a year before Conway returned to the Bath stage, and his departure left Mrs. Piozzi weary of the town and its theatre. "Miss Wroughton, tho' she crossed me at every turn this winter, begs *me* to take tickets now for Mr. Ashe!!! I wonder how she can think of such a thing," she protested to Mrs. Pennington. She was longing for Clifton, but "till July dividends I have no money for *move-about*. Lord bless me! I wonder how other people's bank notes hold out. Mine melt away like butter in the sun." In the meantime, she would heed Dr. Johnson's advice, never to brood after a bereavement, but to throw herself into some new task; to fill the void left by Conway, she finished off the annotations she had been writing in an illustrated folio Bible for his mother,[1] began work on another present for her, an embroidery of a moth, which she hoped to have completed and framed by the time she left Bath.

Another week passed without news from Conway—"a fortnight today— a *whole* fortnight." Mrs. Stratton called, anxious for news, and Miss

Willoughby was inquisitive too, and their enquiries gave Mrs. Piozzi an excuse to drive to Clifton for "a very good gossip with dear Mrs. Rudd and Pennington. *All about Conway.*" A week later she rejoiced to see a "*Letter*—a good kind one—dear to my true heart . . . I was a little sick of a Duck yesterday, but Conway's Letter, and Chicken Broth, did me good." She was now ready to tell Mrs. Pennington something about her plans for the future: she would spend a month or more in Clifton, and would go on from there to Cornwall, where she would spend the winter. Life was not over yet.

Bath April 22d. 1820

Dear Mrs. Pennington will be glad to see the Spring coming forward so sweetly. She will be glad, too, to hear that her true Friends are well; the Little Old Woman and the Tall Young Beau. She will be glad that the Parties grow hot and disagreeable, and that I feel longing for Clifton and the 10th of June. . . . The People are right enough that go abroad. I would go myself, but that I have an Appointment to keep with dear Piozzi, who I brought out of his own sweet Country to lie in the Vault he made for me and my Ancestors at Dymerchion: where I am most willing to keep him Company when I have performed *more* than all the Promises I ever, in any Humour, made his Nephew: and when I have, after paying every Debt, saved a Silver Sixpence or Two for those who soften and amuse the closing Scenes of a Life long drawn out,—perhaps for that very Purpose.

I see where I shall pass the winter Months, escaping Frosts, and keeping clear of Expenses, in a Climate better than Paris, the Latitude very little higher. But if you open your Lips—Adieu!
Dear Conway says his Health was never so perfect, and he uses Horse Exercise, and sends Love to his Friends;—and he is a good Boy. I used to bid my Children when at a Distance, only write three Words,—safe, well, and happy: his Letter is just like theirs. . . .

Be well yourself dear Mrs. Pennington & accept of my *live Legacy* & be careful of him & get him his Shakespeare from those who will hover round her who will be ever yours while H:L:Piozzi.

She went to the Spring Gardens two days later to see the celebrations for the king's birthday, which she described as "very gay. I came home sadly, remembering Conway with me at the same Place last Year. . . . Miss Fellowes came & said Dimond had written to tempt Conway back; for Mr. Warde is going to Ireland." Money continued to be a source of worry. There was a begging letter from Salusbury—she sent him £100—and a demand for £365 for rent, of which she paid £65 and promised £100 more in July: "Oh Lord! Oh Lord!" Then "Colling sent me Horsley's books & poor as I am—I must buy them." But her morale improved on 4 May, when "Dear Conway came, on purpose to see me, he looks in beautiful Health and high Spirits. We dined together and he went off to Clifton. He saw me at work on the Moth." After consultations with Mrs. Rudd, he returned to Bath the following day, and Mrs. Piozzi "supped with my dear Incomparable on Chicken and Asparagus & sat chatting till Midnight. . . . Conway left Bath for London at *five* this morning . . . I mean *tomorrow* morning." After he had gone she "agreed with the Builder about my Castle . . . to be inhabited 27: Jan: 1821." The "builder" was actually J. Riviere, and the "castle" seems to have been a casket of some kind. It was to be mentioned many times in her diary and letters to Conway, but never described; it was eventually delivered to her in Penzance. The next day there was "a long Chat with dear Mrs. Stratton, not unaccompanied with Tears," and "Miss Fellowes made an inquisitive Visit. I told her Nothing." Nor did she tell her diary anything. However, Conway's high spirits and consultations with his mother suggested that he was making some progress with the Hertford family.

After hearing from the duchess of Roxburghe that Lord Hertford had thrown the ball back into Lord William's court, William Augustus needed to find a way to bring some pressure to bear on the man himself. Mrs. Rudd evidently knew the family well, and it must have been on her advice that her son approached two other brothers, Lord Robert and Lord George. According to his letter to Jerdan,[2] they both received him courteously, but "owing to their alleged disunion from their brother," they were unable to help. That letter did not say when those interviews took place, but Conway had been in London for five weeks, and it must be assumed that he had now seen both of them. There was only one other brother left, Lord Henry, owner of Norris Castle on the Isle of Wight, who might have some influence on the wayward William; and as a last resort, there was Lord Castlereagh, the nephew of the Conway brothers. In spite of his elevated position as leader of the House of Commons, an approach to him was not entirely fanciful, as Dorset Fellowes had just been appointed secretary to the Lord Great Chamberlain[3] and would have access to Castlereagh. It was, however, an unpropitious time to approach him.[4]

Mrs. Piozzi told Mrs. Pennington of Conway's brief visit, but gave nothing away about his business; nor did she mention Charlotte, whose name had not appeared in their letters for weeks.

Bath, 5 May 1820

We will see a great deal of each other when Clifton becomes my Place of Residence for six pretty Weeks. After then—old Ocean. Can aught else completely wash away all Recollection of Bath Parties? That fair Assemblage of glaring Lights, empty Heads, aching Hearts, and false Faces?

Who is it says the Conversation of a true Friend brightens the Eyes? I have enjoy'd two chearful Hours *talk* with our best *Speaker,* best Actor, best Companion,—Conway. You seem to express yourself as if half sorry you loved him so

much. I am only sorry that I can't love him ten times more; but we will settle that &
dear Mr. Pennington shall help us, in some Part of those six Weeks. . . .

Here is lovely Weather for frisking up and down, and my empty Pockets will not
overload the Carriage; altho' the whole Family of Immigrants will be packed in,
and on, and upon, my Post Chaise and four. . . .

Salusbury sent me a whimpering Letter, and has already got his £100, which
Heaven knows I owed, and much more, to the Estate and Messrs. Callan and
Booth, Lodging House Keepers [her landlords]. But if I can get five Guineas
o'week for no. 8 I shall bring Matters round in due Time.

That was accomplished when a Mr. Iveson agreed to take the house for
twelve months from 10 June—"turn'd out again at 81 Years old!" She
"pouted" for letters from Conway, and wrote long ones to him, none of
which has been traced, and thought melancholy thoughts as she worked
on her embroidery.

Bath 16 May 1820

I can't stir till 10th of June. I want a sitting Room & four Beds, *that's all*. Three
Beds would *do* because James might sleep at the Bath Hotel, Bessy & her baby
near me, Sophy & Mary in another Room, and I like to be under *Mrs. Rudd's* Roof,
and mean to sleep under it next Saturday three weeks. . . . Sunday's Dinner I hope
to eat with Mr. and Mrs. Pennington at their hospitable Board, and we will talk of
anything and everything but la Partenza [parting], which cannot be before the
same day of July, as till then I have ne'er a Groat. If life is lent me I will be rich that
Time twelve-month; and if it is not lent me, I shall want no Money.

Meanwhile I expect no Letters from our favourite Friend. I have written to him
tho', and told him that you and I were his Hephestion and Parmenio; and if he does
not laugh at his Blue Ladies, we are surely well off. . . .

Callan and Booth, the People I take my House from, have heavy Claims on me
now; so I have let it to Mr. Iveson for a Twelvemonth, and mean to be as smooth as
oyl'd Silk by July 1821. . . . George Hammersley has just left me and taken my
Bankers' Book to Pall Mall to be regulated; and gives me great Credit for my Care
and Exactness in my Money Matters: bidding me make no Scruple with regard to
their House, etc., very good-natured indeed. But as I told him I never yet overdrew
my Banker, and will not (unless something serious happens) begin to do so in the
year 1820. *One* twelvemonth's Short-biting will set all smooth, and you shall see a
merry Face once more on the Shoulders of yours and dear Mr. Pennington's
affectionate H:L:P.

In the three weeks that remained, Mrs. Piozzi sent her embroidery to be
framed and began packing up for a long absence. She did not expect to
return to Bath for another year, and would take to Clifton all the possessions she would need in Penzance. It was a bold venture, at her age, to
uproot once more and go to live, and perhaps to die, at Land's End. She
"packed up Books and Papers & felt Feels of all bad Sorts," while

Conway's silence did nothing to improve her mood. "Three Weeks today &
no Tydings!" she wrote in large, bold pen strokes, and then, more quietly,
"I'll write tomorrow." She "wrote to Hatchett's, half sick, half sorry—or
half sullen," and made a summary of her letter in the margin of her diary:
"Told my engagements; my letter fretful but kind . . . No tydings from Mr.
Bunn, Recollection of *his* low spirits once. Fear of being forgotten: Packing, melancholy. *Verses* A hope expressive of *Castle,* Deaths and sorrows,
conscience. Lancelot Gobbo, hope better at Marazion—moth finished—
Tender reproaches correspondent! no."

The next day she wrote out an instruction to her banker but did not post
it.[5] It was to remain in her possession until she gave it to Conway two days
before she died.

Messrs Hammersley & Co   Bath Monday 29th May 1820

Gentlemen,
   At sight of this Draft be the Period long or short after Date; be pleased to pay to
William August Conway Esqr. or to his Order the Sum of One Hundred Pounds—
and place to the account of, Gentlemen,

                                          Yours faithfully,
                                          Hester Lynch Piozzi

The remaining days in Bath were crowded and emotional. For some
unexplained reason, Mr. Mangin was "stiff, cold & I *think* ashamed," and
Miss Willoughby was in an agony about lovers and lodgings. Mrs. Stratton
called to enquire for our "cruel Conway, & Miss Willoughby called to
lament the loss of Mr. Warde." There was still time for another letter to
Mrs. Pennington.

                                          Bath 6 June 1820

   . . . Three Minutes ago young Eckersall said he had seen Conway in the Street
whilst in London a Fortnight ago, looking very well. If you see his Mother, tell her
so. She will be glad, as I was, to hear that he is *alive* and waiting till Birmingham
Theatre opens. Mr. Warde has taken leave, and all the Ladies wept. Such was the
Crowd that James, my man, could not get in to a Place he could stand upon. . . .

How long, dear Mrs. Pennington, *am* I to live? How many valuable Companions
am I to lose? . . . Thank God Salusbury and Conway—dear Lads—are young, and
likely to last me out. But when they do not write my foolish Heart is fluttering for
their Safety,—naughty Children as they are in neglecting to send me a Letter. I
have heard but once from Brynbella since my £100 went there.

The following day Mrs. Piozzi noted that the queen had landed in
England, and the people were "all raving mad"; then a letter from the

Somerset Herald saying that for a consideration of five thousand guineas, a baronetcy might be secured in the Coronation Honours list, and urged an early decision. She passed it on to Salusbury for comment, and dealt, rather tetchily at first, with some "instructions" from Fellowes, who did not want his portrait to remain at No. 8 while she was away.

Bath Fryday
9: June 1820

I must have explained myself very Imperfectly if Dear Sir James Fellowes has yet to understand that I have *spent too much Money;* and can by no means afford a Journey to Adbury London &c. . . .

Clifton will be my Residence no longer than till the Dividends are paid,—I will then discharge my Rent here to Mrs. Booth, so far as I am able, and get *Tully's Offices* as near the last Page as possible, but Many Matters are behindhand, which a Summer & Winter in the West will bring to a good Level. . . .

I changed my Mind about Thraliana, & shall take her with me; She was packed for Travelling this Morning, & Your Letter is but just come. . . .

Mr. Iveson will have a Loss of the Pellegrini Picture; Miss Fellowes shall have it in her Custody today or tomorrow. I want to tell you that I have an Offer of a Baronetcy for your Friend Sir John; so if he likes Honours better than 6000£—I will sell mine out—curtail my Income, and live retired in a cheap Country throwing up my fine House here entirely: *for his sake*—who is ready at every Turn to Suspect me of unkindness—I guess not why—for I suppose few friends will be found ready to make such Sacrifices.

Meanwhile Long Live the King—who yields up his own Passions & Prejudices *for our good:* & long live Mr. Wilberforce who wishes Passions to cool & prejudice to subside before any Determination is adopted, at a Time when every Determination will be dangerous.

Your dear Father is a noble Fellow; he knew his own Strength & relied on it—against much *grave* Advice;—not *wiser* than his own 'tis plain:—for at 83 years old he has found Benefit from acting up to the dictates of good Sense & Experience in his very difficult Case.

I wish Lady Fellowes and her Sister much Joy; and Mrs. Dorset and Mrs. I Fellowes and all—Birth & Marriage are Moments of Joy—and may such Pleasures ever attend a Family so Sincerely loved & respected by,

Dear Sir,
Yours ever faithfully,
H:L:Piozzi

An Acct: of disagreeables *by Letter* is disagreeable in itself—Anonymous Correspondents are best neglected I suppose—though I do *not* neglect their Advice & rough Admonitions, for I *do* retire from the World, well convinced of its Worthlessness & Deceit.

May you like it better at my Age!
Addio!

Direct No. 36 Royal Crescent Clifton

Having got several irritations of her chest, she wrote to Hatchett's Hotel in more relaxed mood (this one in the Pierpont Morgan Library).

Bath Friday
9: June 1820

So this is in all human Probability the *last* Letter I shall ever write to my dearest Mr. Conway from Bath. The Place where we first met. I wonder the Feel of it does not affect you. It does *me* most sensibly, for the *Place* pleases, tho' the Fools in it have offended me. My nerves are however less unsteady since young Eckersall told me you are alive, & in London, & looking well ten or twelve days ago. Till he called, my Terrors for your safety even overpower'd my Regrets for your Silence, Heart-breaking Creature as you are, both off the Stage & *on*—where I now fear my *Eyes* will never more behold the Figure ever present to my *Fancy*. Ah yes: that Look, that *last* Look in the Character of Fitz James was indeed the parting Glance.—I felt it such, yet struggled against Conviction. Well! Adieu! I will go gossip with Your Mother & Mrs. Pennington till the Dividends are paid—and then away to the Southernmost, & the most Western Point of England: where my Purse & Person find repose—my Mind will soon recover its Tranquillity, & I shall spring to welcome my Dearest Friend when he performs his voluntary, not extorted Promise, of visiting me and my *Castle,* changed somewhat in the Plan and Elevation, but solid & brilliant, the near Verdure beyond all Compare. *Shall* I live to finish, & put you in quiet Possession? such Happiness would surely be too great, and we would keep our Birthdays at Penzance *so* merrily!

Meanwhile I have much to tell, much to consult you about, and a Commission of peculiar Delicacy to entrust you with.[6] If the Soul that now animates this little Clay tenement should be dismiss'd before we meet again—because your *last* Letter dated 20 April *does* profess boundless Devotion to poor H:L:P., & tho' you will not employ three Fingers for five Minutes to give me unspeakable Pleasure—whilst I *am alive*—You will I am confident hold my Commands Sacred after *Death,* so I'll say not another Word upon the Subject *now.*

Among my Rummages—is there such a Word?—I have found a French Rasselas given to Doctor Johnson by the Translator—and bestowed on me by the Immortal S.J. half a Century ago. I *can* give you *that* & will leave it in charge of dear Mrs. Rudd, when setting out for the West. Would God increase my Power, I would yet serve you somehow, but an odd Thing has happen'd on the Brynbella Side, of which the Result is uncertain.—Life—stealing away all the Time—&*You* never coming or writing.—Mr. Mangin said when I complained of slight Insults—Oh Surely Mrs. Piozzi has not an Enemy in the World—Only sharp Shooters replied I; so I will *only* take away the Target and then their Dexterity is useless.

When the Winds rise—says an old Classic Proverb, worship the Echo. I will do so; I will retire from the World before it retires from *me*—and leave the crazy croud for youth to bustle in. The Bibliographic Task will be delightful to me in Cornwall,—may I so contrive the commentary as to lead your Eye to the Text.

She was to embark on another annotation of a Bible, this one for Conway.

The present state of the World horrifies me—not because the Incidents are unexpected; I never had Time to talk with you on *Those* Topics & the hints given in my Writings you have not observed. *No Matter:* If your Mind will honour mine in listening to what I best understand, however, Good will come of it in future & that way my valuable, my matchless Friend may be really and essentially served by his Weekly Monitress—his inviolably attach'd H: L: P.

Miss Willoughby acknowledges very honourably the Pain she suffer'd in saying "For ever, and for ever, Farewell Brutus". I sleep at Clifton *tomorrow.*
Miss Williams gives me a Dinner today. Tomorrow Clifton—direct No. 36 Royal Crescent.

Sir James Fellowes has sent for his Portrait—I gave it a fine new Frame the other day, hope he'll be pleased with *That* & excuse my *Disobedience to his other Commands.* A pretty World you have lived 30 Years in—and are but Three parts thro' yet—& will not come to your Mother's for Comfort.

Mrs. Piozzi's departure for Clifton coincided with the constitutional crisis which had been precipitated by the landing at Dover of Queen Caroline; there was a "fine uproar about the Queen" on the morning that Mrs. Piozzi bade farewell to all her Bath friends, and the story filled "every mouth" at Clifton, where she took up residence later in the day, in Mrs. Rudd's No. 36 Royal York Crescent. This "Crescent to beat all Crescents," as Nikolas Pevsner dubbed it in the twentieth century, was almost brand new then,[7] and Mrs. Piozzi told Miss Williams, who was now a correspondent rather than a daily caller, that "the Height of my Drawing Room, the Terrace under my Window, & the expansive Horizon in full front View reminded me of the Crocelle at Naples—and was the Prospect Sea instead of Land, it would strike everyone with Likeness."
She spent her first evening in "melancholy talk with Mrs. Rudd about Conway," and indeed she was to spend most of the next five and a half weeks with her and with Mrs. Pennington. The next day she read a "tender letter from Conway to his mother," which cheered them both, and later a not-very-tender letter from Salusbury, who "will strip me to the skin I see." She told Miss Williams that he seemed ready, "even hasty," to accept the baronetcy, "thinking possibly my 6000£ will be best secured to him by that means. . . . My Lodgings are lovely, and Sir John says he is coming to stay with me in them, because talking about Business is better than writing. . . . He believes *light* Bags and Purses will be best for me to carry no doubt." Salusbury was highly suspicious of his aunt's growing interest in Clifton and its inhabitants, as well he might be, if he could read her letters. She signed off this one: "Mouse is well, and a dear little Pet. Tall Pet is well too, and writes kindly to his good Mother about their True Friend and Dear Miss Williams's ever Affect. Servant."
Conway's tender letter had evidently reported some progress in his

approach to the Hertford family. Mrs. Piozzi "saw Mrs R—went together
to the Post Office; put in my letter [of Prayers and Wishes of God Speed].
Impossible to hide my agony about the interview—hope however all will
be well—burn'd it by positive Command." [Presumably that was Conway's
letter to his mother.] Salusbury arrived to breakfast the next day." We had
a long business talk—unpleasant of course," and on the Saturday there
was "more disagreeable Conversation & ending in perfect Nihility. Dinner
at Pennington's." On Sunday it was "Bristol Cathedral. Quickening letter
from Cathrow. My poor £6000 gone—Addio! I trust they will leave me the
dividend." By Monday morning Salusbury had left for London to see
Hammersley and arrange for the transfer of his aunt's Consols. *She* "went
to tea with Mrs. Rudd. Dined at Dowry Square—much chat about Salusbury & a little about Conway." It had been an eventful first week in Clifton,
and it was no doubt summed up in her next letter to Conway, which has not
been located ("the 7th I think, since Fryday 5th May"). She would tell him
that the Mangins had also taken up summer residence in Clifton, in the
Mall, a square immediately behind and above Royal York Crescent, and
below Sion Row. Mrs. Piozzi's almost daily walk up through the square to
Sion Row did not go unnoticed by her Bath friends: "Gossiped with Mrs.
Rudd again & saw the Moth. Mrs. Mangin watches me in and out of her
house as if it was the Key Bagnio." Her references to the Mangins
continued to betray a certain edginess. "Mrs. Pennington," she told her
diary, "has fallen in love with the Mangins," and there was a touch of
sarcasm in her observation to Miss Williams that "Mrs. Pennington and
Mangin are mutually struck with admiration for each other's talents."

Conway replied from the Portland Hotel, having moved from Hatchett's,
"still in dreadful agitation," asking Mrs. Piozzi to write to Dorset Fellowes, presumably in the hope of approaching Lord Castlereagh on his
behalf. The Leader of the House, however, was heavily involved in weight-
ier matters, having just reported to the Commons the king's intention to
investigate the queen's conduct while she had been living abroad, and had
been detailed to join the duke of Wellington in persuading her to go back
to Italy. Dining at the Penningtons, Mrs. Piozzi "said nothing of my sweet
letter, but burned it in the night by his express command," and after
church the next day wrote to Dorset Fellowes.

Three weeks in Clifton, enjoying the warm hospitality of the Penningtons and the friendship of Mrs. Rudd, brought Mrs. Piozzi to another
momentous decision: "Clifton really is where I want a Place to live or *die*
in" when she returned from Penzance in twelve months' time. She looked
at another of Mrs. Rudd's houses in Princes Buildings but decided that No.
36 Royal York Crescent was better and hoped that it would be available
when the time came. She would live out her life close to Mrs. Rudd and
Mrs. Pennington. In the meantime, they all fretted for news of Conway.

Mrs. Pennington "is very angry at poor Conway's silence & I DARE NOT SAY HE HAS WRITTEN," but she was placated when Conway dashed to Clifton a few days later to spend twelve hours with his mother, and then "ran to Pennington & me just for a Moment. I gave him Dorset's letter," which she had just received. She did not reveal its contents to her diary, or to Mrs. Pennington, but she seemed happy enough with it. After church the next day she "dined at Dowry Square, walked 2½ miles under the rocks and back again; never had so good a night's sleep."

Her holiday in Clifton was coming to a close; Mrs. Rudd advertised for a tenant to take over No. 36, and Bessy packed up their boxes to go by sea from Bristol docks to Penzance, in the optimistically named *The Happy Return*. Hammersley reported that her Consols dividend had been received, and she noted that for the sake of a baronetcy for her nephew, she would be worse off by nearly two hundred pounds a year. She wrote "more silly Verses about the Castle" and a "partenza" for Mrs. Rudd; and, commenting on the death of a friend, told Sir James Fellowes: "I will go wait for mine at the Land's End, a proper Place enough, if bordering on the Ocean of Eternity. [Clifton] adds to the small but strong Threads that fasten one to Life; . . . it is so beautiful: the Situation so like Naples the View so like that from Brynbella, but too expensive."

16

"Fish and Poultry at Penzance"

IN the midst of her Clifton leave-taking, Mrs. Piozzi received a letter from her "much hurried Correspondent" at the Portland Hotel, which presumably told her whether Dorset Fellowes had been of any assistance in his quest. She answered it immediately, but "very sorrowfully" (according to her diary—the letter itself has not been located), and Conway responded with unprecedented alacrity, to put her mind at rest. The letter from her "sweet William" arrived just as she was leaving for a farewell dinner at Dowry Square. The next day, Wednesday, 19 July, her heavily laden chaise rolled down Sion Hill with Bessy and Angelo, James, and another maid aboard, and after a very good journey—"no Dust, no Rain, no Accident of any sort"—of forty miles, reached Bridgewater, where she wrote a long letter to Conway. The present whereabouts of this letter are also unknown, but in the margin of her diary she made a brief summary, noting that it was her first letter since leaving Clifton and that her spirits were "quite lifted by his." She carried it to Exeter, where she began another, which has survived, and is in the Pierpont Morgan Library.

Exeter Thursday 20
July 1820

Before I sate down to Dinner—nay before I order'd it, my chief Care was to direct & seal, and carry my Letter in my own Hand to the Post Office, lest it should not arrive on Sat: Morn—for Sunday is no Day in London, and I hoped you might be gone to dear *dear* Clifton on Monday Morn: your dutiful Attentions kindly accepted; and your Spirits tranquillized by reflecting on the Propriety of your own Conduct. The uniform Magnanimity which has ever distinguished a Character exalted above the Situation into which Fortune took Delight in placing my incomparable Friend—for *my* Sake, perhaps to rouze me from that Torpor that devour'd every Faculty of my Soul—so that I scarce knew there *was* one in the little Person of H : L : P. Do not ever then learn to hate the Profession in which you first engaged *my* Admiration.

Dr. Johnson said, you know, that Admiration is a short-lived Passion. I have not found it so: but then *we* never knew a Mortal who could heap Fewel on the Flame as *you* have done—he would have loved my Conway—not as I do, because no one but Mrs. Rudd *can* do so: but he would have praised and petted, and made everyone else *appear* as if sensible of your Merits—but have done, Mrs. Piozzi, *do*—and go and see Exeter Cathedral.

Well! so I have done, & a Scene of more gloomy Dignity have I not lately witness'd. . . . The Clock struck me as exceedingly curious—one of the old Charlemagne Clocks it is, shewing the Phases of the Moon, with Minute, and with second Hands. . . .

But here comes the Master of this fine Hotel in Exeter, and threatens me with bad Roads thro' Cornwall, and wretched Accommodations. Such matters fright not *me*. Gravior tuli—be the Accommodations what they may. Like Petruchio "I come to wive it happily at Padua. If *wealthily* then happily at Padua". My Connexion with Penzance resembles his with Katherine—My plan is to save Money—and *your* Promise of a Visit will encourage me thro' greater Difficulties than these.

Welcome for thee—dear Conway, all the past
For thee dear Conway; welcome in the last

So now away—to mean Houses, Mutton Candles, and muzzy Conversation.

Fryday Morn: 21st

Fryday Night—Launceston

The Man was right enough—four Hours have we spent in coming here the last 20 Miles [from Sticklepath, through Okehampton], with *four* Horses, which they forced on us the last Stage, & without which we should never have come at all, through a coarse Country cover'd with Gorse and Furze, barren & Mountainous: worse than the worst Part of my own Skin & Bone country, North Wales—When shall we go home? quoth Angelo. Where's that said I? The lady's pretty Window, says he, Mine's own House—meaning No. 36.

The Sight of the Penzance Mail revived me—that Vehicle will bring my dearest Friend, thought I, to console me in the first Month of the Year 1821—and we will have—if not *Two* one happy Birthday & a few long Evenings together. We have yet fourscore Miles hard Traveling before we reach our Place of Destination. The Duke of Cumberland meanwhile sets all our Bells o'ringing—he is on a Visit at Werrington House in the Neighbourhood & takes away the Horses & plagues us in various Ways.—Here however are we at *Truro* 256 Miles from Hyde Park Corner this Sat: 22d July [after a drive of 80 miles—over Bodmin Moor] while you are reading my Letter dated Exeter—*right* Mr. Conway, as Mouse calls you. The *dear* Portrait sets not out till today from our pretty Bason at Bristol—that (he says) is Mr. Conway in the Box.

Our poor Baby is however very near knocked up, so tedious has the Journey been, & this last Stage *3* Horses—a Boy & a Bidet [a nag?] as they travel in France. The Roads, meanwhile are excellent, but the Country amazes me; Hay cutting *now,* & Wheat scarce in the Ear; everything two Months behind Somersetshire—& wild Commons, with Rocks, & Goats browsing among the Scars: I, who expected Myrtles & all the Beauties of a soft Climate, rationally enough remain surprized. Shall I send this Nonsense to London? Tell me for pity how you are going on—and whether standing still or not. All will end well at *last,* of that no Danger. Their Notice once attracted, je reponds du reste. "For Friends in all the Ag'd you'll meet;

& Brothers in the Young".—but a *Feather* guides the Arrow to its Point;—and some unexpected Accident will effect at last, in a Moment, what you have for Months being studying to attain.

The travellers rested on the Sunday, "fatigued with gentle slumbers," and Mrs. Piozzi added only a few lines to her letter, but found enough energy to forecast her income and expenditure for the remainder of the year, and to note in her diary that £200 due from "little Stock" would go to Booth and Tully, £200 due from the Crowmarsh rents would go to pay Booth and Price. Iveson's rent of Gay Street (£125) would settle little debts, while another £125 from Streatham would pay Booth and "the other little ones." Taking into account her balance at the bank, she had £574 "to last 23 weeks & pay the Castle—so I hope it will too—£11 a week." [This would suggest that the "castle" would have cost £220.] The next day they set off on the last lap of their long drive, and Mrs. Piozzi finished her epistle to Conway with some "Verses made on a Milestone in Cornwall."

> The Journey now begins to advance,
> And take us nearer to Penzance.
> We have met, thank Heav'n, with no Ill Chance
> Thro' this long Distance to Penzance;
> And tho' just now too tired to dance
> Have brought good Spirits to Penzance.
> No Fowl in France, no Trout in Prague
> Beats Fish & Poultry at Penzance.
> And Mangin now may look askance
> His Victim's safe at poor Penzance.
> Indeed a Retrospective Glance
> To Clifton Terrace, from Penzance,
> Would not exceedingly enhance
> The few Delights of low Penzance.
> Yet this blue Sea will pay the Prance
> We made to arrive at warm Penzance.
> Eh! finissons une fois ces stances.
> Les Muses n'habitent pas à Penzance.
> Pardonnez donc la douce folie
> Votre tendre et fidelle amie:
> Your fond & faithful H:L:P.

Badly shaken after a week on the road, Mrs. Piozzi found rooms in a hotel for a few days while she looked for a house to rent, put Conway's letter in at the post office, and announced her safe arrival to other friends.

Penzance 25 July 1820

My dearest Mrs. Pennington will be pleased to hear that we arrived safely at Penzance last night. . . . All we are told about this Place seems true. . . . We shall get a good House, with a Sea View . . . upon the Regent's Terrace, paying 16£ o'month, thro' the whole ten, from 1st August to 1st of June 1821. . . .

Our dear Conway's Name at Length appears in the Morning Post [the *Birmingham Gazette* was waiting for her at the post office], summoning his Troops to meet in the Green Room of the new Theatre, Birmingham. If Mrs. Rudd does not know it, do her the Honour to call with the information. I wish the Ship was come with our Cook, and our Books and our Luggage.

St. Michael's Mount is a disappointing Object, at least to me; and as to the Country we came thro', nothing ever looked so Poverty-stricken, except the very roughest Part of North Wales. . . . Peat Stacks at every Turn shew what Fires they used here last Winter, but till last January Snow had not been seen for many Years, and it lasted but one *Day*. The Tide here is like that in the Mediterranean, just *visible* the Ebb and Flow. . . . No *Mud* offends the Bathers, and no Machine *assists* them.

We have here such magnificent Gardens, and one good House in the Middle of the Row, looking down with true Contempt at the Mouse-holes each side it;—and *that* Mansion I am in chase of, only suspecting that, before we knew it was to be had, I had entangled myself in a Mouse-hole. . . .

> And on this 26th—I shall sit, fret, and dine
> In a Chair-lumber'd Closet, just eight feet by nine.

For I feel myself after all condemned to the Mousehole for three Months certain; £2 15s.o'week, with a View of the Sea, and *then* (if we live to see November), Mr. Paul's comfortable Mansion next door.

A letter from Miss Williams was "the first upon the Table of my dirty Inn, in this dirty Town—of which the roughest part of North Wales—in rough Days too—would have been justly ashamed." But the peasantry, living on barley bread and salted fish, seemed "healthy happy and content, with not a beggar in sight." Penzance, she said, was not like Weston-super-Mare, "a place with only Two Books in it. We have a Geological School, an institute with Professors &c, and a well-furnished Library consisting of very valuable Compartments ranged for Purposes of Science. I shall hope to fill my Time up very profitably, & see not at present how I can empty my much-diminished Purse."

The "mouse-hole" that Mrs. Piozzi was about to move into was in Regent Terrace, which still exists, now mostly as small hotels and boarding houses, but then was a row of twelve houses, with subtropical gardens leading down to the shore one hundred yards away, and a "View of the lovely Bay, the Waves of which are so clean, so blue, so beautiful, I long to go in, but there are no Machines, as at Profess'd Bathing Places." Penzance had no such pretensions, although its soft climate had begun to attract the few visitors who were prepared to make the arduous expedition: it was a hardworking fishing port, an outlet for Cornish tin, and a coinage town, cut off from the rest of the world. There was no regular

View of Penzance and Newlyn, by W. Penaluna, 1817. *Reproduced by permission of the Cornish Studies Library, Redruth.*

stagecoach to the town, and the Penzance Mail that Mrs. Piozzi had passed on her journey was a recent innovation. It carried a letter (PML) from her en route to the post office, Birmingham.

> Regent's Terrace, Penzance, begun
> on Thursday evening 27 July 1820

On this Day, the Day you receive mine, I fancy, do I dearest of all dear Friends—begin a new Letter to you—saying Imprimus that we take Possession of our Nutshell, and sleep in it—tonight. Oh me! and what a Nutshell 'tis, but *clean,* with a full View of the Sea and Land's End[1]—you said it was a shelter'd Bay & So it proves—I half expected to find *myself* where no more *World* was found, But foaming Billows breaking on the Ground.

Old Neptune however is without his Beard here as at Weymouth, or Tenby,—so swift, receding Tide for two Miles almost—as our Bristol Channel exhibits, but a bright blue beautiful expanse of Water, never stormy I am told, even in Winter; & Snow was a new Phenomenon to the Inhabitants of warm Penzance, last year, while we were freezing at Bath. Regent's Terrace is just such a Place as yours was at Bath, & my mansion such as yours there—cleaner perhaps because new built, but scarce as spacious—The Damage £2–15sh. o'Week. We have it for three months certain with Promise of a better—next Door for the last seven Months of Exile. A compleat Ostracism. . . .

I wish my Shakespeare would come, & my Cook—tho' there is no Meat to dress—other Fish to fry. Good night and God bless—I shall have a Letter tomorrow or next day. Fryday Night 28 July.

29 July Sat: No No: no Letter—no Comfort for poor H:L:P, condemned like Constantia in the Deserted Island to Solitude and Seagulls—but without Rock or Sand on which to trace *favourite* Initials & beguile the Time. . . .

I wonder if you recollect a certain Friend of mine, named Augustus, who said in Camden Place, A:D:1818;—I could be happy in a Prison, with dear Mrs. Piozzi and her Anecdotes. The Lady of the House told it to me, for I was not present—You and she had been talking of Cydevant [Johnson?].

Come here in the Winter and *try—1821*—Imprisonment with H:L:P. in her *Castle* by the Seaside.

The Morning Post shows me your Advertisement for the 10th of August [the *Birmingham Gazette* announced that "this splendid edifice will open for the first time on Monday next, August 14th with an Occasional Address to be recited by Mr. Conway"]—Will it be so *Indeed!!* Oh I shall then at least know where to find the Friend who has so long been living on a Milestone.

Sunday 30 Church & devotional Exercises all Day—& roasted Kid for Dinner. . . .

Tuesday 1 August 1820—here comes a Letter from Mrs. Pennington—so 'tis from *her* I am to learn News of You it seems. Cruel Friend! not one short Line under your own dear hand—that hand *how* dear to your poor H:L:P! Well! all she tells is *good* however. You are Well, handsome & Happy. Did I not say this Time Twelvemonth that You would rise up a Phoenix from that Sick Bed?—and the Theatre all Young too, and fresh and gay. Oh brave Mr. Bunn! Give him my Compliments & hearty good wishes. He will join me in lamenting poor old Mr. Davies of Streatham—a 50 years acquaintance to your half-angry, but *wholly* unalterable H:L:Piozzi.

This Letter has been written with dirty Sea Water I believe, but I have got better Ink at last. Your good Mother is really a Comfortable Friend to me: through *her* I am apprized of your dear Health and Safety: & she says you wrote to her in good Spirits—God be praised. The Time is coming I have so long predicted—when that Noble Heart, which rode Oh how triumphant over the Waves of Adversity is to be tried by Sunshine and soft Breezes—the most relaxing Powers of a *prosperous* Sky. To come out *quite* an Angel as I hope for you, the sweet as well as the bitter must be despised. *Eternal* Happiness is alone worth waiting for. *This* World's all Title Page, there's no Contents—but Virtue can build the Pyramids.

Mrs. Pennington's letter, dated Sunday, 29 July 1820, was as wordy as usual, first chiding Mrs. Piozzi for running away and condemning herself to a vile nutshell where fish was the only commodity she would find cheaper than elsewhere. "Oh! that you were once more in good Mrs. Rudd's comfortable mansion at the Crescent at Clifton!" The *Happy Return* was still in the Port of Bristol, and Mrs. Rudd said that the master would not sail until he had taken on his full freight. It could be at least a fortnight before it reached Penzance. On a happier note, Mrs. Rudd had had a letter from her son, "and whatever may be its contents, it has had the power of lighting up *joy and hope* in her countenance. She said she *must not* speak *out*, but she really seems to tread in air, and expressed her belief and trust that there was happiness in view." For her part, Mrs. Pennington could not believe that if he *had* been taken by the hand in a *certain* quarter, he would have taken up an engagement in a *provincial* theatre, always infinitely beneath him in every point of view.

Mrs. Rudd expected to see him shortly, when she hoped to hear more, "if I am favoured with his presence and confidence—which I much doubt." At any rate, he would have "employment for his mind, and for his time, and be enabled to recruit his purse; the deficiencies of which have fallen very heavily lately on poor Mrs. Rudd, as I understand;—but *this* she entreats may remain most strictly *entre nous,* and not the remotest hint dropped on the subject to him, as he would never forgive any communication of this sort."

The Mangins had left Clifton, after spending an hour chatting about Mrs. Piozzi. "My dearest friend, I suspect this gentleman has suffered *unjustly* in your thoughts. . . . He mentioned with a softened voice, in which I totally lost sight of the caustic Mr. Mangin, that it was with infinite concern he felt that they had in some way lost ground, tho' wholly unconscious of any cause. That this man may have felt jealousy of some more favoured object and become sulky and petulant I do not dispute, but *treacherous* I will not believe him. . . . therefore write to him dear friend at your leisure, and let him not indulge the mortification of thinking he is wholly blotted from your regard and esteem. He is too agreeable to be lightly cast off—or only on suspicion."

Mrs. Piozzi thought that letter was "pleasing on the whole" and replied accordingly:

Penzance Wed: 3 Augst.

Charming Mrs. Pennington's beautiful letter was indeed most welcome, tho' it does put me a little more out of Humour with my runaway Frolic than I was before I arrived—and as for Mr. Mangin few People can esteem him as much as I do, because I know him so well. . . . It is difficult not to *like* him, and *love* his agreeable Lady.

Now for Penzance and its Parties. Mrs. Hill made a splendid one, for *me* I rather think, and my black Satin Gown (for no other is yet arrived) was my best Garment. Bessy lent me a Cap of hers, and my youthful Looks were duly appreciated—my Whist playing *applauded*. We had two Tables, one for Shillings, one for Sixpences; a Profusion of Refreshments, and Music in another Room. Oh! if I escape all Temptations to Sensuality I shall live to see dear Mr. and Mrs. Pennington again, and the Hot Wells, and Clifton Terrace, where I shall jump for very Joy. But these red Mullets and Dorees for two pence o'piece will certainly destroy *some* of us. Poor Bessy has been *seriously*, I might say dangerously ill, from indulging in a crab; it made James sick too; all the Family half-killed—for the small Price of a

Groat of Fish, and a Pound to the Dr. Forbes, a real Physician, thank God, and not a Country 'pothecary. . . .

The People know not how to be civil enough, and if my Stomach will reconcile itself to the clotted Cream, I shall come Home as fat as the Pigs of the Country, and such Pork did I never see. Our own Garden affords Potatoes for us all. Onions &c, besides the Flower Pot, perfuming the very Air around with Carnations of every Hue. Myrtles of every Form, and exotic Shrubs with Linnean Names innumerable. The Appearance of our Mansion, *Pleasure Ground* and Kitchen Garden reminds me of Kingsmead Terrace, Bath; but James says the Houses here are by no means so spacious as that where your Compassion carried you when our incomparable Conway was so ill. I hope he has proved himself *irresistible,* and what must be the Heart over which he cannot, if he pleases, triumph?

As to the Birmingham Business, had my Lord Castlereagh taken him by the Hand he would not have deserted his Friend, I am persuaded, or shrunk from an Engagement with the Man who loves *him* & shew'd such Tenderness when only *talking* of our Favourite's Sickness and Danger. I am glad he is going to use his matchless Talents in behalf of that dear Mr. Bunn, who after our Conversation in Gay Street has *had* & ever will have, my best & warmest Wishes.

Oh! if I possessed an unappropriated 100£ in the World, I would go and see him act once again, that I would. . . . I am glad Mrs. Rudd's Heart seems lighter than when we left her; the Rogue has never written to *me,* no, not a Scrap; but she had an *earlier* Pretension to his Regard, I think it is scarce a truer . . .

But I have wrong'd old Neptune; he *can* roar, I hear him now, thank Heaven. Oh! how much more delightful is the Music he makes than that of the pretty Ladies of the Parties, to the rude Ears of dearest Mrs. Pennington's everlastingly oblig'd and faithful Friend H:L:P.

Aug. 3. Fateful Month! but no Clothes, no Books, no Conway's Portrait yet for poor H:L:P.

The next day Mrs. Piozzi "bathed for the first time in the open sea; feel that it does me good," and was even more cheered by a "Letter from mon bel Ami himself—kind, happy, *worthy, charming* Creature that he is." Her reply, which, as she noted, was her fourth letter since leaving Clifton, has not been traced, but she jotted down in the margin of her diary the following summary: "Sorry I so wrong'd him, he so kind. *Old* friends not to be forgotten. Mr. Bunn. Coughs do not come here—no transition of season. all dull & sick from repletion of alkaline food. Bessy recover'd, bel ami, mobs firing London, dreadful. Castle desirable, wait till Jan: settle everything. Verses . . ."

It was now "three weeks since we left dear Clifton. Whole Fleets of fishing Boats in the Bay—but our Happy Return never arrives [it was still in the Avon estuary], with our Tea & Clothes & Books & Cook & *Portrait.* I paid my Subscription to the Library. Shall I get any Books? None appear

& no Ship." Invitations flowed in from the Penzance intelligentsia, who were eager to meet the friend of Dr. Johnson, and especially from Dr. Forbes, who was not only a "real physician" but one of the founders of the library[2] and its honorary librarian—a man after Mrs. Piozzi's own heart. A *Birmingham Gazette* sent by Conway, "all gay and prosperous" carried a glowing account of the new theatre, which she acknowledged in her fifth letter, summarised in her diary as describing "the Place & Society of Penzance, the Food, the Sedan Chairs, &c,—no Ship yet, gives acc. of my Dialogues on my own Death—Conway not humble or obscure; what Bessy said of him; how ill she was, the World coming fast to an End—Paris burning, Prophesies completing, great Bible, sole Work worthy of those fine Eyes—Quotation from the [   ] vous seul & c—*My* Attachment only useful to *his* Salvation, to him, therefore Centre, Circumference &c—A Dieu je vous racommande. Newspapers full of an Antarctic Continent discover'd at east of Cape Horn. Quere whether Smith's Ship, a Trader from Blyth in Northumberland, *could* weather those Seas."

Hot Wells
10th Augst. 1820

What a Treasury of delight & Pleasure have I gained in our renewed Correspondence, my beloved Friend! & I have at last the satisfaction to acquaint you that "The Happy Return," with your little Cook & valuable Luggage, left the Port on Friday last; and as there has been a change in the Wind, is, I trust, by this time safe at Penzance, where I wish I was out of this dust box. . . .

I am vexed you have not heart from dear Conway. I thought he would have been more explicit to *you*. . . . I have been so much engrossed by attention to my husband and the Randolphs that I have not seen Mrs. Rudd since our Favourite was here, & she is, I think, more open & Ingenuous in her Temper.—There would be some sense in the Reserve he thinks it necessary to observe if we were *un*informed on the Subject, as it stands connected with *that* worthy Woman;—but Delicacy with respect to *her* Feelings cannot now be any bar to communication with *us* in this Business,—particularly as, in our former Interview, he entered much more at large as to the Steps he meant to pursue,—His late Visit to me I confess seemed rather the result of Civility than Choice, and there was a polite distance assumed, evidently for the purpose of repressing enquiry. It had its full Effect on me, & we conversed chiefly on general Topics. . . .

I am persuaded we trouble ourselves much more about his concerns than he either wishes or *likes*. The little I could gather, & only from *Inference* is,—that there is no point gained but that of mere *Recognition,* and the satisfaction of having it admitted that he has not brought forward any *unfounded* Claims. It does not appear to me that he indulges in any higher hopes or expectations from this development, & if this point *is* gained, it is so far well;—but I felt so decidedly *checked* by his Manner, I could not ascertain even this;—much more I never anticipated from an application made so late, & under Circumstances so unfavourable as the Situation of Ld. William presents. If he is *unwilling,* or *incapable* of standing forward, it was not likely that the rest of the family would take an active, or warm Interest in the Affair. I hope our Friend will now devote himself steadily to the Profession his talents so eminently qualify him for. . . .

He said I should hear from him from Birmingham, but except thro' the medium of the Public Papers I do not expect it. . . . One must always be pleased when one sees him, but around Absence he throws "such a Death-like Silence & dread Repose" that it is very like Death indeed. . . . This you do not feel,—but you, dear Friend, are much more Amiable than I am, & set less value on the Kindness you shew and feel than I do. . . .

Mrs. Piozzi replied:

Penzance Sunday August 13, 1820

Come! oh come! dear Mrs. Pennington. I see you half-long to be here, and what a Relief, what a Comfort, would your Society afford to your starving H:L:P? Here is no Heat, no Dust, no Cold: I dare say it is a very *negative* Place, but I must not have you tell Tales out of School. Miss Trevenan may justly disapprove my Censure on the *no* Picturesque of her native County: and if you read her my Letters so, I must grow cautious à la Conway. I *have* heard from him, thank God! The Rogue told me Nothing, tho', except how charming you and I were, what admirable Letters we wrote, etc. "Yea, and all *that* I did know before" as Juliet says. Quere, whether he has Anything to tell; unless it be that he has at length calmed his own noble and too-feeling Mind, by Conduct which himself approves.

But at the same Moment with your kind Letter comes our long-expected Ship. Cook says they have been to *Wales;* Swansea in Glamorganshire! The day you receive this one whole Month will have elapsed since I left the full Moon shining in her Brightness on Clifton Terrace. Never have my Eyes seen her since. No, not a starry Night. Yet here is Sun enough, and the Sea is so beautifully blue and clear . . . will you come? There is a Lodging close by my Habitation—one & half Guineas the Week.

Salusbury was threatening to visit her, and she must welcome him, but must not say how much she would rejoice, "should the same Fancy take our tall young Beau by the Brain Pan." As to Mr. Mangin, "if he has at all changed his Mind about me I am sure it must have been my Fault. Sir James Fellowes never writes to me. He as well as Mr. Mangin called himself Friend—but you used to say Friends must love & hate in the same Place. Now these Gentlemen's Prejudices seem rather to run counter to mine. They have, however, *both of them* in their way, & in their day, been undeservedly kind, useful & polite towards Mrs Pennington's much obliged H:L:P."

Mrs. Piozzi began to feel more at home now that she could surround herself with her books, although she was alarmed at their number, and "looked at dear Conway's portrait with resumed delight. Angelo acknowledged it at once—he called me to see it." The only news of the man himself came from the Birmingham papers, which reported that the Theatre Royal had been completely rebuilt after the disastrous Twelfth Night fire seven months earlier, decorated "on the most superb and elegant style," illuminated by twenty brilliant chandeliers, all lighted by gas, and ventilated by a patent apparatus. The dresses, properties, and every contingency of the stage were to be got up with great attention, and the whole was to be conducted by W. A. Conway. He recited an "Occasional Address" on the opening night and appeared as Captain Absolute in *The Rivals*. He was to be heavily engaged at the theatre for the next four months, and was to write to Mrs. Piozzi only once or twice in that time.

Sir James Fellowes, she told Mrs. Pennington, "has written kindly and good-humouredly, and my heart has entirely made up with his. Nothing, as you say, ail'd him but jealousy. Mr. Mangin will write one of these days. . . . I hear no more of Salusbury." But she was more than surprised to receive "a pretty letter as can be from Miss Willoughby," which merited an appropriate reply describing her new surroundings, and adding that "Dr. Johnson said that after the full Flow of London Conversation, every Place was a Blank; I wonder what he would have thought of dull Penzance?"

There was, of course, Dr. Forbes, who admired her books; they read the Preface to *Retrospection* together, and she promised him a copy for the library. Another day "Mrs. Hill brought me a Lady in the Morng. & in the Eveng. some other Lady sent me Fruit & Flowers & Flattery," and "the Clergyman of the Place called on me"—the Reverend C. V. le Grice. Otherwise, "Weather dull & dismal, and no Letters yet. The Queen's Tryal takes up all the Papers & all one's Attention," and she began an embroidery for Mrs. Pennington to avert utter boredom. There was only £300 in the bank, but she sent £100 to Tully and now owed only £38, and £100 to Booth ("blessed be God"). Life was dull from constant privations, endured "just to leave no debts for Salusbury." There was conflicting news of Conway: Miss Fellowes said he was engaged for Bath, and Miss Sharpe said it was Drury Lane, but Mrs. Rudd knew nothing of his plans.

Dorset Fellowes sent Mrs. Piozzi a partridge and a message that his brother did not, it seemed, "like to receive my Letters which cost money and tell nothing." She did her best to make amends with a lively letter about the Penzance scene, with "Rhodendrons now in beauty; Myrtles covered in Bloom, like Italy; and the Arbutus as high as an Apple Tree, very handsome indeed. . . . Old Friends in Leather Jackets, the Books, do not desert me, and new Friends are civil, send me Figs and Peaches, and invite me to their Parties, where we play Sixpenny Whist comfortably enough." But she could not resist a dig at Salusbury, who was never satisfied. The tithes in Caernarvonshire were once worth £500 a year, and the plate and china she gave him was worth £4,000, and "he now has the £6000 I saved for him, & my Income is lessened by the Loss of Interest."

Mrs. Pennington had no complaint about the quality of Mrs. Piozzi's letters:

Hot Wells 21st Sept. 1820

Blessing on you, Dearest Friend, for your charming Letters. They are my *only* Pleasures: the last being somewhat delayed beyond the stipulated time, I began to fidget. . . .

We are quite glad of a respite from this odious trial, which was become wearying & loathsome, & will be more injurious to the Morals of the Country than it is possible to conceive, tho the present Evils are sufficiently apparent:—not a Boarding School Miss, nor Parish Girl, that can make out the Words, but one sees studying these detestable Pages, & devouring the Contents as they would a new Novel. . . .

I am glad you have heard *any*thing of Conway.—I am half resolved not to love, or care for him (if I can help it) for what signifies *caring* for one who will not take the trouble of knowing whether we are alive or dead, contented or miserable? I do not desire frequent, or fine Letters from those who do not like, or *will not* write them.—all I require, from an absent Friend, is some assurance that a kind remembrance & Sympathy is preserved in the Mind. . . . our Tall Beau has "gang'd his aine gait" so long, as the Scotch term it, that I am persuaded he does not *like* to be too closely enquired after, or advised in his Course. I am not inclined to think he has taken an engagement in Bath, because he quitted it under a strong feeling that he was *Ill used* & *worse appreciated* there. I wish he *may* go to Drury Lane & remain. . . .

I wish dear Conway to be wise in time & I think still more since acquaintance has given me an Interest in his worthy & doating Mother's Feelings. His being successful in his Profession, which can only come by his getting a *Stationary* Engagement, is most important to *her* Peace. I am sure it is as much as she can do, in these Times, to clear her Rents & Taxes, & frequent demands on her Purse must be inconvenient, if not Ruinous in the End. But you & I can do nothing in these matters, & with unavailing good Wishes must leave them to take their course.

Mrs. Pennington was treading on thin ice in being so critical of Conway, whose silence grieved Mrs. Piozzi more than she was prepared to admit, and she confined her comments to the hope that Mrs. Rudd "will keep her Houses full, and find me Lodging in some of them next Spring, before the 10th of June, that I may bustle and be busy; and get my little things (as Ladies call everything) from No. 8 Gay Street to 36 Royal Terrace [*sic*] Clifton." Conway was still heavily engaged at Birmingham, acting three or four times a week and supervising productions as well. Bunn's own adaptation of *Ivanhoe,* and *The Marriage of Figaro,* with Conway as Count Almaviva, featured in the first few weeks of the season, and now he was performing *Virginius*[3] twice a week. Mrs. Piozzi told Miss Williams, "The

Tall Beau is Sovereign at Birmingham Theatre I believe, but those who think he watches *me*, & writes to me, are much mistaken—if I hear of him once o'Quarter 'tis as high as my hopes reach, but his last Letter said he was happy, in Allusion to his London Friends & Family Connexion as I understood him. He is a deserving Creature, and has a high Sense of Honour unmingled with Arrogance."

Mrs. Piozzi went on to ask Miss Williams, "Did I tell you that I *had* heard from Miss Willoughby? She too feels shelter'd from the Storms of Life by her Quality Cousins. They will not let her come back to Bath I dare say till she has no Debts there." A few days later she was astonished by another letter from Miss Willoughby, announcing that she was on her way to Penzance. Her relations had apparently advised her to follow Mrs. Piozzi's example and go to live cheaply in the West Country for a year. The same letter repeated the news that Conway was engaged at Bath for the winter, and Mrs. Piozzi was moved to write to him with "Raproches douches et tendres" for keeping her in the dark; and, according to her marginal note, "begg'd a Ticket [for his Birmingham benefit], lamented his Silence . . . threatened writing to Mr. Bunn." The silence was all the more galling, as Mrs. Piozzi was prepared to admit to Miss Williams, because Salusbury was sure that Conway pursued his "old Aunty with Flattering Letters; but such is not the Practice of our high-blooded and high-minded Conway."

October opened on a brighter note when Mrs. Piozzi went to a geological lecture with Dr. and Mrs. Forbes—"well delivered and very instructive," she recorded, "I liked my morning exceedingly." She told Miss Williams that "62 Gentlemen and 44 ladies composed the Audience, and if I did not see the great Sir Humphrey Davy,[4] I saw his Brother, born in the Town as well as himself." Later in the day Miss Willoughby arrived, and they spent the evening together, and a paper from Birmingham, sent by Conway, was a "Consolation for the Night."

17

"Come here, or meet me at Exeter"

Miss Willoughby's main, and perhaps only, source of income was an annuity of a hundred pounds left by her father, and she would certainly be able to live comfortably in Penzance on that. She settled on some "very handsome" lodgings in North Parade at a cost of only fifty pounds for herself and her maid for a full year, and would find it difficult to spend another fifty pounds on food and clothes, but her plan of "Œconomy," as Mrs. Piozzi put it, would make little inroad into any substantial debts she might have incurred. Mrs. Piozzi was puzzled, but rather pleased, that her old companion and former adversary had chosen to live cheek-by-jowl with her in Penzance, to share and enliven the remainder of her own exile, whatever the reason, and took pleasure in introducing Miss Willoughby to her neighbours and acquaintances. Her own plan of economy had almost reached its goal, but she was tied to Penzance until the spring and would enjoy Miss Willoughby's conversation.

She was thrilled when another Birmingham paper arrived with "three sweet words" to say that all was well, and dashed off a letter of thanks "all about the Stage. & a little about the Castle, a little about Miss Willoughby, & a little about Voltaire's Zadig" and another "telling good tydings to Sion." The copies of *Retrospection* arrived too, and were much, "*too* much, admired. I have promised to correct 'em." And there was an "Evng. Cards at Mrs. Johns—neither won nor lost. Pd Chair hire 1s. Bulls and Cowes, a good joke."[1]

It took her only a few days to correct the first volume of *Retrospection,* while she continued to work on Mrs. Pennington's embroidery and read a letter from Sir James Fellowes, which provoked the unexplained comment: "he begins to *R a t* I think." Perhaps he had second thoughts about his executorship. A more cheering letter by the same post from Mrs. Bourdois said that Mr. Iveson had admired Conway in *Virginius* at Birmingham, but that was offset two days later by "a letter two yards long from Mrs. Pennington—she wishes Conway to go to India."

. . . Mrs. Rudd has let her house No. 36 for two months which will tenant it for the rest of the winter. She then looks forward with hope as we all do to your happy return. She says she sent you a wretched newspaper—the only testimony of her naughty boy's existence. I cannot excuse his neglect of *her*—it is carried to an extreme that is unkind and unjustifiable. She feels it keenly, poor woman, but her pride will not let her write a note and remind him of what he seems so well inclined to forget. . . .

I wish anything would take him out of the scene of a provincial theatre—an association in every way degrading and unworthy of him. The family might do it if they would. Lord Hertford could easily procure him an appointment to the Colonies or the East Indies if he would press for it, where fortune and respectability might crown our wishes for him.

Dr. Forbes called, admired the embroidery which she had now finished, and "praised Retrospection & my fine Hand writing in the *Correction* of it."[2] Miss Willoughby dined with her nearly every day, and they read about the queen's "trial." Miss Williams wrote from Wales, where she had been touring with Mr. Wickens, and had called on the Ladies of Llangollen. The news from Birmingham was that Conway had elected to play *Lear* for his benefit, and she wrote to Alfred Bunn asking for a playbill and a ticket; the news from Hammersley was that there was £720 in her account, and she could now write to Riviere for the castle to be delivered, following which she counted her money and her debts "all Day long: hope Salusbury will not murmur if I die tomorrow." She had caught a cold and was feeling low; but worse was to come. Her housemaid, Sophy, caught the typhus that was raging in the town and had struck Miss Willoughby's lodgings. A letter from "Pennington, full of chat," did not raise her morale.

Hot Wells 26th October. 1820

There can be little doubt that the cause which has driven Miss Willoughby to the Lands End is the same that will drive me out of my senses, or more happily, out of existence with vexation, from the *want of a few hundred pounds;*—but I am glad you are likely to have her society for the remainder of your exile. You now have somebody to converse with that *can* understand you. . . .

Poor Mrs. Rudd has suffered a disappointment respecting her house No. 36. The gentleman who engaged it for his family from December died suddenly at Weston super Mare a few weeks ago, but it is let for the present, & she has good hopes it will not be vacant between this & the time when we anxiously hope & trust to see you settled in it. She has at last heard from her son with some partridges—a brace of which, with his compliments he very politely desired might be sent (or she, good soul! chose to send me) but she was not one jot the wiser as to what he is doing, or about to do, than she was before, & fears this Birmingham concern precludes all hope of his getting an engagement in London, as the arrangements there must all be made by this time.

I sincerely wish dear Conway more gratifying applause than can arise from the Birmingham mechanics. It is a wretched waste of talents & graces like his!—but perhaps he is like Caesar who preferred being the first in a village to second in Rome? . . . What the views of our favourite we shall never know from himself, any more than if he were in another quarter of the globe;—to be sure in the East, or West Indies, or at the North Pole, one *might* hear from him but once or twice in the course of one's life. I cannot however but remember that *when* he was in earnest, & really *felt*, his hand was free enough. God direct & prosper him in all his ways,—no one can say Amen to this prayer with more sincerity than your faithful P.S.P., tho' I own I have "took't a chill" on his subject I shall not easily get over.

October ended with the arrival of the "castle," and Mrs. Piozzi wrote to its "Governor" to say she felt contented with it; it was evidently intended for him eventually. She sent a draft to "les deux Rivieres" but uncharacteristically did not record the amount; however, from the state of her balances before and afterward, the object must have cost her between three and four hundred pounds. She confessed to Conway that she was not well, and although Sophia was improving, Angelo had succumbed, and Miss Willoughby had been driven out of her lodgings by the fever. She gave the same gloomy news to Mrs. Pennington, adding that "Tully's Offices are come to the last Chapter, and I shall write Finis to *that* Book, if I live the next Month through. . . . My Heart tells me that H:L:P. has made her last Journey; but 'tis no Matter, and will be no Loss. . . . the People of Penzance do endure the Dregs of the Piozzi very good-naturedly; and Miss Willoughby grows much a Favourite with them All."

She then seemed surprised that her letters should set the alarm bells ringing in Bath, Birmingham, and Clifton. There was a letter and newspapers and "ev'ry thing I could wish from my true friend" in Birmingham, and she replied with a "kind long Letter" and two ten-pound notes for his benefit. She received "a double Letter from Pennington exhorting me to run away from Penzance on Acct of the Fever—Not I truly." Mrs. Pennington also complained once again about Conway's neglect, but knowing how sensitive Mrs. Piozzi was on the subject, added, "For the rest of my life I shall love Conway and serve him—solely for your sake—but if it vexes you that I should so express myself I will for the future be silent on the subject." Mrs. Piozzi replied with a long letter "mentioning Conway & how zealous he was & is about my Health," and also noted in her diary that the queen had been "set free."[3]

Penzance, Sunday 12 November

I am very sorry, dear Mrs. Pennington, that I said anything about this odious Fever; it will perhaps hurt the Place, and in no Wise benefit me. . . . We are surely in the Hands of the same God at Penzance as Torquay. . . . I cannot leave my Habitation, which I have taken for a long Term, and must abide in till the Term is over, nor will I go back without having done what I came hither to do. My Friends are but *too*, too solicitous. They have all heard this nonsensical Story, and every Day brings me Letters full of pathetic, and I believe *sincere* Admonitions. . . . I wish you would all be more moderate in your Kindnesses. My Establishment is not a little Cloke-bag to put on my Shoulder, and carry from one Place to another. . . . Be *quiet*, dear Friend, as I say to Miss Williams and Conway, who are half wild, God bless them!—and their Loss would be Nothing to what they fancy it. Yet 'tis all I can do to keep them from the Door.

The World is all unhappy. This vexatious Affair of the Queen has been a *Tryal* to Everybody. I wish to know how the Bishops of Salisbury, Bangor and St. Asaph give their Votes. Lord Liverpool's Observations were the best. If there was Nothing *wrong* between the Lady and the Courier, what *was* there? Conversation was difficult, and Talents there were none. . . .

I do believe there is always Fever of this Sort in these low Situations, and when we *do* move, if it be not to Dymerchion's burying Ground, it shall be to the lofty Crescent at Clifton. Torquay may do for some of those future Years dear Mrs. Pennington talks of. . . . If you like to tell Mrs. Rudd I still hope to come early in the Spring, do tell her so. Her Son is a good Child, and will ever be an Honour to her and your really obliged and troublesome H : L : P.

She told Miss Williams that it was all she could do to keep Conway from "quitting Business & Benefits & flying 400 miles after an old Woman of fourscore. He had more need to run to his own Uncle,—Lord Hertford— who is ill and has much to leave, whilst poor H:L:P has not an unappropriated Guinea. What's left is my own now but £6000 was a monstrous Cut upon it—and unlucky because that foolish Concert Ball & Supper had run me so far behind. When all Debts are paid and the Days begin to lengthen, I will put my Luggage aboard the Ship called the *Happy Return* and get away to the Heights which agreed with me so when I was there last May or June."

The typhus outbreak had run its course, and the queen's "acquittal" gave the populace something else to celebrate: "Penzance run mad for Love of the Queen, menacing their Neighbours' Houses, Windows &c. Riots. The most beautiful Illuminations I ever witness'd—the Ships all hung around with Lamps, & St. Michael's Mount beyond all Praise. Letter from Hammersley about the Money Stuff."

Penzance 15 Nov. 1820

I feel terribly afraid, dear Mrs. Pennington, that my State of Anxiety when I wrote last, betrayed my Pen into some Impatience of Expression . . . and the Interest Dr. and Mrs. Randolph were obliging enough to take in my Concerns deserved more Thanks and Compliments than I had, at that Moment Leisure to pay. . . . The

Weather is changed, and the Fever quenched, and H:L:Piozzi become less of a Nuisance to her friends. . . .

This Town may defy any Place of its Size, or twice its Size, for a Burst of real feeling displayed in Honour of the late Event. All the Ships in the Harbour have Flags during Daytime, Lamps blazing thro' most of the long Night. "Queen Caroline for Ever" round every head in Ribbons. . . .

16th Wish'd Morning's come. The Windows unbroken. The gay Fellows from Newlyn and Mousehole, who increased our Mob, had all gone Home to bed after drinking "The Queen and Count Bergami for Ever" till they could scarcely reel to their wretched Habitations. But St. Michael's Mount was a beautiful Sight to see. Lamps in pyramidical Form to the Top, where Tar Barrels were placed, and gave a glowing Light to the Scene, resembling the Bay of Naples.

Mrs. Pennington protested that Mrs. Piozzi had scared them all, and was then half-angry when they were frightened. "Above 200 miles distant, was it possible to hear of fever and typhus in the town, and even in your own house, and not be alarmed?" And in spite of her avowed intention to keep her own counsel about Conway, she could not resist one more gibe.

You have much more Confidence in Mortal Man than I have, dear Friend—I am wickedly Sceptical—on these Points my Faith goes no farther than my Sight, which as you know is often directed at a Mill Stone. . . . I do most sincerely hope your "tall Beau" will be all you predict of Comfort, both to his Mother and you, his best and kindest Friend;—but such negligent Conduct would never be any Comfort to your P.S.P.

Mrs. Piozzi had just received "a kind Letter from my kind Friend at Birmingham" and once more took up the cudgels on his behalf, urging Mrs. Pennington not to be too hard on him or Salusbury. Time was surely running out for her; indeed, as she observed, five of her oldest acquaintances had died since she came to Penzance. "Am I to outlive everybody?" she asked.

Penzance Fryday 24 Nov: 1820

. . . I will live, if I can, but every Day counts now, aye, and every Pulse, too, and 'twere Folly not to feel it. . . . Do not be sorry that I have arrived at more than three-quarters over, but pity those who have many Arches to pass, with broken battlements on their Side, enough to giddy their Brains. Salusbury's Path seems clearest of Difficulties, but he is in Danger of Drowsiness; Conway's Walk is above all Men's dangerous. And neither of them, poor dears, have, in their early Stages, experienced the Advantages of an *authorised* Hand to lead or guide them. You will see them both—good fellows in their Way—whether they love *me* enough or not, I'm sure you will. Conway *certainly,* I believe *both,* do think better than she deserves of theirs and your H:L:P.

She finished writing to Mrs. Pennington, and she noted in her diary that she was planning another letter, "about Exeter," and the following day, Tuesday, 28 November, "I wrote to Mrs. Rudd, and enclosed a Draft, one Month's Run; wrote to her Son, saying 'Come here, or meet me at Exeter.' " The draft was for fifty pounds—a generous deposit to secure her tenancy of 36 Royal York Crescent. The letter to Conway, which has not been traced, must have given at least an indication of the business which was so important that Mrs. Piozzi was prepared to drive over a hundred miles to discuss it. In her next letter to Dowry Square she turned her attention to matters of State (the queen was that day driving in triumph to Saint Paul's Cathedral) and studiously avoided mentioning Conway. But Mrs. Pennington was not prepared to ease off the pressure; in spite of her resolve to hold her tongue, she returned once more to the attack.

Hot Wells 4th Decr. 1820

Impossible, dearest Mrs. Piozzi's letters can arrive too frequently, especially when, like her last, they afford a prospect of her more speedy return. I have seen Mrs. Rudd, who desires me, with her best respects, to say how rejoiced she is to hear a better account of your health & the state of your household & that you may rely on No 36. being ready for your reception on the 12th of March. For my part I rejoice in the power of dating a new month, as it is so much nearer the time when we may reasonably hope to meet again. . . .

I am astonished you do not hear from Brynbella. *Men* who do not give themselves the habit of writing letters, or feel they do not do it well, are generally bad correspondents, but Lady S—— writes easily & prettily. I dare say Sir John will make a very respectable steady country gentlemen; a little dull, perhaps—but yet I think (as you say you have found him) sufficiently on the *qui vive* where his *interest* is concerned. Conway will always be *charming*—what else, the destinies must decide. I dare say he *was* alarmed & shocked at reflecting on his negligence, when he heard of the situation you were in. It would have given him an *awkward feeling,* after a silence, on his part, of 5 months, to have seen his good mother's name, or yours, or even *mine* with an Obit. in the papers.

I am glad you get *kind* letters from him; better late than never; but why he did not write before, or why he writes *now,* is equally inexplicable to me!—and it will ever appear to me the most extraordinary thing in the world that he should think it *too much trouble* to keep up the only intercourse that absence permits, & to support an interest that does him so much honor. I hope his benefit proves productive, which is most to the present purpose. The theatre at Birmingham closes this week—but not a word touching his *own* emoluments, or future destination has he communicated to his doting parent!!! . . .

My letters, dear friend, can be nothing but a dull commentary on yours. The weather is so bad I seldom leave my own fireside. . . . My acquaintances are all on the Hill, & no one comes down to us, nor can I, without more expense & hazard, get to them. I was tempted the other evening to go & see Mr. Mathews' "At Home" & was amused & really amazed at the versatility of his powers, & the truth & spirit of his imitations.

Mrs. Pennington's continual harping on Conway's silence was all the harder for Mrs. Piozzi to bear as each day went by with no word, and when their "anniversary" arrived, it was Dr. Forbes who gave her pleasure, sending "Verses and Books expressive of his Admiration" of her *Retrospection;* there was an interesting diversion the next day when "Miss Willoughby dined with me on a Woodcock; read me the whole Story of her Father's Quarrel with Mr. Burke concerning the French Revolution." Mrs. Piozzi did not mention that story in her next, rather delayed, letter to Mrs. Pennington, though she ranged far and wide in her choice of subjects to write about, and showed her displeasure by not mentioning Conway at all:

Penzance Dec 14. 1820

My dear Mrs. Pennington says her Letters are mere Commentaries upon mine. What Text shall I find *next* to excite her eloquent Flattery? Lord Kirkwall's death is what most readily presents itself to a woman just twice his Age, who little dreamed of living to lament him. Poor dear K! My Heart is heavy at the Thought. And when Recollection, or Retrospection places him before my Mind's Eye, it is with a Pint of curious Constantia Wine under his Coat, or shooting Dress, to please dear Piozzi in his last Illness. So kind! Well! sure the People will have done dying some Day! Never was Sight so wearied as my own is by reading Newspaper Lists.

Mrs. Mostyn writes chearfully. Living abroad loosens all old Attachments, and gives no Opportunity of forming new ones. 'Tis the true Mode of keeping the Mind free. . . .

Tell me sometimes about the Weather—in the *World*. Here it is mild, soft, and just now silent; stormy enough at Times, but never clear. . . .

I have Comfort to hear my fair Daughters praised even in *this* odd Place. They patronized some poor Families, when such Philanthropy was less common than now, and are remember'd with grateful Tenderness. Such recollections are among the Hothouse Plants which bloom in the open air of Penzance. . . .

The Houses here are so constructed that, except in one particular Wind, we live smother'd. Coals are however not cheaper than Elsewhere; Meat and Fish bear no Price, but we pay for every drop of Water—salt or fresh—because it must be *carried*. The Place is replete with Objects of Curiosity, nevertheless, and Lady Keith gained immortal Fame here, by descending 35 Ladders, of 35 Steps each, into a Tin Mine. Not the most extraordinary of all the Tin Mines, for there is one under the Sea: a submarine Residence of many wretched Mortals, who seldom see Light, save such as their Patron Sir Humphrey Davy supplies them with. . . .

Meanwhile you have been amused by Mathews. Even I, who naturally hate Buffoonery, was much diverted by his Story of the Yellow Soap, which dear Sir George Gibbes never wearied himself with repeating. . . .

Mathews was on tour again after his London season, and Mrs. Pennington had seen him in Bristol, since when he had appeared in Birmingham, where Conway's engagement had come to an end. In September he had appeared at Oswestry and had entertained, and been entertained by, the Ladies of Llangollen. He wrote a graphic description of both occasions to his wife:

> The dear inseparable inimitables Lady Butler and Miss Ponsonby were in the boxes here on Friday. . . . Oh, such curiosities! I was nearly convulsed. I could scarcely get on for the first ten minutes after my eye caught them. Though I had never seen them, I instantly knew them. As they are seated, there is not one point to distinguish them from men: the dressing and powdering of the hair, their starched neck-cloths; the upper part of their habits, which they always wear, even at a dinner party, made precisely like men's coats. . . . They look like two respectable superannuated clergymen. I was flattered, as they were never in the theatre before. . . . I have today received an invitation to call if I have time as I pass, at Llangollen.

That was not convenient, but the ladies accepted Mathews's invitation to join him for dinner near Oswestry, and he duly reported home:

> Well, I have seen them, heard them, touched them. The pets, the "ladies" as they are called, dined here yesterday. . . . I shall never forget the first burst upon entering the drawing-room to find the dear antediluvian darlings attired for dinner in the same manified dress, with the Croix St. Louis and other orders, myriads of large brooches, with stones large enough for snuff boxes, stuck into their starched neckcloths. . . . I longed to put Lady Eleanor under a bell-glass and bring her to Highgate for you to look at.

Mrs. Piozzi would have enjoyed those descriptions even if she did not care for his buffoonery. She would not have been amused to know that Mathews may have seen some of her own words, which were intended only for Conway's eyes.

The Proposal

It is probably true to say that little credence has been given by those who are at all familiar with Mrs. Piozzi's life to the suggestion that she ever proposed marriage to Conway; Clifford did not even mention it, and no clues have appeared in the letters and diaries so far to shed light on the allegation—until Mrs. Piozzi's dramatic call for Conway to dash to Penzance or meet her in Exeter. The story of the proposal first appeared in the *New Monthly Magazine* of April 1861 in a long, authoritative, but unsigned review of the first edition of Hayward's biography. In discussing the controversy about Mrs. Piozzi's relationship with Conway, the reviewer, who was referred to in Hayward's second edition as a "distinguished man of letters," claimed personal knowledge of one piece of evidence which had not hitherto been disclosed:

We ourselves heard the late Charles Mathews say—and no one who knew him will question his veracity—that Conway himself had shown him Mrs. Piozzi's offer of marriage, and asked his opinion and advice. Mathews told him at once that he could not honourably take advantage of it. *"That,"* said Conway, "is what I myself felt; but in a matter so important to one so poor as I am, I also felt that my own decision should be confirmed by the opinion of a friend. I now know what to do." This, we repeat, we heard from Mathews himself, at the time the circumstance occurred, and we therefore believe it.

Though the writer accepted the story as genuine, he put no great store by it himself, suggesting that Mrs. Piozzi's judgment may not have been "as sound as it had been in better days." Leaving that question aside for the moment, we might ask whether the facts as presented are plausible and what were the credentials of this witness. Unfortunately, his identity has not yet been discovered: he might well have been the editor himself, Harrison Ainsworth, who was also the proprietor of the journal, but he would have been only fifteen in 1820, the year when the incident would have taken place, and it is unlikely that Mathews would have revealed the story to such a youngster. However, it will be noted that the reviewer used the words "we heard Mathews say," meaning that he was not addressed directly but was in the company of others at the time. Considering Ainsworth's family background, it is not difficult to imagine that he might have been present on some occasion when conversation turned to the rumours about Conway and Mrs. Piozzi, and he cannot be ruled out as the writer of this review, and a reliable one at that.[4]

The reviewer also said that he heard the story "at the time the circumstance occurred." When, exactly, was that? If the proposed meeting at Exeter was as momentous as seems likely, the proposal may have been put in Mrs. Piozzi's letter of 28 November, and shortly after that date there was an opportunity for Conway to meet Mathews, who arrived in Birmingham about ten days later for a short engagement after the conclusion of Conway's season. However, it is also possible that the events took place earlier in the year, when Mathews and Conway were often in each other's company in London and at Ivy Cottage in the months of April, May, and June. That is the time when Conway urged Mrs. Piozzi to burn two of his letters, which may have touched on this delicate subject as well as his business with the Hertford family. And the occasion when the reviewer heard the story was more likely to have been when Mathews and Conway were both in London than when Mathews was on tour in December. Thus the balance of probabilities suggests that if Mrs. Piozzi *did* make the offer, it was when she was in Clifton in June; and this does not diminish the significance of the Exeter conference, when the proposal might still have been on the table. To put it no higher, the revelations of Mathews and his chronicler are not contradicted by other circumstantial evidence.

Finally, there remains the question of motive—assuming that Mrs. Piozzi was still capable of rational thought, of which there can be no possible doubt. Having handed over the six thousand pounds to an ungrateful and grasping Salusbury, she made no secret of her conviction that she had done enough for him and that whatever was left was hers to dipose of to more deserving causes, principally to her two pets, Angelo and Conway. Indeed, she was still waiting for Conway to respond to her invitation when, in a letter to Miss Williams on 16 December, she complained that "Salusbury never tells me anything but how much he wants Money," and almost in the same breath that Conway "is an excellent Young Creature of Infinite Merit, and has not yet obtained half his due Share of this World's Good. . . . *My* Assistance all evaporated in last Year's Benefit."

Her existing will left to Salusbury everything which was not held in trust for her daughters, but if she were to remarry, that will would be nullified. She had no intention of depriving Salusbury of what he already owned, but there were her belongings at Gay Street, and perhaps books and papers at Brynbella (which were not safe in his hands), and other sources of income that could be used to make some provision for her favourites. It happened that two days after last writing to Miss Williams, she worked out what it would cost to live in Clifton instead of Bath, and, allowing £750 for housekeeping, £300 for rent, £200 each for coals and beer, and £100 each for clothes, medicine, carriages and chairs, journeys and accidents, Madox and Fortnum, and "give and throw," the answer came to £2,050. That figure did not alarm her, and although she did not set down her corresponding income, it must be assumed that it was adequate. The Crowmarsh and Streatham rents amounted to about £650, so that her remaining investments (which may have been held in trust) must have brought in £1,400. When she died, the Crowmarsh rents would go to Lady Keith. Streatham Park, and perhaps other assets, would revert to the trust, but there might have been enough to make a modest provision for her "pets" in a new will.

In the meantime, she longed for letters from Clifton, where she assumed Conway had gone, and saw Miss Willoughby every day, until to her surprise he wrote to her from London, three weeks after her "Exeter" letter. Her diary did not reveal his news, but in fact he was engaged for a season in Bath early in January, and their meeting was unlikely to take place. She wrote next day to the "belle Veuve & her Boy."

Christmas brought the news from Mrs. Pennington of "the entire destruction of the Kingston Assembly Rooms by fire. . . . Those very rooms in which, near to the same time last year, you made above six hundred people so happy! Everybody, I believe, but me and Conway, who you certainly desired should have been *most* so; but he was so wretched, and infected me with his misery, so perversely does everything go in this world." The fire had spread to Upham's shop, and Mrs. Piozzi was glad that she had paid all his bills. She reported to Mrs. Pennington that "Miss Willoughby is in the highest Favour here. She plays Country dances, Waltzes, etc., . . . for the Boys and Girls to dance, after winning their Money—or that of their Parents—at Sixpenny Whist; and she makes Riddles and Charades to amuse us all, and is very entertaining." As the year ended she was working on some scheme to benefit Angelo and Conway, and "wrote to Hammersley *private* about Puss & pretty one. I sent him a neat Statement of Debtor & Creditor." Perhaps the idea was that if she could not change her will, she would try to divert all she could to them in her lifetime. She told Booth that she would have to "quit No. 8 Gay St., as too expensive for poor H:L:P" and closed her diary with "Adieu old Year 1820! Cold farewell compared that of 1819."

18

"Your precious Portrait"

THE new year opened with snow and gales and roaring seas, and the mails all stopped; but a letter from Sir James Fellowes got through, and Mrs. Piozzi told him that "those who said no Snow was ever seen at Penzance, dealt in Fiction and Fable; here is a heavy Snow this Moment, and but that the Sea is open enough, I should call this a Polar Winter." She confessed that she had never found the courage to look in *Thraliana* since her arrival in Penzance, "so little does looking back delight me. At eighty-one Years old 'tis Time to begin reconnoitring, when we know Retreat is impossible."

The *British Stage* announced that Conway, "who (according to report) has married Mrs. Piozzi, was about to open at Bath," almost exactly twelve months after the rumour first circulated in theatrical circles in London. The *Courier* reported a terrible accident to a coach on the way from London to Bath, and Mrs. Piozzi was convinced that Conway was among the injured, but Mrs. Pennington's next letter reassured her on that account.

Hot Wells Jany. 8th 1821

Two very different Subjects Dearest Mrs. Piozzi present Themselves for the commencement of our New Year Correspondence. In the first place I have to announce to you the Death of our worthy old Friend Mrs. Lambart. . . . In the next place I have to report a Visit from our Conway—no longer qualified to play "Master Slender", but growing to what I should suppose the celebrated Mr. Barry[1] was, in his best Days. He told me he was on his way to Bath, where I cannot feel delighted he has accepted an Engagement, as he was, or *thought he was* ill-used there last year. I am, however, glad for his poor Mother's sake, he has secured Employment anywhere. After toiling four months as Stage Manager & first rate Actor, Birmingham again treated him scurvily at his Benefit. Tho profuse in Applause they did not distinguish him above the 2d. rate Performers, & he got from them only 106 pds!!! Detestable Mechanics! I hope he will waste no more such Powers on them.

He will now enter Bath without Rivalship, for Warde is not there; and without *particular Patronage,* for People like so much better to give their Applause & their Money voluntarily, than to have either extorted, that it often does more harm than

188

good; and we shall see how this fine Creature gets on single Handed;—but I do think he is a most unfortunate Wight, for *with* Patronage or *without* he always seems to miss the only Fruits of his Labour that is of any real importance.

Shall you & I go over to his Spring Benefit, & sitting snug in Mrs. Dimond's Box mark how the Game goes, without being Players in the Party? You will not want to know if I was very Cruel in the Interview. The Rogue pretended to come with *trembling* apprehensions of my Wrath—which was all stuff. He knows well enough he has only to appear—"Look in his Face & you forget it all". However I did remember to shew him that he had taken something of the fine Edge from that warm Feeling I had in his favour. "Anything so noble! so manly! so graceful! so *handsome* as his figure at this time I really never saw"—so said my maid Sarah, who opened the Door to him; but he is certainly afraid it should make too powerful an impression, for I could not prevail on him to dine with us; however he has *half* promised, if his leisure will permit him to return for two or three days to Clifton in the course of this week.

That letter from "the fair Pennington," which Mrs. Piozzi dismissed sardonically in her diary as "3 scrapes, a kiss & your humble servant," is the last one from her to be quoted by Knapp, and it is the last in the Princeton collection, although she wrote several more during the next few weeks. Mrs. Piozzi's later letters to her have survived, the next being dated 13 January, in which she wrote: "I can't cry because his Benefit brought only £106. The People in London get very little. Mrs. Hoare says she saw excellent Acting to completely empty Benches. . . . Miss Willoughby dined with me Yesterday. She says Coriolanus is an unfavourable Character for Actors to appear in just now, when insulting Language to our Peuple Souverain will perhaps be treated as it was in Rome. I shall be happier when I see the Newspaper, and learn how our Friend has been received; but do not fright Mrs. Rudd about it, perhaps she may get good Intelligence before the common Prints of the Day come out. If the Play should be disapproved, every kind, good-natured Acquaintance will inform her."

On the same day, Mrs. Piozzi wrote to Conway at the Theatre Royal, Bath, and this one *has* survived,[2] unlike the twelve she had written to him between 4 August and 22 December, the present whereabouts of which are unknown:

Penzance Saturday
13 Jan. 1821

Dear Partial Friend! and how well you know the Heart of poor H:L:P. It did beat dreadfully when that Coach fell between London and Bath just at the Moment I concluded that you were stept into it—and all the Passengers hurt—was the Expression. Oh! but I suffer'd more when receiving a Bath Newspaper with a Piece cut out, apparently speaking of the Theatre.

For what could Overturns or Sword or Home
But mangle and torment that beauteous Frame;
More cruel bitter Words; they murder all our Fame.

It was a false Alarm; but I will have a Paper of my own in Future, Meyler's Paper; and be obliged to no one. My Health won't bear now to be trifled with; tho' while Things go smoothly Complaints would be graceless, and we will try for a happy New Year—by endeavouring to deserve it. *You,* on whose Merit I build more than half my Happiness; *do* deserve every Consolation in *Fortune's* Power; and what is placed in *mine* I will take care of.

The Frost suited my Mountain-born Lungs better than these horrid Fogs, which while they conceal disagreeable Objects, magnify them. Dear Mrs. Rudd's House No. 36 shall be inhabited to *her* liking and mine, after the 12 March if it shall please God to grant me a good Journey & *Deo volente,* you know, *etiam in Vimine.* I have learned at Penzance how *that* Saying became popular. St. Piran, Patron & Protector of our Tinners here in Cornwall, was supposed to have sail'd hither from Ireland in a Kitchen Cullendar, & he actually sleeps at Mousehole with these Words for his Motto—Vimene, a Basket, being more heroic, I trust, than a Kitchen Utensil. Mousehole! you exclaim: why *is* there such a Place? ay truly, & a wretched Place it is:—only 28 people—Inhabitants—who can write & read, & *they* study Tom Payne's Works; & Pen Addresses to the Queen—Craft's Hole & Cats Hole were silent, & I felt sorry; because the first of these was so nam'd from producing 13 Cuckholds out of 12 Dwellings only—those Dwellings a Hut with one Room apiece.

Now who says I live on Fish—like an old Witch—hovering thro' Fog & filthy Air—*for Nothing??* but I must go on adding to my Stock of Ideas while Life is lent to me—for who knows at 81 how soon that Power may be taken away? Let me at least if admitting ludicrous Fancies keep out all unworthy ones: suffering no sullen Reflexions on the Past to pollute a Future warmed by Friendship so pure as ours—Tho' I do confess a Moment's Vexation when reading yesterday how some Lady gave a Fete at dear *dear* Offley Place Hertfordshire,—so many years considered as the certain Property of poor Hester Lynch Salusbury—see the Biographical Sketch in your own Hands ["The Abridgment"] & see Thraliana too; which I brought here, but have never dared look at, my Spirits being so low. What Wonder! residing in a Chair-lumber'd Closet just 12 feet by 9. That Closet filled with Smoke, & not a soul to speak to on any literary Subject—save now and then Miss Willoughby.

Your precious Portrait is my only true & comfortable Companion at ev'ry Meal, and I shall drink your Health to the Darling Creature by & by; and Success to Coriolanus—"Well Madam, I'm going, going to the Capitol"[3]—Incomparable Conway! how present is that Scene to my Eyes!! But I want to *hear* the Welcoming Shout of Rapture once more to greet your long-sigh'd-for Return to their Boards. "A Shout that tore Heav'ns Concave" best would please me.[4]

The Pennington seems to expect much from your next Meeting with the Bath Folks: I have a Letter from her filled with lavish Encomiums on Your Looks, Manners etc. Two Months ago *it was another Story*—since when we have corresponded more distantly; tho' I did not quote Juliet upon her, and say

Is it more Sin to wish me thus Mistook
Or to disparage my Friend with that same Tongue
Which thou hast praise'd him with above Compare
So many Thousand Times??

—but never heed her.

The Mind of Mrs P—— is like a Pail of clear Water, shewing the Faces of her Acquaintance as in a Mirror—but touch the vessel, shake it ever so little, it reflects nothing but Wrinkles and Deformity. I have known her more Years than you have Months; and think very highly of her Abilities: mais les Qualités du Coeur sont les plus essentielles, celles de l'Esprit sont les plus brilliantes. On se fait aimer ou haïr par ses Qualités—says Abbé Girard; on se fait rechercher par ses Talents. Des qualités excellentes, continues he, jointes à des variés talents font le parfaite merite. Il font un Auguste moderne, un Conway, says H:L:P. One would go round the World for such a Character.

Well! I have been down to the Quay just now to see one of the Ships that surrounded our Globe, commanded by Captain Cook; she was Endeavour then, but having discovered some Straits or Sound, which they called Prince of Wales's Strait, she took that Name, & has been purchased in her old Age by the United States of America, who loaded her with Timber t'other Day—meant for the Port of London—but a hard Gale of Wind drove her to Penzance; while (as you say) the light Craft paddle successfully along, blow Wind which way it will—of large Vessels here the Wrecks have been very dreadful.

In the great Ocean to which we are all hastening, the good Ship *Christiana*, Captain Bold Honesty Commander, will cleanest & safest get into Harbour—& such a Harbour! Why will you wish me still to remain out at Sea? But there are, and have been longer Lives than mine, retaining every Faculty.

A Cornish Gentlewoman in this neighbourhood, Zenobia Steevens by Name, held a Lease by her own life *only* for 99 years, and riding ten Miles to give it up, the Duke of Bolton to whom her House belonged, kindly permitted her to stay in it, unpaid for, as long as she should live, & inviting her, good-naturedly to drink a Glass of Wine. *One* if your Grace pleases, was the reply; not two: because having to gallop hence these short Evenings upon a young Colt, I'm afraid of being giddy-headed.

Farewell! Be in Spirits; Tout ira bien: Enjoy *my* Birthday & your *own* & trust in God that the year 1821 shall *not* be that which deprives my dearest Mr. Conway of his truest Friend, Invariable, Immutable H:L:P.

Write just a scrap, but *mind,* nothing except your Business. Then, you'll be to Bath—as is the Osprey to the Fish who takes it—by Sovereignty of Nature.

Bessy and her Boy are well—as we call well—he daily verifies all you said of him,—but we *pant* for Clifton, *literally* as well as figuratively. Your Bible is in great forwardness, Castle-Lock'd fast.[5] When shall I put it in the Governor's Hand?—on Sunday 15 March I suppose—we may count the Weeks now.

Hammersley's Bank seemed to have been dubious about Mrs. Piozzi's recent instructions, for on 12 January she repeated them, writing to "*Hugh* Hammersley *private* concerning Puss & the pretty one," noting that according to George Hammersley's statement, her balance was £1,403.12.0. On Tuesday, 16 January, "Miss Willoughby came to Breakfast wth Congrats; calling today—as it really *is*—my Birthday. No Letters, No newspapers." When the *Gazette* did arrive, she would be happy to learn that Conway's Coriolanus was warmly welcomed, and that Mrs. Pennington was probably right in thinking that without Warde (*and* the partisan Mrs. Piozzi), he might fare better. Mrs. Rudd wrote to say that No. 36 would not be ready before 2 April, but until then she could have rooms in her own home at No. 10 Sion Row. In Mrs. Pennington's next letter she apparently expressed concern that Miss Willoughby's politics might lead her friend astray: "You are a comical lady in your fears lest Miss Willoughby should make me a Radical. Salusbury seems, by his letters, to have fears lest she should be hovering over my death-bed, to his disadvantage. I hope to hold fast both life and loyalty one little while longer, and cannot believe she will help hurry either of them away. Poor Miss Willoughby! were it not for her I should not have known Milton from Shakespeare by this time: for to no other creature here are those names familiar."

A letter from "Tulip flos floris—Positive, comparative & superlative"[6] called for more words of encouragement, in a letter to "Tulip the poor," which is now in the Pierpont Morgan collection.

Penzance Tuesday
6: February 1821

Dear tender-hearted Friend! for you say I must not call you Romancer—let me at least thank you for the Partiality my Mind considers seriously as so very great an Honour. Be in better Spirits: The Pendulum now vibrating as you describe will make its Stop at *Love*—it will indeed. When you last saw or heard from him, as old Menenius says, *He had not dined:* but natural Affection however choked by the World's Thorns, will spring up in green some Time. . . .

This Nonsense will come into your Hand upon Thursday, & that Day Month shall I put my little Troop in Motion. Before then I must absolutely go to the Land's End and see the Place where no more World is found, But foaming Billows breaking on the Ground. It is a difficult Drive as People tell me; a Gentleman of the Town however says he will go with Miss Willoughby and me. His pretty Wife may trust him; for our *Youth & Beauty* will not I think endanger his future Peace: he is the Attorney of the Town, a Handsome man, certainly; because Miss Willoughby fancies him like Mr. Warde, and Bessy says he resembles Mr. Conway.—The man resembles neither, but Human Beauty of one peculiar Cast is common at Penzance, where the Inhabitants have the same System of Features, high & low & all the same Tone of Voice. I wonder'd at first, but now I find that they are all related: curious enough!

The *Happy Return* takes, in a Week or Two my Luggage back to Bristol. Dear Mrs. Rudd will have a fine Plague with us, but like you She is all Kindness & true Good Will.

I see the Foundling of the Forest advertised [Conway had appeared as the Count de Valmont]. Its author [William Dimond] must think time creeps sure till some of *his* pieces are exhibited. When my favourite Hero of the North comes out I think Miss Jagger [the miniature] will get a sly Salute or Two, but if you would call on Roche the deaf and dumb Man he would court you to sit & then I could when rich enough, purchase myself a *constant* Companion.

The Runaway I have been reading and talking to for 8 long Months sets out on his Sea Voyage soon under safe Convoy of his Guardian Angel, St. Michael, to whom our Mount and Bay are dedicated—leaving me almost ridiculously wretched—but 40 Days now will shew me the Original. I hope you will find me not much worse with regard to Health. The warm Sea Baths agree with me.

Well! if I live as long as Harry Jenkins I shall never run into an Angle of the Island again—though Success so far attended my Frolic, that I *do* return owing but 50£ in the World, instead of 7 or 800.

And so God bless my true & honourable Friend—who will I hope live long & happily; and die 60 Years hence in the Arms of *his own* H:L:P.—the Daughter I shall perhaps one Day embrace.

> Meanwhile the manner of the mounting Lark
> Thy fellow songster Conway mark.
> Up to the sky let thy loud Fame resound,
> Thy humbler nest build on the ground.

So sung Pindaric Cowley—but in true Sadness and in sober Love, when I pray for choicest Blessings on that beauteous Head I always *do* think more of Fame than of her heavy-loaded Follower Fortune. *She* comes so late into the Inn you know, and is so liable to be robbed on the Road. 'Tis so that *Learning* is content to drive the Baggage Waggon of Genius; but tho' always plodding in the old Ruts—like your *old* Friend—is always in Danger of being overturned by naughty Boys that Lay Heaps of Rubbish in the Highway and deface the Milestones.

Talking of naughty Boys, puts James into my head;—he really behaves too bad to talk about. Doctor Forbes asked me today if my fine Footman was married to the Baker's Daughter yet?—Adieu dearest & *truest* & tenderest of all Friends, to poor H:L:P.

The Salusburys have got a new baby—*William* Edward. God guard him & the dear *William* just 30 years older than he through the thick Brakes and Briars of this workaday World.

Mrs. Pennington was evidently still "angry with Salusbury for his Jealousy of every one I love, & angry at Conway for not calling on her"; Mrs. Piozzi was prepared to accept her strictures of the one but not the other.

Penzance
February 10th 1821

Thanks dearest Mrs. Pennington for your kind Letter speaking the Words of Truth and Soberness—We will send Hams & Bacon by the Happy Return most certainly;—the Butter here is Poyson, whether in Pot or Pan.

All you can say of poor dear Miss Willoughby is true to a Tittle. Sir John is very ill-natured in detesting Everybody who contributes to my Comfort, and I hope not *quite* correct in supposing that neither you, nor she, nor Conway would endure my Company for an Hour but for Interest. Sophia Hoare's Civilities will make him very angry indeed when he hears me say I delight in them: but he deserves such sort of Vexation.

So you see Horace Twiss[7] is the Man at last who when public Virtue finds herself Sick and Squeamish; holds the successful Smelling Bottle to her Nose— and are they not all Actors on both Sides? Surely they are. *That* Titmouse began his literary Career by criticising & ridiculing H:L:P in Magazines, Reviews &c; and afterwards begged my Pardon at a Party Mrs. Siddons gave one night at Westbourne. We shook hands and drank each other's Health, & I wished him the Success his Audacity deserved. . . .

But there's a Passage in the Bath Paper that interests, and *ought* to interest me more than Marriage or Merriment. A Woman dying in the Act of Supplication to Almighty God—past 80 years old, found dead at her Prayers. I used to say that no Death ever pleased me, but here is one at last with which my Heart would be content with indeed. Why did she not take me with her? If however the next Month carries me to Clifton, and treats me with a Sight of *True Friends,* I shall think leaving me behind was merciful, and feel replete with Gratitude.

Conway has written to me very kindly. What will his Benefit do for him I wonder! He seems by what I read of such Affairs, to be the Man that holds up Dimond's Theatre—of my best Wishes he has been Three full Years in full Possession.

George Hammersley had told her that "Conway's a favourite at Bath," and the Luwyches told Miss Williams that they enjoyed him in *The Foundling of the Forest.* Mrs. Piozzi passed the word on to Dorset Fellowes that "Conway is in high favour at Bath, the papers say; so indeed do private letters. That young man's value will one day be properly appreciated; and then you and I will be found to have been right all along." His benefit was one of the few beacons on the road ahead; if only she were spared to see it.

My dear Miss Williams will not be sorry when I say *packing* has hinder'd me from writing to her: The Things which go by Sea must be sent early, and I have five Weeks yet to see through, before I see myself in a Place to be called by Courtesy, *Home.* What a Blockhead I was to come hither, and what a Booby I am to go hence again, crosses my Mind every Moment; dancing about so on the very Edge of Life's Precipice: I will dance no more, but stay at Clifton (if it should please God to set me safe there) & end my Days among the Invalide & Superannuated Preparers for their last Journey.

A "Silly Letter from Miss Williams," apparently asking for more information about her future plans, provoked Mrs. Piozzi to a "snappish" reply.

What *Plans,* my dear Miss Williams, would the People hear of? Does planning future Life accord with the Age of 82? I left Bath in June last for Clifton, and happen'd to like a House there: Sir John Salusbury seem'd to like it too, and Mr.

Lutwyche liked it—and I will go thither when 'tis ready for me, & wait in a Lodging till we make it so. Is this a *deep Plan* worth People's stopping you in the Street to enquire? It is all I can tell, and more than they have any Business to ask. The Acquaintance I have made here are more kind & less inquisitive, and if the Place had agreed with me, here I would have stayed, but my Lungs now require a high Situation.

There was more to Clifton than altitude, but Mrs. Piozzi was tired of public probing into her affairs.

The Penzance folk had made much of her last few weeks in their midst, and George John's offer to take her and Miss Willoughby to Land's End was much appreciated, though even that prospect did not keep her from "thinking of my Preparation for the *World's* End & fancying my Death close at Hand."

19

"Sickness and Sorrow"

MRS. Piozzi described her adventure in what she thought would be her last letter to Mrs. Pennington from Penzance:

> On last Wednesday, a memorable Day, Mr. George Daubuz John undertook to show us the Land's end, and we did stand upon the last English Stone, jutting out from the Cliffs, 300 Feet high, into the Atlantick Ocean, which lay in a wide Expanse before us towards the Land Columbus first explor'd, Hispaniola. Dinner at a mean House, affording only Eggs and Bacon, gave us Spirits to go, not forward, for we could go no further, but sideways to a Tin and Copper Mine under the Sea. Aye! 112 Fathoms from the strange Spot of Earth we stood on, in a direct Line downwards, where no fewer than three score Human Beings toil for my Lord Falmouth in a submarine Dungeon. . . . This Place is called Botalloch, whence we drove Home our half-broken Carriage but not even half-broken Bones; having refreshed at the House on which is written "First Inn in England" on one Side, and "Last Inn in England" on the other.[1] By "us" and "we" I mean Miss Willoughby and H:L:P., but we took our two Maids, Bell and Hickford, on the Dicky, and James rode. Four Horses were not too many for such an Exploit, tho' one of them was a Waterloo Warrior.

It seemed that James's next ride, from Penzance to Clifton, was to be his last in Mrs. Piozzi's service. Not only had he misbehaved with the baker's daughter, but he "been among the w——s, and how can I make school-mistress to a lad of 18?" And he had " 'beaten the Maids a Row' like the fierce Fellow in Shakespeare."

> This has been going on a long While, but I forebore to speak to you about it till it suited me to say—do, dear Mrs Pennington, get me a Footman. Not a Fellow to wear *his own Clothes;* I must have a *Livery* Servant, who will walk before the Chair, and ride behind the Coach. . . . My little Plate, so small in Quantity, is easily clean'd but *clean* it must be. For I will not live in a State of Disgust when I have a decent Mansion over my head, and James too dirty and slovenly, even for a wretched smoky Closet like that I inhabit at Penzance; he is a sad Fellow. . . .

> We will go to Conway's Benefit certainly, if I get home time enough: Miss Willoughby will wish herself of the party most truly. But for *her* I should have pass'd many a dreary hour.

Mrs. Piozzi wrote again the following week, in answer to Mrs. Pennington's request for her travel plans.

The day of our Arrival how can I *certify?* My hope is to see you sometime on Tuesday 13; but Lord! I was so ill on Friday Night I hardly felt anything like Certainty of ever seeing myself out of Penzance alive. Never mind that, though; and say Nothing about it; for the People make such an Ado I dare not confess that anything ails *me,* like other old Women. It is really troublesome to excess. . . .

Clifton will be nearer both to Books and Men. Dr. Randolph must be careful of his valued Life. No one respects his Abilities, or would regret the Loss of them, more sincerely than H:L:Piozzi, whose Comfort it is that she is likely soon to escape the truly uneasy Sensation of outliving Friends and Enemies, and standing alone upon the Stage of Life, till hiss'd off for being able to furnish no further Amusement. After having been At Home on the Boards, like Mathews, the Buffoon, for so many silly Years. Bear me however Witness, that I am all but weary, and only kept from confessing myself so because I think it is wrong. . . .

Everybody seems to approve my sitting down at Clifton, as neither in the blaze of Society nor the Obscurity of Solitude. We will make out the Close of the Game as we can; and if you ask me to Dinner on Wednesday the 14th, a Refusal need not be apprehended from your poor H:L:P.

The last letters Mrs. Piozzi received before leaving Penzance, from Mrs. Lutwyche and Mrs. Stratton, both spoke of Conway and his forthcoming benefit, and gave her heart to face the long and arduous drive to Clifton, in a carriage which was not up to the task. She spent the morning of Thursday, 8 March, packing and paying—"gave away Money with both hands"—and limped to Truro, where makeshift repairs were made to her vehicle. "Bad Roads, bad humour, bad Accommodation at Launceston" were followed by a bad night—"Headache & nervous," and on the road to Exeter, Mrs. Piozzi was alarmed when Angelo followed her into a dirty house, full of smallpox. That night, climbing into a high bed with the aid of a light stool, she slipped and hurt her shin badly but went to the cathedral service the following morning, before setting out for Taunton, where they arrived late at night "by a Miracle, the Carriage breaking at every Step." More repairs were needed to see them through the last lap, on the Monday, to "No 10. Sion Row—Heaven be praised! here we are, safe & sound in a lovely Country, & *with kind Friends*—and all well."

The next day her first callers were the Penningtons: "They both appear much broken. Evening Dear Conway came to tea and his mother—passed a sweet afternoon." She was in heaven, surrounded by the friends she loved best, gossiping with Mrs. Rudd at every opportunity. She was amused by a "Comical Letter from Cecy Mostyn" from Florence, and comforted by a sweet one from Hugh Hammersley, confirming that she had six hundred pounds in his house. She looked at a school for "Darling," read *Kenilworth,* which she lent to Mrs. Pennington, and after a week reported to Miss Willoughby in Penzance[2] that she was where she wished to be, "on the sweet Gloucestershire Downs—numberless old acquaintance & some *new* kindly expressing pleasure at my return." Conway was occupied onstage in Bath all week, but returned to his mother's on Sundays.

> Our friend is not younger; he won't play Master Slender now: his enquiries after you were very kind indeed & he rejoyced for *my* sake that Penzance was *your* chosen retreat. Oh! how he regrets his Leperillo! . . . The benefits are thin, we hear, but that for which *we* are interested gives good hope: Monday 26th will be the day, & Mirandola with the Chevalier de Morange the night's entertainment. . . .

> I have seen the *future* footman—he will at worst be better than poor James, I suppose, who has gone to Bath now on a frolic: Bessy tearing her hair & Mrs. Pennington will be eloquent in her expressions of wrath & anger. . . .

> The ship things all came safe, & Mr. Divie Robinson—to whom I sent 60£ as you know before my leaving Cornwall, has never taken care to let me have it, and I have to live, without wine or *waiter* for James returns no more from Bath Theatre—the loadstone of attraction.

She told Miss Willoughby of her mishap and made light of her injury, but the next day she was worried enough to call in Dr. Dickson. He said the leg was all right, but she was not so sure; in fact, she wrote in her diary, "I suppose this Leg is to be my Death; God's Will, not mine, be done!" She also told Miss Williams about her injury, but urged her

> for God's Sake do not write to Wales & tell of such Nonsense; or I shall have the Salusburys here in a Minute—before I am got into my house, under the Idea of obliging me most exceedingly:—whereas nothing could possibly vex me half so much—or put me into such Distress. I have asked them for July, when the Dividends will be paid—and that will be quite Time enough for me to receive Sir John's Instructions of *who is to visit me and who is not.*

> If you ask for my private Box at the Theatre we shall meet—I know you are asked to Miss Fellowes's to meet me, and I am sorry I am engaged.

The leg continued to worry her, though she pretended to "care less & less concerning the Result." There was no fracture, and her bruises and contusion ought not to have caused any greater concern than would be sensible for a person of her age living in those days. But she had almost made up her mind that the injury would be the cause of her death, which could not be long delayed. Yet she happily paid one pound for a year's subscription for library books, and threw herself into "the 1st Vol. of

Melmoth,"[3] the second volume of which wearied her. She rejoiced that her box of books and manuscripts had arrived safely from Penzance, and read in the *Bath Journal* that "seldom have we seen a performance to rivet the attention of the audience more closely" as Conway's Carwin in *Thérèse, or The Orphan of Geneva*.[4] With only a few days to go before the benefit, Dr. Dickson advised her to stay indoors. "I never stir," she complained, "and shall soon suffer for Lack of Exercise—but 'tis no Matter, I will die the Death they bid me die." A letter[5] from Sir James Fellowes arrived on the Saturday before the benefit, which called for a prompt reply:

Your letter only came last Night—My dear Sir James Fellowes, though a tardy Correspondent is always a kind one. True it is, that your Sister has seduced me to dine with her on Tuesday next; and rejoyce in our Friend Conway's Success, which I hope to witness on Monday Evening. . . . Sleeping at Russell St. however, would not do. I have asked Miss Williams to dine with Mrs. Pennington and me at the Elephant and Castle, where I will set up my Repose, and keep my l.e.g.—my elegy—in good Repair. . . . Since my Arrival at Sion Hill,—for there I occupy a Lodging until my House in the Crescent is ready,—two Parcels directed by dying Friends have given me a mournful Sensation; they are Letters written by me to them in distant Days, I know not how happy. You will have to look them over after my Death.—My Intention, however, is not to be in Haste; though Salusbury seemed to apprehend his Journey would be long and expensive if I died in Penzance, but now he could come to the River Severn to look after the Demise and the leg I see (legacy); but he must stay away till I have put my house in order.

I wish you had seen Miss Willoughby & I drinking your admirable Father's Health upon St. Valentine's Day. She was a great Comfort to me at that savage Place, but dear Salusbury was as jealous as he was of Mrs. Pennington last Winter at Bath, or of Conway.

The next day Mrs. Piozzi "wrung Dr. Dickson's consent to go to the play & to Fellies for dinner tomorrow—I did go to the play and saw dear Conway more inimitable than ever." Conway took the title role in *Mirandola* for his benefit, before a poor house. At the Elephant and Castle Mrs. Piozzi rose late the following morning, found that her leg was no worse, "wrote to Mrs. Rudd & said so." It was her first appearance in Bath for many months, and many friends (including Sir Walter James and Conway, and "Tradesmen out of Number") paid their respects. That evening at the Felloweses' dinner party, "Conway was the hero adored by all," and Mrs. Piozzi was gratified to observe that Sir James Fellowes was "very civil" to him. Fellowes recalled that occasion himself, and confirmed his high regard for Conway, in a letter to Hayward many years later, when he handed over his Piozzi material:[6]

On the day following the date of this letter [above], which was the last I received from Mrs. Piozzi, I called at the Castle and Elephant at Bath, and found her with

Mrs. Pennington. She was in high spirits, joking about the l.e.g. She dined with my father and sister, at No. 7 Russell Street, and was throughout the evening the admiration of the company, amongst whom were Mrs. Pennington, the lady so often mentioned in Anna Seward's correspondence as the beautiful and agreeable Sophia Weston; Admiral Sir Henry Bayntum G.C.B., a distinguished naval officer at the Battle of Trafalgar; Mr. Lutwyche, and Mr. Conway, the actor, who was held in high esteem for his excellent private character.

Conway took breakfast with Mrs. Piozzi the morning after the party, and stayed with Mrs. Pennington while she called on Miss Sharpe, and "bought a cucumber for Dowry Square." Later she and Mrs. Pennington returned to Clifton, where they dined, "play'd at Whist, won my chair hire." Life returned to normal.

Thursday 29 March Dr Dickson called—says my leg is mending—gave me leave to walk out, a very little. I walked and was no worse for it. Sate at home writing letters all day long. The Wine is arrived. . . .

Friday 30 March Dear Conway came for five minutes last night, Breakfasted today & ran back to Bath to act Calas tomorrow & Young Marlowe in Goldsmith's play on Monday next. . . .

Saturday 31 March Dr. Dickson saw the Leg again; says it is going on admirably. It may be so!! God's Will be done! I read Melmouth; a Bath Herald at Night from his Admirer Conway. Dr. Dickson 1£ of course every Visit—He bids me take Caster Oyl.

That was the first indication that she was suffering from any other disorder, but she made no mention of her health in a note to Miss Williams that day, except that, after saying that she had left Mrs. Stratton and Miss Sharpe *in their beds,* she added, "So runs the World away, & so away from the World runs, dearest Madam, yours ever H:L:P." In a postscript she wrote, "I suffer'd nothing from my Visit to Bath, & our Friend Conway gained nothing. He scarce cleared 30£ when all Expences were paid, I hear."

A few days later she had just noted with satisfaction that her own finances were in order (there were five hundred pounds at Pall Mall, and she would have a thousand pounds when the dividends came in July), when Salusbury dropped a bombshell.

Brynbella 3rd Apl. 1821

My dearest dear Aunt

        I should think your last kind & welcome letter must have crossed on the road one from Harriet to you—& therefore do not know whether you owe us a letter or not—I always however feel indebted to you for many more than I can ever repay—I feel very glad that you are return'd to Clifton *safe well & happy* & ought to be very thankful you are able to write word that you are so. I hope I may conclude from this observation that you are now quite free again from pecuniary embarrassment & resolved to continue so. The greatest pleasure I have is derived from perceiving that whatever depression takes place in the agricultural districts, you will not suffer, neither in income or your spirits.

It is easy for those who have fortunes arising from funded property, to make them minds perfectly quiet about the "National Misfortune of having Bread too Cheap"—but indeed dearest Aunt, I cannot do so—when I find my income reduced in the tithes alone £300 to £400 annually! & when I have been obliged in consequence of rascally tenants to take farms in hand amounting to nearly 300 acres & taking into consideration the extraordinary difference in the price of every kind of grain, you will not, I am sure (knowing my original income) wonder at my being in many respects very much distress'd in circumstances, as well as depressed in spirits, by this very unexpected change; nor will you be much surprized when I tell you that I feel persuaded (unless times change for the better) of the necessity of breaking up my establishment at this dear place; & retire to some other residence where I can live upon a reduced income——I have taken no further notice of Mr. Cleaver's letters since you told me to set him at defiance—& indeed if this Catholic question is decided in their favor, the tithes everywhere will be much reduced in value—& then the pale-faced precentor, as you call him, will repent having been so difficult to please—God bless you my dear Aunt & take care of yourself. Pray excuse this letter all about myself—but one is too apt to think so much of ourselves.
Adieu—Harriet sends her most affectionate love. Believe me ever to remain my dearest aunt your most affect. & sincere nephew.

John S. P. Salusbury

Mrs. Piozzi's diary comment was remarkably restrained: "I recd a saucy [=impudent] letter from Salusbury—care the less about my Debts," but her next letter to Miss Williams left no doubt as to what her response would be.

Monday 9: April
No. 10 Sion Row, Clifton

I thought dear Miss Williams would like *official* Intelligence concerning her Friend's Leg—so since my charming Doctor Dickson was going to Bath & beg'd Commands from me, I courted him to call at kind No. 43 and make *true Report*.

He came back saying how well *You* looked considering past Sufferings; and how good you were & how partial. . . .

This fine Air does agree with me certainly; but I should not have tumbled down at Exeter, it was a very foolish Trick indeed.

I have heard from Salusbury—a Letter full of *bitter* Lamentations concerning the Price of Corn—mingled with somewhat like reprehensory Advice to poor H:L:P not to run in Debt any more, with a sarcastic Addition of happy whose Income is in the *Funds* & so forth. His Tythes have fallen, I dare say—dismally—but Lord! I suppose if this Catholic Bill passes there will soon be no Tythes at all. . . .

Here is beautiful Weather—I suppose that will increase the national Misfortune of having Bread too cheap. It is a shame to hear Country Gentlemen lament such a Situation of Things as a Calamity: we who pay Baker's bills on a Monday Morning are glad of it—& thankful.

In her diary she put a brave face on Dr. Dickson's call. He had "visited my Leg & scraped & hurt it—& I said he was too faint hearted & fearful of making me squeak," and afterward there was a "sweet letter from our own incomparable Conway. God bless him." She wrote to Salusbury that night—it may be assumed that she did not mince her words—and showed her letter to Mrs. Pennington the next day before posting it. Her almost daily doses of castor oil were proving ineffective, and Dr. Dickson brought in a surgeon (to administer an enema?). She passed a comfortable night afterward, but knew that it was "very foolish to fancy myself mending." She sent a note to Mrs. Pennington to say that "our kind and skilful Dickson is just gone. He only waited till things were in the state they should be, I perceive; and today he brought the tall man again, who performed the *operation* and praised my courageous endurance. This for your own kind heart's private information. *Mine* is completely satisfied of their skill and management. . . . All that was done yesterday and today (rough usage on the whole) has raised, not lowered, the spirits of your ever obliged and faithful H:L:P."

Still resilient, she attended a "gay party" for fifty people at the Penningtons for whist and "Commerce" two days later, and on the Sunday afterward Conway took breakfast "and a bad dinner" with her. He had now completed his season at Bath and had been engaged for the summer at the Haymarket, where he would once again face the London critics; and whatever fears he may have harboured on that score, Mrs. Piozzi was delighted to hear of his progress. The surgeons had forbidden her to go to church that day in case a touch on the leg should cause more damage, but they did sanction a gentle walk to the Crescent to look at her future home on the Monday. She went to bed in the evening feeling rather worse, and the next three days' entries in her diary were scrawled, almost illegibly, and the following three days were blank. It was probably the first time in nearly eighty years that she had not put pen to paper. She had not the strength to comment on Salusbury's next letter.

Brynbella 17th Apl. 1821

My dearest Aunt,

I found your letter on my table after my return from Chester, where I have been with dear Harriet for these last ten days on a visit to Mr. Myddleton. My last letter to you certainly was a *complaining* one, & I regret most sincerely that I should have written to you at a time when my mind was depressed at the thoughts of leaving this place, that I forgot how little interest anybody (who lives in this world) takes in the welfare of others; or should certainly not sent you such a long account of my own distressing circumstances. It is not, however, my intention to teize you with a repetition of the *complaints* contained in my last—& will therefore conclude the subject by stating to you that I merely hinted at the probability of my being forced to leave Brynbella in consequence of my family being increased, and my income very much diminish'd; . . . thinking you might offer some advice, or at least express some regret at my Fortune being so much reduced as to render it necessary for me to adopt a measure, which of course must be so painful to my feelings.

I have now, however, resolved to make immediate arrangements for letting this beautiful residence as soon as possible; and must look out for an eligible tenant who will do as little injury to the place as he can help—in the meantime I must contrive to find a house in Chester, which will suit my family & from whence I can come & see after this Estate as often as occasion may require. . . .

You have never told me what accident you met with on your journey from Penzance—but I hope you did not receive any serious injury; pray tell me in your next. I believe Miss Williams's tale of woe concerning Col. Wynne of Garthewin is too true—but it is equally true of many other families in this neighbourhood, who are less able to raise money to pay off so unexpected a claim. . . .

Pray remember me kindly to Mrs. Pennington

That letter was the last straw, and when she did summon up the strength to write, it was the words "Sickness & Sorrow" across the spaces for Monday, 23, and Tuesday, 24 April. Of all the bitter disappointments that she had ever experienced, there could have been none more galling than Salusbury's abandonment of Brynbella. There was surely nothing left to live for now. And yet the next day the old indefatigable bounced back, a little shakily:

Wednesday 25 April Leg quite well. Mrs. Pennington has broken my spectacles.

And then, barely able to hold her pen:

Thursday 26 April More Doctors—less Health, every day

Friday 27 April Sir George Gibbes called. Mrs. P.——ready to ring all the Bells for Joy—I guess not why.

So ended Mrs. Piozzi's diary. Mrs. Pennington's show of cheerfulness had not deceived her; indeed, she had told Sir George, "I almost dread your professional efforts in my favour, for I *would* not recover, and long to flit away."[7] As she lay dying, her bitterest regret must have been her decision to adopt John Salusbury Piozzi in the first place, and then to hand over her estates prematurely. And now even that was not enough to support him. She refused to have him sent for. If she could put back the clock, there is no doubt as to who would be her beneficiary now; but all she could find for *him* was the draft for a hundred pounds that she had made out twelve months earlier.

Conway was so alarmed at the sudden decline in her condition that he took it on himself to warn Salusbury that the end was near. Desperately afraid of being guilty of interfering in family affairs, he chose his words with even greater care than usual:

Sir,
    I am prompted to address you by a very melancholy occasion. My kind and very highly valued friend Mrs. Piozzi, whose health has been visibly on the decline for several weeks, owing to a severe accident she met with on her return from Penzance, is at present so much reduced as to afford, I fear, no reasonable hope of her recovery. The only person near her who has any direction of her affairs is Mrs. Pennington, and she appears so much afflicted and agitated that she may possibly omit giving you timely notice of the circumstance. I therefore venture to do so, and entreat you will not lose an instant in setting out, if you hope to see poor Mrs. Piozzi alive. Mrs. Piozzi has taken apartments at my mother's, with whom I at present reside—but as taking any step in this business might appear in me unseemly and officious, I rely upon your honour, Sir John, never to name me as the source of your authority for setting out. My motive for addressing you is good to some, and harm to none, and I therefore stand acquitted to myself for my conduct.
            I have the honor to be, Sir,
                Your very obedient Servt.
No. 10 Sion Row   W. A. Conway
Clifton Apl. 30

Mrs. Pennington had urged Mrs. Piozzi at least to let her daughters know how ill she was, and then, unaware of Conway's initiative, she also wrote to Salusbury:

                                        Clifton No 10 Sion Row
                                        Tuesday 1st May 1821

My dear Sir,
                        I am extremely sorry to be the medium of intelligence that cannot fail to give you the most painful feelings. Our beloved Mrs. Piozzi has been some time indisposed, but her disorder has taken so unfavourable a turn, and is attended with such alarming symptoms, that it is not right you should any longer remain uninformed,—tho' it was not until this day I obtained her permission to address you on the subject. She has the best medical attendance this place affords, and I believe I may say there can be none better,— and we have the satisfaction of a friendly visit from Sir George Gibbes. They all agree in opinion, that tho' perhaps not immediately dangerous, her case is very alarming from her advanced age. . . .

Mrs. Piozzi desires me to inform you that Mrs. Hoare has volunteered coming to her, and we expect that lady tomorrow; whether any other part of the family accompany her, I know not. They are to occupy the house she has unfortunately engaged for 12 months in the Crescent,—the same you visited her in last summer. If you should meet the ladies here the dear invalid trusts it will be in perfect harmony, as she finds herself much too ill to bear discussion on any subject; indeed for the greater part of her time she is in a state of stupor from the effect of anodyne medicines she is taking to quiet the irritation of her bowels, and stop the hæmmorage from those passages,—the seat of her disorder. I feel that I should have explained to you, in the first instance, that the leg has no share in this general derangement of the system, as you might naturally incline to think was the case. That is quite well, miraculously so! as it should seem at her time of life, when such accidents often baffle all attempts to cure, in younger subjects,—and we vainly flattered ourselves it was an uncontestable proof of the purity and strength of her constitution which has unhappily for us, suddenly given way from other causes.

Her faithful servant is indefatigable in her care and an entire devotion of time and attention on my part will, I hope, prove that there is something more than profession in the long tried and disinterested friendship of,

Dear Sir,
Your obedient humbl. Servt
P S Pennington

I beg my best compliments to Lady Salusbury and I beg to assure her Ladyship that I never leave our interesting invalid for more than two to three hours. Her mind is perfectly satisfied and tranquil,—exactly in the situation we could wish,— She desires to be most affectionately remembered, and that her kindest love and good wishes may be registered in the hearts of all at Brynbella. . . .

It is very unlucky dear Mrs. Piozzi could not get into her house before she was confined by this attack as her present lodging is very limited and inconvenient.

Salusbury may have already set out before that not-very-urgent summons reached Brynbella, but he did not get to Clifton before his aunt died, with Queeney, Sophia, and Susan at her bedside; Cecilia was, of course, too far away.

20

"Be kind to my remains"

MRS. Pennington was deeply impressed by the Ladies' display of grief at the bedside, and she told Miss Willoughby[1] that she had been misled all those years about their lack of affection toward their mother.

> It is my painful task to communicate to you, who have so lately been the kind associate of dearest Mrs. Piozzi, the irreparable loss we have all sustained in that incomparable woman and beloved friend. She closed her various life about nine o'clock on Wednesday, after an illness of ten days, with as little suffering as could be imagined under these awful circumstances. Her bedside was surrounded by her weeping daughters: Lady Keith and Mrs. Hoare arrived in time to be fully recognised; Miss Thrale, who was absent from town, only just before she expired, but with the satisfaction of seeing her breathe her last in peace.
>
> Nothing could behave with more tenderness and propriety than these ladies, whose conduct, I am convinced, has been much misrepresented and calumniated by those who have attended to *one* side of the history: but may all that is past be now buried in oblivion! Retrospection seldom improves our view of any subject.

Considering that Mrs. Piozzi was not yet in her grave (she was buried beside her beloved Piozzi on 16 May), and that Mrs. Pennington was hardly intimate with Miss Willoughby, those comments might appear hasty and uncalled for, even if they may have contained a grain of truth. The daughters were without doubt charming and gracious ladies, but of the three who were there, only Sophia had shown any warmth to their mother during her lifetime, and none of them had seen her, except at her initiative, since she married Piozzi.

Mrs. Pennington also contrived to suggest to Salusbury[2] that his aunt had taken Mrs. Rudd's house at above its market value, and advised that as there was little chance of finding a subtenant for the duration of the agreement, he would do better to accept Mrs. Rudd's terms of one hundred guineas to terminate the tenancy. Mrs. Pennington then went out of her way to complain about Bessy.

> Bell returned so much out of Humour & continues in so sullen and irritable a state that I have had very little communication with her, nor any Information

respecting the Beloved Remains after they left Clifton;—but it is ever the way with that Class of People; if they do not feel it any longer for their Interest they soon lose sight of that Respect and Attention which had no other Object.

Those comments revealed as much about Mrs. Pennington's character as Bessy's. She seemed not to recognise that after perhaps twenty-five years' devoted service, Bessy had suffered the greatest loss of all by the death of her mistress, and was now homeless and unemployed. But the relationship between Mrs. Pennington and her friend's housekeeper had never been comfortable. Piozzi once said, in front of one of the maids (it might have been Bessy) that Mrs. Pennington had become too much of a hanger-on; and the maid, resenting her interference one day, let slip an unguarded retort, which sparked off the fatal row between the Piozzis and the Penningtons. Even if Bessy was not the maid involved, she would have known all about the incident and the subsequent breach. Years later she had named her baby Angelo in honour of the master, and was more one of the family than a servant. She was now holding her ground until her late mistress's intentions were clear. Salusbury had known Bessy ever since he arrived at Brynbella at the age of four, but his response to Mrs. Pennington's intelligence was as unfeeling and revealing as hers: did the servants realise, he asked her, that they were now "living at their own cost"?

In her reply, Mrs. Pennington was able to report that the servants had by then left No. 36. "The young man[3] very modestly retired on receiving his discharge: I have fortunately procured him a good Service with my Friend Lady Collier, which gives me pleasure, as I really believe him very deserving. Mrs. Bell's affliction seems to have rendered her quite *Savage!*—she has never called on me since her return from Wales!—and today, I am told, she goes off with the little Boy & Sophy to Bath." A month later Mrs. Pennington wrote another long letter to Sir John:

Hot Wells 6th July 1821

Dear Sir,

I address you in consequence of a Letter just received from Mrs. Mostyn dated Lucca, who thinking it probable you may be in this part of the Country in your Office of Executor, & not doubting, from my attentions to her lamented Mother, but that the most friendly Intercourse subsists between you & me, she requests me to say, with her kind Love, how much she shall be obliged if you will reserve her something that was her Mother's. . . . It may seem that the application is superfluous, but I am rather inclined to embrace this opportunity of writing to you as I feel sorry we somehow parted on less friendly terms than we met.

Many motives attach me to you. I very sincerely esteemed your worthy Uncle. . . . . I loved you when a boy, and you were dear to the Friend I best loved. I am well aware of the vacillating Principle that had too much Influence on *her* Conduct—I suffered so much and so long from it, but let you and I only remember her better Qualities, & unite in doing them all the justice in our power against a World ever ready to depreciate a Character that stood so highly distinguished as hers. Mrs. Mostyn remembers you with the most liberal kindness and sets us an excellent Example. She seems to feel only for the Friend and Parent she has lost, and to sink into generous oblivion all remembrance of the Disappointments she has experienced, for I presume you are not to learn that at her Marriage the Estate you now possess was as much pledged to her and to her Children as the Tea-kettle and Lamp was ever promised to Lady S., or *given to me*. Your not seeming to credit my assertion on that point hurt me extremely.

All her friends, she said, knew that Mrs. Piozzi had promised her the teakettle, but now the word had got around that Sir John had refused to part with it and denied that his aunt ever intended it for her. She was afraid that he included her in the "hangers on and toad eaters" whom he said more than once Mrs. Piozzi was surrounded by. If the truth was that Lady Salusbury had set her heart on having the tea-kettle herself, she would settle for any other token of remembrance that he could present to her. But there was something else:

I am surprised and vexed that my letters are not to be found—I am sure there must have been numbers of them left at Bath, and I understand that the first time you returned to Clifton, after having *slightly* examined the papers there, that you said you saw several in my hand-writing. It was then I requested they might be returned, which you politely said you should do with reluctance, or something to that purpose. It is very unpleasant to have ones private affairs and crude opinions exposed to chance, and I still hope they will be found. I have a larger, and perhaps better collection of dear Mrs. Piozzi's letters than any other correspondent, and am in fuller possession of her opinions on all subjects, *private, public and literary* possibly than any other person in the kingdom, which I shall carefully preserve. Dr. Whalley says was any publication intended, they would be a most rich and most valuable addition, and altogether form a collection of letters more eagerly sought after, and more agreeable to the general taste than any that have been ever published.

I am glad you settled with Mrs. Rudd. She has only let part of it & it is not likely she will let it to any advantage until the Winter—I am also glad to hear Mr. Conway has got the Shakespeare & really thank you for relieving me from a sort of responsibility that lay upon my Conscience. That no Memorandum was made on *my* subject I am confident was because she considered it as a gift passed away from her, & not being under her Sight at the last was not thought of.

Sir John's reply was brief, restrained, and final:

17 July 1821

Dear Madam,

I think it right to acknowledge receipt of your letter; but refrain from entering into particulars, lest any observations I might be induced to make should give you offence.

With best Compts. to Mr. Pennington etc

It is significant that Mrs. Piozzi had left no directions about the tea-kettle; she probably resented her friend's wheedling and may have never really intended her to have it, not knowing where it would end up after Mrs. Pennington died. Far better, she may have thought, to leave it in the family, but whatever may have been her intentions, Mrs. Pennington's clumsy and tactless letter to Salusbury was unlikely to succeed. On the other hand, Conway, who asked for nothing, received everything that Mrs. Piozzi wanted him to have. A few days after she died he sent the draft to Sir James Fellowes with the following note.[4]

Sir,
    As [you are] one of the Executors of my late revered Friend Mrs. Piozzi I take the liberty of placing in your hands the accompanying Draft, which was presented to me by that lady only two days before her Death. I am very ready to acknowledge the acceptance of many acts of kindness during her *Life*, but must decline appropriating to myself what I consider a *posthumous* benefaction, which more properly belongs to her Heirs.
    Be good enough to dispose of the same as you may deem right.
    I have the honor to be, Sir, Your very obedient Servt.
                          W. A. Conway
Bath
May 7, 1821

Salusbury wrote to him later confirming his aunt's bequests, and on 23 July Conway replied from 12 Dean Street, Soho, in suitably deferential tones,[4] acknowledging their safe arrival:

Sir,
    Particular business summoned me from Clifton almost immediately upon receipt of your letter, and I have since been entirely occupied with the opening arrangements of the Haymarket new theatre; these circumstances will explain and apologize for any delay in addressing you.

Allow me to offer my sincere acknowledgment for your polite and liberal attention to the wishes of my late patroness. The books have been safely delivered to me, and are indeed valuable! the other articles mentioned in your letter were presented to me by her own hand; one of them before her journey to Penzance, and the other within a few days of her lamented demise.

The latter item must have been her gold alarm watch, which she would not part with until the end. Among the books were Malone's *Shakespeare*, a copy of Johnson's *Prayers and Meditations*, with additional manuscript prayers, and Mrs. Piozzi's name on the flyleaf, and a folio edition of Young's *Night Thoughts* (the handsome edition she thought she could not afford), all of which together with those she had given him earlier, were to remain with him until he died. The annotated Bible and the "castle" have not been traced; the precious portrait would have been reclaimed by Mrs. Rudd.

When Mrs. Piozzi gave Conway the draft, she may also have returned his letters; if not, Salusbury would surely have destroyed them on sight, but they have disappeared anyway, except for the few notes that he wrote from Princes Street and were probably locked away at Gay Street. Mrs. Pennington did get her letters eventually, but not the teakettle. Salusbury found that his aunt's estate fell so far short of his expectations that he was obliged to withdraw his acceptance of the baronetcy, though he could afford to stay at on Brynbella. Mrs. Piozzi was now beyond caring what happened to her possessions; what mattered first and last was that posterity should

> Be kind to my remains; and oh! defend
> Against your judgment your departed friend
> Let not the insulting foe my fame pursue
> But guard those laurels which descend to you.[6]

She died knowing that Conway was about to make another bid for success in London after an absence of six years. He made his first appearance at the Haymarket on 6 July in *The Provok'd Husband,* and would have been gratified to read that the *British Stage* thought he was "much improved since we saw him last; the formality of his manner has been partly corrected, and he treads the stage with far more ease and self-possession than he formerly did. We hope he will not again quit the metropolis, for he is always a sensible, and sometimes an excellent, actor. His Lord Townley was a very impressive performance." Unfortunately, notices like that were more than offset by the attentions of *John Bull,* which had been launched earlier in this coronation year by Theodore Hook to promote the interests of the king and to besmirch even more the name of the queen and her supporters. It was "the most infamous newspaper that was ever seen in the world. . . . Its personal scrurrility exceeds by miles anything ever written before."[7] There was more drama and farce in public life than in the theatre: the queen was denied admission to the Abbey for the coronation of her husband, but showed herself to the crowds when and wherever possible. "At Drury Lane on Monday (30 July), Kean played Richard before the Queen: we never saw an actor and an audience better suited," wrote *John Bull.* The same theatre mounted a lavish reproduction of the coronation two days later, the queen having prevailed on the management "to gratify her insatiable curiosity by as good an imitation as possible, in a place where as money levels all distinctions, she *must* be let in."

William Augustus Conway had the dubious honour of being mentioned on the same page, in a report on the Haymarket complaining about the "new player thrust upon us in principal characters headed by a fantastical person, of the name of RUDD, who with the deplorable coxcombry of such persons as PETER PROCTOR alias BARRY CORNWALL has re-christened himself with the romantic name of HENRY AUGUSTUS CONWAY." Theodore Hook had found another stick with which to beat the unfortunate actor, who he thought was parading under false colours, and Conway must have feared that sooner or later *John Bull* would hear about his approaches to the Hertford family. On other occasions, "MR CONWAY (as they call him) was by no means successful in JAFFIER, but the contortions of his face were highly entertaining." And "Mr. CONWAY is too tall for an actor . . . it appeared as if Jaffier had been plotting against Lilliput, or Pierre and Belvidera had been betrayed into Brobdignag."

Week after week, *John Bull* picked on Conway: his Mr. Oakley awakened "the most unpleasant reflections—there was never anything so bad. His consummate affectation, his barbarous pronunciation of the English language, and his entire incapacity to express any passion or feeling, kept us in a continued fever of disgust." The *New Monthly Magazine* was much kinder: "he has a noble person, a strain of brilliant declamation, and no small power of depicting agony and sorrow . . . he is still deficient in ease; he seems scarcely to know what to do with his height; and his hands move about fantastically, as if he had no command over them. He is, however, a great acquisition to any theatre." At the end of the four-month summer season, the *British Stage* agreed that "Conway as usual has been treated in a scurvy way by the braves of the press, but he has earned a good opinion of those who judge for themselves, and regard with due contempt the vile personal abuse that has been heaped upon him."

Hook's jibes were too ludicrous to be taken seriously, but these personal attacks so undermined Conway's confidence that even the most sympathetic notices failed to encourage him. He seemed doomed to be the centre of controversy, and if he could not succeed in the metropolis, he saw no future on the stage. Mrs. Piozzi would have certainly urged him to stand and fight, but he could take no more, and after the Haymarket was never seen on the English stage again. Macready, who had also been savaged by Hook, wrote in his *Reminiscences* (pp. 295–96), that "poor Conway allowed himself to be the victim of this man's abuse, and wanting in strength of mind to endure the sneers and personal attacks with which he was constantly assailed, retired from the stage, which afforded him a respectable income, and which could ill-afford the degree of talent he possessed."

Sheer poverty drove him back to the Haymarket that year, to take a job as prompter at four pounds a week, which would hardly cover his expenses; and while he was there, death removed the two noblemen who might have rescued him from penury—the marquess of Hertford had died in June, and in August the former Lord Castlereagh[8] had cut his own throat. Conway was the guest of his friend William Jerdan shortly after that sensational event, and evidently told him how these deaths had dashed his hopes of ever securing their patronage; whereupon Jerdan had offered to find a way to approach the new marquess on his behalf. He asked Conway to set out his story in writing, and his letter[9] must surely be one of the longest he had ever written, and certainly is too long to reproduce in full.

Oct. 13th 1822

Dear Sir,

I gladly avail myself of your kind permission to renew, through this medium, the subject of our last conversation, and though experience forbids me to entertain any *sanguine* hope from your promised interference, my most sincere acknowledgments will be yours for your friendly *endeavours* to serve me. In that conversation I spoke of Lord William Conway as my father, and I must now inform you that, owing to peculiar circumstances, he has never supported or assisted me, and though not *formally* disowned, I am not acknowledged by him. My various letters soliciting that act of justice, or an interview to enable me to demonstrate my claims to it, remain unanswered. On one occasion I traced him to an inn at Ringwood, and in a note which I prevailed upon the landlord to place in his hands, implored an audience, if only for a few minutes.

Conway went on to describe his approaches to the late marquess through the duchess of Roxburghe and to William's other brothers, Robert and George, since when he had apparently made another abortive approach to the marquess.

My *last* effort was through the assistance of a particular friend, a gentleman eminent in the literary world, whose knowledge of my straitened circumstances and natural claims upon the Hertford family induced him to seek an interview with the late Marquis for the purpose of pleading my pretensions. On account of ill health the Marquis declined *seeing* him, but intimated his willingness to receive a *written* communication. Such communication was accordingly made, but I did not receive an acknowledgment. I send you a copy of it, and the request which preceded it, that you may be able to appreciate the strength of that application, which was not honoured even with a reply.

I fear these details will have been sufficiently tedious, but in justice to myself I could not be less circumstantial. My hopes now lie with Lord Henry[10] and the present [and third] Marquis, to neither of whom I have the honour of being known. By your strong representations, perhaps, these noblemen may bestow a closer consideration on my very hard lot, than it has hitherto been deemed worthy of. Their lordships may be humane enough to feel, and candid enough to allow that though Lord William chooses to estrange himself from his connections, it is most unjust that *I* should be the *sole* victim of his peculiarity. For though his legitimate children may not have a large share of his personal attention, they are at least supported by his *purse,* and enjoy the full benefit of that *rank* in society to which their birth entitles them; while I am not only without any mark of *personal* notice which might give me a decent respect with the world, but I am also without the slightest *pecuniary* aid that would enable me to live without it. Little sanguine as repeated reverses have taught me to be, I cannot forbear to entertain *some* hope that their lordships will commiserate, when reminded that while every member of their numerous family, legitimate or otherwise, enjoys some provision from the wealth or influence of their connections, I alone of their blood am doomed to neglect and penury—am abandoned to struggle as I may with adversity, without assistance or encouragement—left to battle or beg my way through the world unregarded and unrelieved!

He hoped that their lordships would either be able to make him a small allowance to supplement his earnings from the theatre, or else would find him a public office to which he could apply his industry. But if neither course were acceptable, he hoped they would use their seniority within the family to persuade Lord William to grant him an interview.

Such, sir, are my opinions and feelings upon this disagreeable subject, and such the *expectations* I have ventured to build upon them. . . . I know it cannot quicken your zeal, though it may *hasten* your *endeavours* to be informed that now that the theatre is closed I am without any prospect of provision for the passing day. Of course I shall attend your answer with some solicitude, and hope that it will convey a permission for me to see Lord Henry.

Jerdan passed that on to the new marquess with a covering letter:

As the editor of a Literary Periodical work it has happened to me to form the acquaintance of a very estimable individual, and to have taken that interest in his welfare which I think his merits and misfortunes can hardly fail to inspire. That individual, my lord, is Mr. Conway, who is known, as I believe, to your lordship, as he certainly is to Lord William Seymour, to Lord Robert, and to the rest of your lordship's family.

In his distress he has entrusted me with the story of his birth and struggles in life; but I hope your lordship will do him the justice to believe that this was not done until necessity overcame the long cherished sentiments of delicacy, pride, and honour. . . .

To your lordship, as the head of the family, I am, from your general public character, emboldened to appeal without fear of misconstruction. I write to solicit the favour of an interview, in which, should there be no insurmountable obstacle in the way, I am persuaded I shall be able to impress on your lordship the extreme hardship of the case, and persuade you even to overstrain a point to become his advocate and benefactor. That he has not been successful on the stage is not his fault, for to ability he joins industry, perseverance, and respect for himself. May I be allowed to say, that that stature and personal appearance which gives dignity to a noble station (and which he inherits from his parentage) is not auspicious to dramatic effect.

Still, my lord, Mr. Conway is in need of a little help, and this is so honourable to his discretion that I do hope that what your lordship's interest could do with a

breath will not be withheld from one who has such peculiar claims, indepen-
dently of his deserts, to consideration. . . .

I will not close my letter without expressing my opinion of the value and
integrity of Mr. Conway. Had he no pretensions, I aver that I would deem it an
act reflecting lustre on any nobleman to take him by the hand; and sincerely do I
pray that his father in acknowledging him will place him above the calamities of
life, beyond which his humility looks for nothing.

In his autobiography, Jerdan claimed that Hertford House responded
favourably to his request for an interview, but the marquess's illness
caused the arrangement to be postponed, and his subsequent death
crushed all hope of furthering Conway's cause.[11] Conway himself had
really placed little store by Jerdan's mission, and still faced the problem of
earning a living, but so strong was his aversion to acting that he turned
down an offer from the Bath management at the end of 1822, saying that he
would rather break stones for a shilling a day than return to the stage for
fifty pounds.

That resolve was broken some months later when former colleagues,
among them Charles Mathews, who was making his first visit to America,
and James and Henry Wallack, who had already established a foothold in
the New World, urged him to try his fortune over there. James, a prominent member of the Drury Lane company, had first crossed the Atlantic in
1819 to escape the overshadowing fame of Edmund Kean, and two years
later, Henry, a member of the Covent Garden company, had followed suit,
engaged to appear at the Park Theatre, New York. James was to divide the
remainder his career between New York and London, becoming one of the
first transatlantic commuters.[12]

In September 1823 Conway wrote a farewell letter to Jerdan from
Liverpool:

My passage is now secured on the "Columbia" packet . . . my luggage on
board, and I am summoned to follow it tomorrow morning. As this, then, may be
the last time of my addressing you, accept the assurance of my *unfeigned
respect* and *devoted regard*. Accept also my warm acknowledgment of the zeal
and promptitude with which you have on many occasions stood forward to
vindicate my *professional* and improve my personal pretensions.

21
The New World

NEW York was then a small town at the tip of Manhattan Island, supporting only one theatre, managed by Stephen Price,[1] who preferred to tempt English stars across the ocean rather than cultivate native talent. Kean had lived up to his wild reputation when he made his first visit in 1820, and the critics were eager to see Conway, whom they regarded as one of the Kemble school. His treatment at the hands of the London press had not gone unnoticed, and their New York rivals were ready to make their own judgments. "The crowning event of the [1823–24] season," wrote George Odell,[2] was to be "the first appearance in America of the famous William Augustus Conway . . . on 12 January in the character of Hamlet," a part he had rarely played before and was given a great reception. In his curtain speech he said that he had been induced to try his fortune in America by several distinguished actors who had enjoyed the judgment and liberality of its audiences, and by "other circumstances too inconsiderable to be detailed." In its review of the performance, the *American* recalled that whereas Kean was apt to "outrage the meaning of the author by frantic starts and uncalled for bursts of passion,"

> Mr. Conway is guilty of no such extravagance; his whole soul seems absorbed by the intensity of his melancholy and sensibility. . . . His voice is flexible and fine-toned and of sufficient compass; his articulation distinct, and his manner of reciting and reading almost faultless. We never heard the meaning of Shake-speare more distinctly rendered.

Notices like that, as George Odell observed, "must have been balm to his galled and weary spirit," although the *American* did add the usual caveat that "his height rises above six feet, and his figure is somewhat large; hence his manner of treading the stage, though manly and imposing, is not graceful." After a month at the Park Theatre, his benefit raised fifteen hundred dollars, "an astonishing sum, indicating the success of the engagement . . . leading the management to the brilliant if expensive idea of combining the talents of the new star with those of [Thomas Abthorp] Cooper."[3] They played to packed houses for another month before going

Interior of Park Theatre, New York, November 1822, watercolour by John Searle, showing Charles Mathews and a Miss Johnson on stage. *Courtesy of the New-York Historical Society, New York City.*

on to Boston, Philadelphia, and Washington, and on this tour Conway switched from the Mark Antony that he had played for most of his career to Brutus, modelling his performance on Kemble's interpretation, with great success.[4] Next to Brutus, Jaffier was considered to be one of Conway's best parts: "indeed *Venice Preserved* should not be performed in America except those two actors be present."[5]

After the summer recess, Conway went on alone to Charleston, South Carolina (which boasted the earliest theatre in America) and Savannah, as far south as New Orleans, which he reached in March 1825. There Edwin Forrest, then a very young and unruly member of the Camp Theatre, who was later to become the foremost tragic actor on the American stage, had the opportunity to study "the distinguished visitor's methods"[6] and to apply what he had learned when he made his New York debut the following year in support of Edmund Kean. But before then, Conway and Forrest were to appear together in Albany, New York, after the Englishman had spent the summer in Newport, Rhode Island, and Forrest had followed along with the Camp theatre company on their annual steamboat tour up the Mississippi.

Back in New York, Conway shared a winter season with Cooper, and in the summer of 1826 he joined Henry Wallack, who had established the city's second theatre, the Chatham Garden. In the autumn, New York's third theatre was opened in the unfashionable Bowery, where Conway and Forrest shared the leading roles. By this time Forrest had discarded anything he may have learned from Conway and drew the greater share of the applause by emulating Kean.

Macready, by now at the top of his profession, had delayed his own American debut until public demand had reached almost breaking point, and arrived in New York just before the Bowery Theatre opened. He went there to see a performance of *Julius Caesar* by a company which, he wrote in *Reminiscences* (p. 319), "was composed of some of the best actors in the country."

> I was very anxious for poor Conway's success in the States, holding him in great esteem as a thoroughly gentlemanly man, and entitled to credit for considerable talent. The part he acted in was Brutus. . . . The performance was even, perhaps too tame, and correctly described by that chilling word "respectable". Forrest was the Mark Antony . . . the "Bowery lads", as they were termed, made great account of him. . . . He had received only the commonest education, but in his reading of the text he showed the discernment and good sense of an intellect much upon the level with that of Conway; but he had much more energy.

Macready was not the first to detect that after Conway's earlier success with the American theatre public, he was now facing the cold winds of competition. And in reaction to the popularity of the new generation, his performances had become tame and lifeless. Indeed, the always sympathetic *Albion* of 3 February 1827 offered some words of advice:

Mr. Conway is an actor of great merit. He does not (lately) do his fine talents an ample justice. He has apparently persuaded himself that the public is unjust or that some newer idolatry has pushed him from his pride of place. This is a mistake. The public is not unjust, and there is nothing hurtful to him in this new idolatry. His dramatic character will wear well. His own acting, though not marked with the fiery bursts of Kean's genius, nor the elaborate finish and passionate vehemence of Macready, has about it a sustained dignity, an elegant deportment, marvellous accuracy of conception, and beauty of execution. His manner belongs to the Kemble or classical and not to the romantic school. It is a manner which will do much to rescue the American stage from the coarseness into which it is liable to be flung from an intemperate admiration of Kean.

That was written just before Macready opened his own tour with a three-week engagement at the Park Theatre, and had magnanimously invited Conway to support him. They had not acted together since Macready had usurped him in the English provinces, and Conway rose to the occasion, excelling as Jaffier to Macready's Pierre, Falconbidge in *King John*, the Prince in *Henry IV, Part 1*, to mention only three of the highlights. Macready took his benefit in *The Fatal Dowry*, and two nights later generously agreed to play his favourite Cassius to Conway's Brutus for the latter's benefit. New York had now seen four of the leading actors of the day, and the *Mirror*[7] took a tilt at its rival theatre critics:

You hear of Kean's fire and genius, and Macready's talent and elaborateness; and that Mr. Conway is cold, classical and finished; and Mr. Forrest is fiery, furious and unfinished . . . until you are absolutely sick of it. . . . Bah! We content our selves with noticing that Mr. Conway (whom we greatly admire), and Mr. Macready (of whom we could not sufficiently express our admiration though we tried) are at present delighting and astonishing the admirers of the drama at the Park theatre.

The *Albion* asked why the revitalised Mr. Conway did not engage himself permanently at the Park Theatre, and two weeks later rejoiced when he reappeared there.

One desirable effect this will have upon the rest of the company. His manners may serve as their model, and the palpable effects of gentlemanly deportment may inoculate them with a wish to resemble him. There is a rude carelessness about many of our actors—a sort of *slouchiness* which is inexcusable and offensive. These people affect to represent gentlemen and noblemen and ladies on the stage, in dresses which none of these classes ever wore, and with manners which no refined society would ever tolerate.

The season ended before any impression could be made on that rag-tag-and-bobtail company, and then, apart from a benefit performance of *Julius*

Caesar in June in aid of a former colleague's family, Conway, "whose generosities are common," was never seen on the stage again. Macready's visit, and Conway's latest notices, ought to have restored his confidence in his future, but the occasion seems to have had the opposite effect. For all his success in the profession, Macready shared Conway's distaste for the theatre, and in the many talks they had offstage, was unlikely to have fired Conway with the enthusiasm to carry on. The visit demonstrated once more to Conway that he was never so successful as in a joint engagement, and reminded him that on his own he was not a crowd puller. Unfortunately, neither Macready's *Reminiscences* nor his diaries touch on this engagement,[8] though they must have reminisced about the theatre and about Mrs. Piozzi, for when writing about her, he mentioned the draft which Conway returned after her death, and only Conway could have told him about that. This was the last time Macready saw Conway alive, and his recollections of their conversations and his final verdict on Conway's acting would have been invaluable.[9]

"Man overboard!"

The next time that Conway's name appeared in the papers was in reports of his death by drowning, on 24 January 1828, after boarding the coastal packet *Niagara* in New York, bound for Savannah, and having apparently thrown himself overboard near Charleston Harbor. He was travelling with all his worldly goods, which were shipped back to New York for the attention of the British consul, James Buchanan, who was soon engrossed in his papers.

In a letter to the *Albion* dated 12 February, Buchanan explained that although his official duties were limited to watching over British commercial interests and to protecting "living subjects of our Gracious Sovereign," he felt an irresistible claim to afford protection to the memory of a former British subject who might, by some, be branded with infamy. He had formed the impression, from reading Conway's letters, that he "had been a prey to melancholy, previous to his leaving England . . . too deeply seated in his soul to be removed by coming to the United States—and which ultimately broke down his mind, and drove him from his profession, wherein he was labouring to secure a provision for an unprovided mother—a profession, too, which it was proved he would have been successful, as it appears by his bankers' accounts he had saved a handsome sum at the close of his theatrical career in this city."

Conway's papers evidently included letters from home, as well as *copies* of those he had sent. Buchanan quoted from one, which quite explicitly was "a *duplicate* of a letter dated 7 December 1827, and forwarded to England but a few weeks before the catastrophe":

You mention, dearest Mother, your having heard that I act seldom, and am preparing myself for holy orders; in confirmation partly of which, I will inform you, that events beyond my controul [*sic*] having entirely separated me from my profession, I am applying myself to the study of Divinity, in order to ascertain how far I may reasonably calculate upon success, should I seriously embark in the undertaking. The study is profound, extensive, and in great degree new to me; but I bring an unlimited devotion to the task, and that is the main step towards achievement in every pursuit. But, should all my endeavours prove ineffectual, the paths of commerce are open to me,—and perhaps employment in a particular branch of academical instruction: Of business I cannot be expected to know much, but it is not of very difficult acquirement; and observation has shown me, that good sense combined with principles and industry, rarely fails of some share of success, in a land of commercial enterprise. The agreeable prospect to which I have so long and eagerly directed my attention, of being able, of my labour and economy, to secure a comfortable retirement in this country, to where I might one day invite you, is, by the change, utterly annihilated; for, succeed as I may in my new pursuit, I cannot hope to be able to accomplish this, at least for a length of time. Abandon, therefore, dear Mother, I beseech you, the intention communicated in your letter, of crossing the Atlantic. What wise or beneficial purpose could it possibly answer? we might see each other it is true, but under circumstances so disadvantageous, that it were better we never met again. I am provided with no means for your reception; I am without a home to invite you to, friends to make your acquaintance with, or a single source of comfort or amusement to present for your acceptance. Reflect, also, upon the length, fatigue, and, at your time of life, even hazard, of the voyage, to be repaid at last by no enjoyment. Oh, dear Mother, I am as anxious to behold you as you can possibly be to see me: but be not offended if I say, that I look farther than you into the consequences. Should it be the will of Providence that my life is prolonged, and I am enabled, by my future efforts, to succeed in such a manner as may give me the means of inviting you to partake of my hearth and board, it will be the most blissful moment fate can have in store for me,—and gladly, joyfully will I say "Come". But till then, continue to reside among your neighbours and friends; and may the Almighty grant my fervent petition, and give you health, tranquility, and long life.

At this point, Buchanan observed, Conway asked his mother to remember him to a number of friends, and concluded:

I have more to say, but my paper compels me to reserve it to a future opportunity. Alas! I speak of the future as we are only authorized to do of the present. I have feeling and forebodings, but I confine them to my own bosom. Let us, in our separation, be patient and resigned. I do not, at this season, bid you discard hope, for it is the advent of our blessed Saviour, whose coming brought hope and joy to all. But let us, under every event, console ourselves with the certain conviction that while we live we live for each other, and that nothing but the last mortal stroke which separates soul and body can sunder the tie that has, through life, so closely united us to each other.

My Mother's most affectionate child
W. A. Conway

With hindsight, a sense of premonition may be detected in those last words, but on the whole the letter is rational, lacking in self-pity, and confident of success in a new career. The consul had heard that "a few in this city have made it a point to sneer at his performances," and thought this may have been the reason for his retirement from the stage.

In the course of his investigations, Buchanan next interviewed the captain of the *Niagara,* who told him that

> when Mr. Conway came on board he observed his singular manner and dress, the lower buttons all off his vest—wearing only a pair of old thin slippers and altogether unsuitably clothed for the season or for a voyage; that during the passage he was extremely retired, sat generally in a corner of the cabin, seldom saying more than merely returning a short answer to questions asked, or to some civilities proffered; very usually reading in his prayer book, and at other times much engaged in writing.

> Upon the morning of 24 January the captain mentioned to the passengers that if the wind held they would see Charleston by 12 oclock, upon which Mr. Conway requested Capt. Besher to inform him when they came near the Bar. At 12 each day the passengers generally lunch, and on that day Mr. Conway partook of a biscuit, a piece of cheese and a little spirits and water. He then went on deck, when the captain, according to his promise, informed him they were near the Bar. The Captain and passengers having gone down to dinner, and observing that Mr. Conway was not at the table, the steward was sent on deck to call him, to which he replied to the steward that he had "taken what was sufficient for ever he would require". The steward had but just returned without particularly regarding the reply, when all were roused by the call on deck "a man overboard". At the time the ship was under a press of sail—although every effort was made, yet the captain was aware all would be, as it proved, unavailing.

The captain also told Buchanan that Conway "had his valuable gold watch, his pocket book, and all his cash on his person when he rushed overboard" but did not explain how this was known, and "fortunately he had not his prayerbook, as he usually had in his hand, in which was found a bill of his bankers in New York, which he had endorsed payable to his mother." It appeared also from Conway's accounts he had not long since remitted her one hundred pounds sterling. The consul was curious about the work that had occupied Conway on the voyage, and found some notes in his hand, setting out the Greek, Latin, and English versions of some passages in Saint Matthew, extracted "for the consideration of those who maintain that our Blessed Saviour did not call himself the *Son of God.*" There was also a commentary by Conway on some verses of the "21st Chapter of John in which he, with great clearness, refutes the opinions of several able commentators, and manifests a mind of no ordinary cast and intensity of thought."

By now Buchanan was so eager to learn more about Conway that he paid a visit to the hotel where he had been staying in New York, the fashionable American Hotel on the corner of Broadway and Barclay (now the site of the Woolworth building), facing Park Place and the theatre. The staff remarked on Conway's "unassuming retiring disposition, never even drinking a glass of wine—after dinner taking a solitary walk and invariably returning to his studies," and his regular attendance at the Episcopal church. The consul discerned that Conway's view of religion was "not of a gloomy cast," but he had "met with little encouragement" in his studies. The Episcopalian church later denied any knowledge that Conway was preparing for Holy Orders. Buchanan concluded:

I feel that I have stated sufficient to rescue the character of Mr. Conway from the aspersions unfeelingly cast upon him. And if I have stated more, though interesting to some, I should become his biographer rather than the protector of his memory. . . . How little do we know of human murder; such acts are either rash or are the effects of insanity. Observe the feelings he laboured under to afford support to his mother. Would he have leapt overboard with his gold watch, his money and other valuable articles, in other than an unsound state of mind? I dwell on this, as many, very many, have charged this truly amiable man with a deliberate intention of the act, chiefly founding their uncharitable opinions upon the fact of his asking to be informed when the ship approached Charleston. I conclude, Sir, with "alas, alas, poor Conway".

Yr. humble servant, J. Buchanan

James Buchanan had done more than his duty on behalf of his countryman, and it would be churlish to ask for still more; but it would have been invaluable, with hindsight, to ask whether Conway had left a forwarding address, or whether he had disclosed why he was sailing south. Nor did the consul investigate Conway's movements leading up to his departure. In fact, he spent the summer in Providence, Rhode Island, and at his favourite resort of Newport, Rhode Island, where he kept to himself and his studies, and he returned to New York probably in October. From the American Hotel he replied to a letter from Anne Mathews which had just caught up with him. (This is the letter[10] in which he explained his aversion to writing.) It was written just two weeks before his last letter to his mother and conveys the impression of a contented soul. He was cross because Charles Mathews owed him a letter and some money, but pleased to hear from his wife and to be reminded of Ivy Cottage and the cheerful hours he had spent in the "agreeable society of its hospitable owners."

Though living at present in the centre of this large and populous city, I am leading a life of perfect retirement—so secluded from the stirring scenes of business or pleasure that I can give little account of either. I am, as I am sure you have heard, separated from my profession, and I go so rarely to the theatre now that I do not know how they are getting on.

After commiserating with her on the death of her mother, he did conjure up some theatre gossip:

There have been numerous dramatic arrivals from Gt. Britain this autumn, but the greater portion of their names are new to me. Mr. Cooper after a long residence in this country has embarked for England and is to appear at Drury Lane. Mr. Kean we hear has gone over to Covent Garden. We have also been informed of the wedding of Miss Tree to Mr. Bradshaw, Miss Paton to Lord Lennox, and Mrs Coutts to the Duke of St. Albans. When are we to hear of St. Cecilia changing her name? Of course you will understand me to mean Miss Stephens.[11]

Conway sent his compliments to her husband and their son, complained of "fingers benumbed with cold, paper not good, pen worse, ink execrable, thicker than Builgiudunns [?] beer" and signed "with perfect respect and sincerity, your faithful servant." There was little indication of serious depression there, but the writer of an obituary in the *Providence Literary Cadet* of 10 February 1828, who knew Conway well but has not been identified, saw him in New York that winter and found him "moody and melancholy, care-worn and distressed."

On 1 February, before the news of Conway's death had reached the *New York American,* a poem appeared at the foot of page 2, without comment or explanation, which began:

THE FAREWELL

A wanderer, doom'd to dwell
On foreign shores a solitary man,
To home's lov'd scenes lamenting thus began
The parting, and farewell.

I leave my happy home,
The streams and meadows I have loved so long,
And the fair city with its joyous throng,
O'er the rude waves to roam.

There followed six more stanzas bidding farewell to father, mother, brother, son, and "thou whom next I love," and a final stanza which read:

But see! the white waves swell
Ah blest companions of my early youth,
Dear object of my fondest love and truth,
Sweet home, and friends, farewell.

CONWAY

That poem was reproduced by most of the papers which reported Conway's death, some, like the *Boston Statesman,*[12] pointing out that "the signature has attracted attention, but whether the author was the gifted and unfortunate tragedian is of course mere conjecture." Nor, it must be added, even if it were, was it strictly autobiographical, but its publication gave credence to the view that it was a public suicide note. That would imply that Conway had embarked, with all his belongings, on his journey southwards, intending to jump overboard before reaching his destination; and while it seems unlikely that his death was accidental, it is inconceivable that it was premeditated so melodramatically. The poem is certainly poignant, but even if it were written or submitted by the actor, might have less ominous implications.

Clearly Conway had turned his back on the stage, and had withdrawn from society in general, but his last letter to his mother demonstrated a determination to succeed in some new profession; and as the *Albion* observed, he had "pursued the grave and solemn nature of his studies with an ardour that proved his sincerity" and without encouragement from the local clergy. Perhaps he hoped for better support elsewhere, but the truth will never be known. The *Albion* could only lament the fate of a man "in the prime of life—very tall and of fine personal appearance; his head and face were remarkably good, and quite indicative of his character—and in private life he was one of the most honourable, urbane, and polished men we ever met with."

Epilogue

THAT is not the end of the story, which began, as I wrote in my Preface, with a study of a theatrical family whose ostensible founder was William Augustus Conway. *His son,* Frederick Bartlett Conway, who carried on the tradition, was born, according to the reference books, in 1819, which seemed most unlikely to me, having found no trace of that event in the letters or diaries. His obituary notices in American newspapers in 1874 described him as a native of Bristol, England, and his date of birth was given as 10 February 1819, but I searched the local parish registers in vain for a baptismal record which might support those details. However, I did locate Mrs. Rudd's will. She died in December 1830 after naming two guardians and leaving her "large Bible" (undoubtedly the one Mrs. Piozzi gave her), the Harlow portrait, and the residue of her small estate in trust, to "Frederick Bartlett Conway, son of the late Augustus Conway, who sometime since was drowned in America, until he shall attain his age of 21." The same Frederick Bartlett Conway was married in Bristol in July 1840, declaring himself to be of "full age," and was therefore born before July 1819. In the absence of better evidence, therefore, we must accept that the event occurred in Bristol, probably in Clifton, in February 1819— which poses further questions.

Conway was not mentioned in Mrs. Piozzi's diary between his benefit on 23 January and his appearance in *The Æthiop* four weeks later, during which time there may have been more drama at Clifton than on the stage. Hazlitt, in May of the previous year, had asked once again why Conway did not marry, and if he had married since then, Mrs. Piozzi would surely have known and would have welcomed his son. The reader will recall that she had remarked that "I wish you had a son, though; you promised to keep my Portrait for him, and I think you will never part with the Repeater till *he* takes it with him to the University. What an immeasurable Length of Time that seems to my Friend as he reads this!" The mother may have been one of Mrs. Rudd's servants and, like herself thirty years earlier, deemed to be an "unsuitable" wife for the father. Perhaps she died in childbirth, or shortly afterward. Conway would certainly have ensured that the baby was baptised, but all we know is that he gave the child his name. Within a few months he was paying court to Charlotte, and may have been

225

naive enough to think that she would accept the baby as a stepson, as Mrs. Fox accepted Harriet Willoughby.

Whatever the truth of the matter, we can now see Conway's quest for a wife, his efforts to secure recognition from his own father, and his despairing return to the stage to earn a living in the light of his own responsibility to provide for a son. The boy was only three and a half when Conway sailed for New York, and his warm reception in the States encouraged him to stay there for a few years, perhaps with the intention of sending for his mother and son later; but when eventually the theatre palled as it had in England, there was no going back.

Mrs. Rudd never accepted that her son had ended his own life, and she brought her grandson up to love and respect his memory; whatever he may have learned about his father from other sources did not deter him from following in his footsteps. He went on the stage himself in 1840, and after ten years of modest success in England (he was seen as Malcolm to Macready's Macbeth in 1847), he emigrated to the States, where the Wallacks welcomed him as the son of his father. He was not as tall as William Augustus but was equally fond of the "high and noble parts, toga'd Romans and the like,"[1] and some years later with his second wife, Sarah Crocker, he founded the first professional theatre in Brooklyn.

That is another story, but we must give him and his daughter Minnie credit for their contribution to this one. Minnie married Osmond Tearle and became his leading lady, and when their company was chosen for the Birthday Festival of 1889 at Stratford-upon-Avon, she presented her grandfather's portrait to the Memorial Theatre, where it has been on public view in the Picture Gallery ever since. Mrs. Piozzi would not have been in the least surprised to be told that the portrait which was once her sole companion in a smoky room in Penzance would be seen by countless thousands of pilgrims, for as she often predicted, it would be "semper Augustus, Conway for ever!"

There had always (apart from the years immediately following Piozzi's death) been a man in her life with whom she enjoyed a special relationship. Her first mentor and hero, Dr. Collier, was soon followed by the mighty Dr. Johnson, and after he became more of a burden than a guardian, Piozzi was the white knight who rescued her from a hostile world and, as her husband, fiercely protected her interests. It did not matter that he had no pretensions to scholarship; he was a romantic to whom she could give her "virgin heart" after years of marriage to the stolid Thrale. Her morale was at a low ebb when Fellowes happened along and agreed to be her Boswell, and Mangin played his part, too, as a sparring partner. Marooned in Penzance, Mrs. Piozzi freely acknowledged that "both of them, *in their way and in their day,* had been undeservedly kind, useful and polite" toward her, but their heyday had been ended by marriage.

Another chapter in her life had closed when she saw Brynbella for the last time and, utterly disillusioned with Salusbury, was ready to take up another interest. It was Mrs. Stratton who unwittingly gave her the idea of "adopting" Conway when she reported his fascination with her *Anecdotes;* the friend of Garrick and Mrs. Siddons was not to be outdone by the likes of Mrs. Stratton, or Miss Willoughby with her Mr. Warde, or the now-fading Miss Wroughton. Patronage soon turned to affection, and as Mrs. Piozzi tried to spoil him as she had her nephew, Conway became both her pet and her hero.

As to his affection for her there can be little doubt: she had taken him up when Hazlitt had reduced his morale to rock bottom. He was overwhelmed by the attentions of a lady who was a celebrity herself, and one of the most talented women he had met. His reluctance to correspond with her was probably compounded of a deep-seated aversion to writing and embarrassment at the impression he had made on her, of which he was probably unaware until the avalanche of words hit him in the summer of 1819.

The publication of a few of those letters started a hare which has never been caught until now, when this belated attempt to "discover" Conway has, I hope, illuminated that last inevitable friendship. Much of his life still remains in the shadows, but what shines through is an image of a really gentle man: too sensitive and introspective an actor to appeal to the masses, but who in private life was, as the *Albion,* said, the "most honourable, urbane, and polished of men." Mrs. Piozzi's "dear tender-hearted Friend—you say I must not call you Romancer" had a way with older women, but he was not so fortunate with women of his own age, and he remained unmarried, in spite of his charm, good looks, and sociability. He may have been Don Giovanni on the stage, but in real life he was no philanderer, and in fathering a son he was more likely to have been the seduced than the seducer.

McCarthy saw Conway as Mrs. Piozzi's "son, father, uncle, tutor, hero, a Perseus to her Andromeda," but it is difficult to perceive signs of the father, uncle, or tutor in the material that has been presented here, though there is at least a hint of the *bridegroom*. Jerdan, who must have taken his cue from Conway, thought that it would be an exaggeration to say, at her period of life, that she was "enamoured of his friend; but there was a warmth in her conduct and expressions towards him which would have warranted such a phrase, had she been a few years younger." If Conway could have entered her life instead of Piozzi in the 1780s, he might have filled the same role, but as it was she could offer marriage only in some vain hope of providing him with financial support after she had gone. She may, for the same reason have encouraged his pursuit of the Hertford family, recollecting the happy ending of her comedy *The Adventurer,* but with Johnson's *Life of Savage*[2] also in mind, she was equally anxious that he should not neglect his profession in the process.

By the beginning of 1821, when she really had reached the age of eighty, she accepted that Conway would take nothing from her, and as her life was drawing to a close, she felt a need for protection herself; she hoped to find it at Clifton, under the wing of his mother, and died there with her hero close at hand.

Appendix: The Conways and the Seymours

THE history of the Conways and the Seymours and their titles is long and complicated. The Seymour name was derived from the Norman Saint Maur, and Conway from the river and town in North Wales. The names were combined in 1699 under the terms of the will of the earl of Conway, when he bequeathed Conway Castle and the Ragley estates in Warwickshire (which became the family seat), to Sir Edward Seymour (1633–1708), Speaker of the House of Commons in the Long Parliament. His son Francis (1679–1732) was created Baron Conway of Ragley and later Baron Conway of Killultagh in County Antrim. In 1750 his elder son Francis Seymour Conway (1719–94) was granted the earldom of Hertford which had been in abeyance since the death of its first holder, the Duke of Somerset, who was beheaded in 1552. The younger son Henry Seymour Conway (1721–95) became a general and later field marshal, who, as a member of parliament opposed the war with America.

The six younger sons of the earl of Hertford, including William, the putative father of William Augustus, were entitled to the style the Hon. (Christian name) Seymour Conway, until, in 1793, the earl was created marquess, whereupon they were styled *Lord* (Christian name) Seymour Conway. There were also six daughters, one of whom married Robert Stewart and was mother to Viscount Castlereagh.

By the time William Augustus laid claim to a connection with the family, the second marquess had reached the age of seventy-six. He had been Lord of the Treasury and Cofferer of the Household, and a lifelong friend of the Prince Regent; his wife Lady Hertford had been one of the royal mistresses. After his succession to the marquessate in 1794 he reversed the order of the family names, so that his younger brothers became known as Lord Henry Conway *Seymour,* Lord Robert Conway Seymour, etc. (Later the family adopted the form Seymour-Conway.) Henry and Robert were joint Clerks of the Crown, while Edward had been a canon of Christ Church, Oxford, and Hugh an Admiral. George and his sons also held appointments of State, but there is no record of William's preferments if any. He seems to have distanced himself from the rest of the family, and continued to be known as Lord William Conway. He married in 1798 and had two legitimate sons to provide for.

The second marquess died in 1822, leaving estates bringing in an astounding ninety thousand pounds per annum, and his successor, Francis Charles (1777–1842) increased the family's wealth by marrying Maria Fagniani. She was legally the daughter of a marchese, but both the Duke of Queensbury and George Selwyn believed themselves to be her real father and left their fortunes to her. She lived in Paris with her son, Richard, and devoted herself to the upbringing of his illegitimate son, Richard Wallace (1818–90). Her son became the fourth marquess in 1842, but when he died unmarried in 1870, his vast wealth went to Wallace, including the collection now known by his name, while the title and rundown estates went to a cousin, the grandson of the above Lord Hugh Seymour.

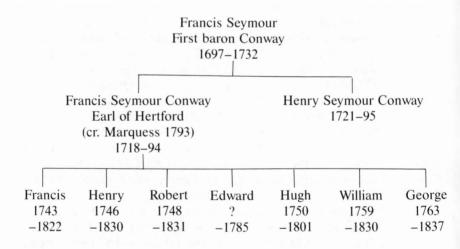

The Males of the Conway Seymour Family

Notes

Introduction

1. James L. Clifford, *Hester Lynch Piozzi (Mrs. Thrale)*, 2d ed. (Oxford: Clarendon Press, 1987), p. xv.

2. Katharine C. Balderston, ed. *Thraliana: The Diary of Mrs. Hester Lynch Thrale (later Mrs. Piozzi), 1776–1809*, 2d ed., 2 vols. (Oxford: Clarendon Press, 1951).

3. Letter from HLP to WAC dated 29 May 1819, in Historical Society of Pennsylvania, *Notable European Women*, case 13, box 19.

4. Edward A. Bloom and Lillian D. Bloom, eds., *The Piozzi Letters: Correspondence of Hester Lynch Piozzi, 1784–1821*, vol. 1 (vols. 2 to 6 forthcoming) (Newark: University of Delaware Press, 1989).

5. "Love Letters of Mrs. Piozzi." *Bath Journal*, 30 January 1843.

6. Alfred L. Nelson and Gilbert B. Cross, eds. *Drury Lane Journal: Selections from James Winston's Diaries, 1819–1827* (London: Society for Theatre Research, 1974).

7. (Edward Mangin), *Piozziana; or, Recollections of the late Mrs Piozzi, by a friend* (London: Edward Moxon, 1833).

8. Edward Mangin, *Miscellaneous Essays* (London: 1851) (an unpublished letter to the editor of the *Bath Herald*, 24 January 1843).

9. *Athenaeum*, March 1843, p. 259.

10. The MS of these "Biographical Memoirs" is in the Princeton University Library, MS. 3891.8.313.

11. See, for example, "Autobiography and Letters of Mrs. Piozzi," *Edinburgh Review*, April 1861, pp. 501–23.

12. Charles Elliott Norton, "Original Memorials of Mrs Piozzi," *Atlantic Monthly*, May 1861, pp. 614–23.

13. These volumes are now in the Hyde Collection, Somerville, New Jersey. In 1861 they were in the possession of Duncan C. Pell of Providence, Rhode Island. Hayward, in his biography, repeated some of Norton's quotations from the autobiographical notes, and referred to them as either the "Conway MS" or the "Conway Notes."

14. E. F. Ellet, "Mrs. Piozzi's Love Letters," *Athenaeum*, 12 July 1862, p. 50.

15. "Letters of Mrs. Piozzi to William Augustus Conway," *Athenaeum*, 9 August 1862, pp. 169–72.

16. Dutton Cook, "Mr. Conway and Mrs. Piozzi," *Gentleman's Magazine*, April 1888, pp. 536–50.

17. Hester Lynch Piozzi, *Anecdotes of the late Samuel Johnson, LL.D.*, ed. S. C. Roberts (London, 1786; Cambridge: University Press, 1924). p. xlviii.

18. Hyde, *The Thrales of Streatham Park*, p. 313.

19. McCarthy, *Hester Thrale Piozzi: Portrait of a Literary Woman*, p. 261.

20. Edward T. James, ed., *Notable American Women, 1607–1950: A Biographical Dictionary*, vol. 1 (Cambridge: Harvard University Press, Belknap Press, 1971), pp. 569–70.

21. John Rylands University Library of Manchester (Ryl. Eng. MSS. 616), which holds all the later diaries except that for 1820, which is in the Rare Book and Manuscript Library, Columbia University, New York.

22. Of these, I have traced only *Retrospection* (at the Beinecke Library, Yale University) and the "Journey Book" *(Observations and Reflections)*, now in the Hyde Collection.

Chapter 1. Mr. Conway

1. William M'Cready (1755–1829), Irish-born actor-manager.

2. The only source which mentions a precise figure is the *Oxford Companion to the American Theatre*, ed. Gerald Bordman (Oxford: Oxford University Press, 1984), citing Allston Brown, who wrote that "Conway was 6ft 4in high, well-proportioned, and possessed great muscular power."

3. William Charles Macready (1793–1873), the foremost tragedian of the second quarter of the century.

4. Pollock, *Macready's Reminiscences*, 1: 35–36.

5. Ripley, *"Julius Caesar" on stage*. Chapter 3.

6. or *point devise* (to perfection).

7. [Hester Lynch Piozzi], *Three Warnings to John Bull before he Dies, By an Old Acquaintance of the Public* (London: R. Faulder, 1798). An antiradical pamphlet based on her narrative poem "The Three Warnings."

8. *Reminiscences*, 1:110.

9. Robert William Elliston (1774–1831), actor and manager: a larger-than-life character who learned his craft at the Orchard Street theatre in Bath between 1793 and 1804, when he took over the leading roles from Dimond. He later managed theatres up and down the country, and leased the Theatre Royal, Birmingham, in 1813, and Drury Lane in 1819.

10. *Isabella*, or *The Fatal Marriage*, Garrick's adaptation of Thomas Southerne's play, was one of Sarah Siddons's most popular vehicles.

11. This was the first performance in Bath of *Don Giovanni, the Libertine*, billed as a new operatic drama in two acts, with music by Mozart, arranged for the English stage by Mr. Bishop. It had been performed six months earlier at Covent Garden, when it was entitled *The Libertine*.

Chapter 2. "The Abridgment"

1. Probably *Retrospection*, which she had already annotated for Conway.

2. In 1752 the Gregorian calendar was adopted in England to replace the Julian version, which had an accumulated error of eleven days. These were "cancelled," and at the same time the New Year was deemed to begin on 1 January instead of 1 April.

3. Polly Hart was a former mistress. This, like all later quotations not otherwise identified, is taken from "The Abridgment," by kind permission of Lady Eccles.

4. Dr. Arthur Collier (1707–77), her former tutor and confidant.

5. Balderston, *Thraliana*, 7 December 1779.

6. Hyde, *The Thrales of Streatham Park*, pp. 85–86.

7. This account has been discredited by present-day authorities, who are unaware that its only published version was copied from Norton's article in the *Atlantic Monthly*. In the "Abridgment," Mrs. Piozzi preceded her reference to the Globe Theatre with an account of the demolition, in the early 1760s, of the wall of an alley leading to the site of the old theatre. Her mother remarked that the debris looked like the ruins of Palmyra (the excavation of which was in the news at the time) before the plot was grassed over. Years later, when the brewery was put up for sale, Mrs. Thrale was surprised to discover that the joke had persisted, and the plot was called "Palmyra" in the deeds. In his article on Mrs. Piozzi's autobiographical notes, Norton omitted the next two paragraphs, in which she referred to the sale and other matters, before telling Conway about the remains of the Globe Theatre. The omission of those paragraphs creates the impression that, according to Mrs. Piozzi the foundations of the theatre were on the site of "Palmyra." Hayward copied the Norton text and perpetuated the fallacy which has persisted to the present day. In the *Survey of London*, vol. 22 (London: Athlone Press, 1956), the editors, Howard Roberts and Walter Godfrey, took the view that "Mrs Piozzi was confused about the position of the Globe, which was west of her dwelling-house, not on the east side of Deadman's Place where the garden was made." The sponsors of the Globe Theatre "reconstruction" accordingly dismissed as unreliable Mrs. Piozzi's recollection of the hexagonal remains.

8. The Misses Thrale, *alias* the "Miss Thrales."
9. In her published edition of the *Letters,* HLP reworded this one, and omitted the two that follow. See R. W. Chapman, *The Letters of Samuel Johnson,* (Oxford: Clarendon Press, 1952). 3:172–73, 175.
10. See Clifford, *Hester Lynch Piozzi,* pp. 229–30.
11. It was apparently an Italian translation, published in 1603, by the Swiss Calvinist Giovanni Diodati (1576–1649). Mrs. Piozzi gave a different version in her autobiography for Fellowes: she said that Piozzi had advised her to leave it behind and be content with an English Bible.

Chapter 3. Mrs. Piozzi

1. Balderston, *Thraliana,* January 1785.
2. *St. James's Chronicle,* 8 January 1785.
3. Bertie Greatheed (1759–1826) one of the Della Cruscans, whom the Piozzis had met in Florence.
4. Sarah Kemble was a friend of the Greatheeds, having been sent as a teenager to stay with Bertie's parents at Guy's Cliffe, Warwickshire, in the vain hope that she would get William Siddons out of her head.
5. Balderston, *Thraliana,* 27 March 1788.
6. Ryl. Eng. MSS. 649.
7. Recently unearthed by Margaret Doody in Ryl. Eng. MSS. 652. See her New Introduction to Clifford's biography of Mrs. Piozzi, 1987, p. xxxii, where she suggests that the character is a self portrait of HLP.
8. In 1768 this was the first theatre outside London to be granted Letters Patent, which licensed it to present plays unaccompanied by music.
9. William Wyatt Dimond (1749–1812) was the leading man at Bath when Mrs. Siddons began her career there.
10. In a postscript to a letter from HLP to Miss Weston dated 27 June 1790, Hyde Collection.
11. These celebrated ladies, the Honourable Eleanor Butler and Sarah Ponsonby, had eloped and set up home together at Plas Newydd.
12. Dated 11 November 1798, Princeton University Library.
13. Thrale had left the Oxfordshire estates to Queeney, but under the terms of the marriage settlement, his widow was entitled to the revenues. The ambiguity had never been cleared up, and the adoption of John Salusbury Piozzi had provoked Queeney into legal action.
14. To John Salusbury, 14 May 1813, Ryl. Eng. MSS. 591.
15. Letter to Sophia Weston, 14 October 1792, Princeton University Library.
16. Dated 12 October 1805, Ryl. Eng. MSS. 574/22.
17. *The Penitent.* HLP's memory was surely at fault here. Mrs. Siddons does not seem to have appeared in that play in Bath, in January to March 1808, and certainly not with William Dimond.
18. Mrs. Siddons blamed Garrick for the failure of her London debut in 1775. Gabriel Piozzi first came to England about that time, and Garrick died four years later.

Chapter 4. Bath Cat

1. As in previous chapters, unattributed quotations are taken from "The Abridgment."
2. Letter to the Reverend Dr. Robert Gray, later bishop of Bristol, 27 November 1814, Ryl. Eng. MSS. 371.
3. Elizabeth (Bessy) Jones was born in Halkyn, near Holywell, in 1793, and had probably been in the service of the Piozzis ever since they settled at Brynbella.
4. Sir James Fellowes (1771–1857) graduated M.B. in 1797 and M.D. in 1805, and served with the armed forces overseas. He made a study of epidemic diseases in Spain, and in 1815 wrote "Reports of the Pestilential Disorder of Andalusia, which appeared at Cadiz in the

years 1800, 1804, 1810 and 1813," and had just retired as chief medical officer to the army. His parents, Dr. and Mrs. Fellowes, lived at 13, The Vineyards, Bath.

5. Edward Mangin (1772–1852), of Huguenot-Irish ancestry. His ample means allowed him to devote most of his life to writing, mostly in Bath, where he was a leader of the literary set but left no works of great significance.

6. HLP's "Commonplace Book." MS in Hyde Collection.

7. The play was *Riches, or The Wife and Brother,* by James Bland Burges, based on Massinger's *The City Madam.*

8. William Henry West Betty (1791–1874) had been a child prodigy whose popularity at one time rivalled even Mrs. Siddons's. He continued to act after he grew up, but the "Master Betty" craze had passed.

9. Samuel Whitbread (1785–1815), son of Henry Thrale's closest rival in the brewery trade, was a social reformer, pacifist, and advocate of Catholic emancipation.

10. That letter, dated 27 December 1816, was quoted by Hayward in *Autobiography, Letters and Literary Remains,* the second volume of which has a section entitled "Miscellaneous Letters, mainly to Sir James Fellowes." It includes letters to Dr. Gray, Dorset Fellowes, and Harriet Willoughby, who turned them over to Sir James after HLP's death. He later showed them to Hayward, and they are now dispersed, some to Harvard, and others to the Huntington, Pierpont Morgan, and Yale libraries. All the extracts which follow may be found in Hayward.

11. The approach road to the Southwark Bridge, opened that year, was driven between the sites of the Rose and Globe theatres.

12. William Beloe (1755?–1817), sometime prebendary of Saint Paul's Cathedral, rector of All Hallows, London Wall, and assistant librarian at the British Museum. An anonymous postscript to the book written by a friend who had seen it through the final stages of production, was later identified as the Reverend T. Rennell. A second edition was brought out in 1818, unchanged apart from a new postscript denying all responsibility for the views expressed by Beloe, and adding that "even if he had seen the passages which have been deemed objectionable," he could not have prevented their publication.

Chapter 5. Patroness

1. Harriet Willoughby was born in 1782, before Fox married Mrs. Armistead, his mistress of many years, in a union he did not acknowledge publicly until 1802. Mrs. Fox accepted Harriet as a step-daughter, and her father left her an annuity of a hundred pounds a year when he died in 1806.

2. Margaret Williams (1759–1823), sister of Sir John Williams of Bodylwddan. She lived in Upper Park Street, Saint James's Square, Bath.

3. Letter from HLP to WAC dated Penzance, 27 July 1820, Pierpont Morgan Library, New York.

4. The first edition sold poorly, and when the remaining stocks were sold in 1821, the preface was greatly abridged, with the apologies to WAC omitted.

5. Otherwise known as "corn dollies." Straw plaiting was a local cottage industry.

6. HLP was to remind WAC of this incident in "Love Letter VI" dated 3 February 1820, the original of which has not been located.

7. HLP to WAC 28 May 1819, quoted in the *Athenaeum,* 12 July 1861, p. 179.

8. *The Wonder: A Woman Keeps a Secret!!!,* a comedy by Mrs. Centilivre.

9. Miss Penley, from Covent Garden.

10. Letter HLP to WAC, 15 June 1819, Historical Society of Pennsylvania.

Chapter 6. "Transcendant Conway"

1. On the death of John Palmer in 1818, his share passed to his son, who showed little interest in the theatre; its management was now in the hands of Matilda Dimond and her son, William, and their acting manager, Charles Charlton.

2. The former Lady Caroline Ponsonby, daughter of Earl Bessborough and wife of William Lamb, Viscount Melbourne. Best remembered for her wild behaviour and her affair with Lord Byron.

3. With his long white beard, he even looked the part.

4. Conway had played *Don Giovanni* nearly every week in Bath in the 1817–18 season.

5. J. C. Trewin, *Mr. Macready. A Nineteenth Century Tragedian and his Theatre* (London: Harrap, 1955). p. 41.

6. J. W. Cole, *The Life and Theatrical Times of Charles Kean,* 2 vols. (London: Richard Bentley, 1859).

7. B. S. Penley, *The Bath Stage: a history of dramatic representations in Bath* (London: W. Lewis, 1892).

8. An ancient city in Campania, Italy, which bore a superficial resemblance to Roman Bath.

9. Guido da Siena, Italian painter (fl. 1250–75).

10. Alfred Bunn (1797?–1860) author of *The Stage: both before and behind the Curtain,* 3 vols. (London: Richard Bentley, 1840), which described his experiences as lessee of both Covent Garden and Drury Lane between 1833 and 1838. He had previously been associated with the Drury Lane management under Elliston.

11. Ryl. Eng. MSS. 596/1–5.

12. The opening lines of Addison's *Cato.*

13. R. Merry, leader of the Della Cruscan poets. HLP wrote the preface and contributed some poems to *Florence Miscellany.*

14. Now in the Beinecke Library, Yale University.

15. The Reverend Thomas Sedgwick Whalley, D.D. (1746–1828), HLP and Fanny Burney first met him in Bath in 1780.

16. Hannah Maria Bourdois (1772–1865), Fanny Burney's niece, lived at Batheaston, two miles away.

17. George Henry Harlow (1787–1819) was only thirty-two when he died earlier that year. It was he who painted the portrait of Conway in 1815 in the character of Hamlet (see frontispiece). Like Sir Thomas Lawrence, he had once been a child prodigy and, before his untimely death, had carved out a niche for himself as a theatrical portraitist. Engravings from his portraits were in great demand—the equivalent of today's publicity photographs. His group depicting Sarah Siddons as Queen Katherine, and John Kemble as Cardinal Wolsey was the Royal Academy "picture of the year" in 1817. It included other members of the Kemble family in various characters from *Henry VIII,* and Conway as Guildford, all painted from memory or his notebooks.

18. S. T. Roche was also a miniaturist. His studio was in Pierpont Street, and Jagger's in Milsom Street.

19. The Regatta letter was one of hers that she included in her *Letters to and from the late Samuel Johnson* and which had achieved a celebrity of its own.

20. Quoted in the *Athenaeum,* 9 August 1861, p. 169, where it is incorrectly dated 1818.

Chapter 7. The Correspondence

1. Autograph letter dated New York, 23 November 1827, in Harvard Theatre Collection.

2. Nathaniel William Wraxall, *Historical Memoirs of my own Time from 1772 to 1784,* 2 vols. (London: 1815).

3. Did HLP reveal to WAC Johnson's fear of insanity?

4. John Junius Booth (1796–1852), an English actor who emigrated to the United States. His three sons were first-generation American actors—John Junius (1821–83), Edwin Thomas (1833–93), and John Wilkes (1839–65), who assassinated President Lincoln.

5. The Simon Gratz Collection, Historical Society of Pennsylvania, Philadelphia includes seven letters from HLP to WAC.

6. James White, HLP's young footman.

7. Eliza O'Neill was the Juliet.

8. Angela Catalini was a popular opera singer.

9. This was Harlow's oil painting portrait of Conway in the role of Hamlet. See frontispiece.

Chapter 8. "Fev'rish for Want of Rest"

1. Mrs. Piozzi was fond of the image of the "towering tulip." She had read that a tulip bulb named "Semper Augustus" had been sold for seven hundred pounds in the "tulipmania" of the seventeenth century. The bulb's striking coloration—red-and-white striped on a blue-tinted base—was unfortunately caused by a virus, and despite its optimistic name, the strain eventually died out.

2. Thomas Hamlet (ca. 1770–1853), a celebrated retail goldsmith and jeweller. A desk seal he made for George IV in 1823 was in the sale of the duchess of Windsor's jewels in 1987.

3. The story is corroborated in *Piozziana*, p. 45. Mangin recalled that he had been summoned by HLP to call on her "at an early hour," when she asked him whether she should destroy this diary of more than fifty years of her life. Unaware that she was probably teasing, he begged her to keep them safe and trust in the discretion of her survivors. "Her answer was that for the present they were rescued from the flames, and so saying she replaced the volumes in the cabinet. I did not see the inside of one of them, and, of course can say nothing of their contents, but cannot doubt that they were in all respects, most interesting."

4. Riviere and Son were goldsmiths and jewellers in Bond Street, Bath.

5. What a fib! In *Piozziana* (p. 9), Edward Mangin described the miniature that HLP had given to *him* three years earlier! "She gave the ingenious artist Roche of Bath many sittings; and enjoined him to make the painting in all respects a likeness; to take care to show her face deeply rouged, which it always was; and to introduce a trivial deformity of the lower jaw on the left side, where she told me she had been severely hurt by a horse treading on her." She had also presented a miniature of herself to Sir James Fellowes.

6. Captain Vallobra, or Vallopra, had been escorting Miss Willoughby for some time, but Mrs. Piozzi had recently noted in her diary that he had called on her and "renounced all connexion with Miss Willoughby. Poor little Fool!"

7. A novel in four volumes by Samuel Richardson (1689–1761).

8. The version in the *Anecdotes* reads: "It was . . . the first two volumes of Clarissa that he prized: 'For give me a sick bed and a dying lady, and I'll be pathetic myself.' "

9. Pastiles were used to fumigate clothing against lice, the carrier of typhus fever.

10. The Gloucester House and Steam Packet Hotel was near the Hot Wells House.

11. *Historical and Posthumus Memoirs*, H. B. Wheatley, ed. London: 1884, 4: 30.

12. The copy that HLP annotated for WAC has not been located.

Chapter 9. Weston-super-Mare

1. "Memoirs of Mr. Conway," *Theatrical Inquisitor* (London), May 1814.

2. Elizabeth Lambart (1730–1821), widow of General Hamilton Lambart sometime M.P. for Kilbeggan.

3. This letter, and those that followed over the next few months, are now in John Rylands University Library of Manchester (Ryl. Eng. MSS. 568, letters 130–150, 153–54). The rest of their resumed correspondence, dating from 17 January 1820, which Knapp quoted in *The Intimate Letters of Hester Piozzi and Penelope Pennington*, is in the Princeton University Library.

4. PSP to HLP, dated Dowry Square, 23 July 1819.

5. On the other side of the card she wrote a more successful anagram:

Willoughby
Oh I will be ugly
Her Lover departed and courted a Miss Brook

Well! if he does hang over the brook, said she
There shall be no weeping willow by.

6. Lucius Sergius Catilina (ca. 108–62 B.C.).
7. The index in the British Library attributes both works to Alfred Bunn. In the preface to *Conrad* he sheltered behind anonymity, but acknowledged that his "obligations to Mr. Bunn are inexpressible; in addition to the benefit which the tragedy derived from the emendations of his elegant pen he gave every advantage of scenery and music which it could have derived from a London theatre."

Chapter 10. "No more examining the Postman's Hand"

1. This must have been at the Theatre Royal, Bristol, in March 1818, when the *Bristol Journal* also found Conway's performance distracting.
2. Shuttleworth owned the lodging house in Princes Street.
3. Elsewhere HLP also reveals that she believed WAC to be two or three years younger than he was.
4. "Miss Jagger" was HLP's pet name for the miniature she gave WAC.
5. Ryl. Eng. MSS.596/11. Only one page has survived.
6. An allusion to Philip Astley, the horseman who founded Astley's Amphitheatre.

Chapter 11. "22 Weeks since we parted"

1. It was three years later that Conway told his friend Jerdan of his efforts to secure recognition and confirmed his story in a letter, dated 13 October 1822, which Jerdan reproduced in his *Autobiography* (London: 1852–53). Jerdan (1782–1863) was an editor of several periodicals, notably the *Literary Gazette,* and one of the founders of the Garrick Club and the Royal Society for Literature. He had known Conway for some years. In 1815 both had sat for Harlow, whose untimely death Jerdan mourned in a long obituary which spilled over into two issues of the *Literary Gazette* in March 1819. He singled out Harlow's portraits of Sarah Siddons, Conway ("full of spirit and force"—evidently not the "Hamlet" pose), and Charles Mathews, as examples of his "superlative ability."
2. Being an *Irish* peer, he was not disbarred from the Lower House.
3. Mangin's sarcasm was lost on HLP.
4. Kemble earned the nickname "Emperor" for his strong rule over Covent Garden. It is astonishing that HLP did not yet know of WAC's association with him.
5. Richard Carlile (1790–1834), a radical, had already been imprisoned for publishing obnoxious literature, namely the works of Thomas Paine. In November 1819 further charges were brought against him, and WAC evidently attended his trial, which lasted three days, at which he was fined and sentenced to three years' imprisonment. It was widely held that reporting of the trial would itself be unlawful.
6. WAC's letter to Jerdan of 13 October 1822 did not record the dates of any of his approaches to the Hertfords.
7. Miss O'Neill married William Belcher, a wealthy Irish M.P. the following day, and gave up the stage.
8. Since the days when the Piozzis were regular visitors to Clifton, a lock had been built across the Avon to create a floating harbor in the center of Bristol. A bridge carried the Bath road close to Dowry Square.
9. A new comedy, *A Short Reign and a Merry One,* from Covent Garden.

Chapter 12. The Gala

1. It was picked up by Percival Merritt in a New York bookshop in 1925 and later presented to the Beinecke Library. It was this letter that convinced him that the seven "love letters" were genuine.

2. William Tryon (1729–88) was the British-born governor of North Carolina from 1765 to 1771, when William Pennington was controller of customs. Both of them returned to England in the 1780s.

3. William Dorset Fellowes was Sir James's brother.

4. Theodore Hook's *Tekeli* was advertised, but not performed, the theatre being closed on account of the king's death.

Chapter 13. "Une petite Traitresse"

1. Charles Hicks, M.R.C.S., surgeon, fl. 1808–42. His patients were mostly wealthy or aristocratic.

2. HLP evidently thought that Mrs. Rudd's own pedigree was superior to that of the Strattons.

3. Sister of Dorset and James Fellowes.

4. As already mentioned, WAC had left Birmingham more than fifteen months earlier than the date of this letter.

5. That injunction was rendered in print as "EXALT THY LOVE: DEJECTED HEART", which gave rise to Mrs. Ellet's complaint that the altered punctuation and emphasis distorted the meaning of HLP's words. The line comes from a poem by Thomas Parnell (1679–1718) entitled "A Fairy Poem in the Ancient English Style," the last verse of which runs: "Exalt thy love-dejected heart. / Be mine the task, or ere we part, / To make thee grief resign."

Chapter 14. "Adieu pour jamais"

1. HLP's letter of 13 February 1820 is now in the Tutt Library at Colorado Springs. It was found in an extraillustrated copy of Boswell's *Life of Johnson* compiled in 1901, and is the only Piozzi letter in their possession.

2. He or she has not been identified.

3. Lord William Conway and Walter James went up to Oxford in 1777, Conway to Christ Church and James to Trinity.

4. The original has not been traced.

Chapter 15. "Longing for Clifton"

1. Now in the British Library, inscribed: "This Book is the property of Mrs Susannah Rudd." HLP wrote on the flyleaf: "It was an imperfect copy bought cheap for love of the *Prints* in 1819 & intrusted to my care, who restored the text and wrote notes to it for Love of the Possessor and *her* heirs: not those of H:L:P. 10 April 1820."

2. Letter to Jerdan, 13 October 1822.

3. The Lord Great Chamberlain is an officer of State whose duties include the management of the Palace of Westminster; not to be confused with the Lord Chamberlain, an officer of the Royal Household, which post was then held by Castlereagh's uncle, Lord Hertford.

4. Shortly after his accession, George IV had declared that he would never agree to his estranged wife Caroline's coronation as Queen Consort. He issued a proclamation forbidding her name to be printed in the Liturgy or mentioned in prayers for the royal family, and had asked Parliament to dissolve their marriage. The queen responded by threatening to return from her Villa d'Este to take her place at the coronation. As Leader of the House, Lord Castlereagh was in the eye of the storm.

5. A copy, in Sir James Fellowes's hand, is in the Hyde Collection.
6. The nature of this commission has not come to light.
7. The development was abandoned during the Napoleonic wars, and the crescent was not completed until 1818.

Chapter 16. "Fish and Poultry at Penzance"

1. Land's End proper is not visible from Penzance, being obscured by Penlee Point on the headland to the west of Mount's Bay.
2. The Penzance Library, now in Morrab House, was founded in 1819 and has been a treasured institution ever since.
3. Sheridan Knowles's new tragedy, which was to remain popular throughout the century, was first seen a few months earlier at Covent Garden, with Macready in the title role. There is a curious reference in Alfred Bunn's *The Stage* (1840) which is full of contradictions. He wrote that he recollected "the late Mrs. Piozzi, with whom I had the pleasure of being acquainted in the latter years of her life" saying that plays set in Rome rarely succeeded, except when played by Kemble. "I was describing to her the presentation of *Virginius* by Mr. Conway (then my stage manager), in whose welfare she took a lively interest; and remarking that it ought to take in more money than it did, she replied, 'I perfectly remember Mr. Garrick about the middle of the last century, electrifying his auditors of old Drury Lane by his delivery of two words *thou traitor* addressed to Appius Claudius; but Virginius was nevertheless the least attractive of Garrick's performances'. The pecularity of the expression 'somewhere about the middle of the last century' delivered as if we had been of the same age amused me as I was then 'somewhere about twenty-two', while the garrulous and delightful old lady was within a few days of her eightysecond, having that morning invited me to the celebration of the eightysecond anniversary of her birth."
Conway appeared in *Virginius* in Birmingham several times between 15 September and 9 October 1820, when Mrs. Piozzi was in Penzance, and long after her Gala. Bunn's visit to Gay Street must have been in 1819, when Conway was ill, but is not recorded in the diary. The Roman play he had in mind must have been *Brutus*, or *The Fall of Tarquin*. Garrick could not have appeared in Sheridan Knowles's *Virginius*.
4. Sir Humphrey Davy (1778–1829), scientist, inventor of the miner's safety lamp.

Chapter 17. "Come here, or meet me at Exeter"

1. The queen's trial, as it was popularly called, was in fact a bill presented in the House of Lords "to deprive her Majesty Queen Caroline Amelia Elizabeth of the Title, Prerogatives, Privileges and Pretensions of Queen Consort, and to dissolve the marriage between his Majesty and the said Queen." It turned into an investigation of the queen's alleged adultery with Count Bergami, and provided the whole country with much salacious gossip for months. The joke that Mrs. Piozzi enjoyed hearing and retelling was that "since her Majesty has possession of all the John *Bulls*, her Husband ran to Cowes by way of Retaliation." (Letter to PSP dated 15 October 1820).
2. A copy of *Retrospection* which was listed in a Penzance Library catalog in the 1850s, may have been the copy that Mrs. Piozzi presented; but I could not locate it during a visit in 1987.
3. In other words, the bill had been thrown out.
4. An inquiry as to the possible identity of this writer, placed in *Notes and Queries* in June 1988, has failed to elicit any response.

Chapter 18. "Your precious Portrait"

1. Spranger Barry (1719–77), was in Garrick's company at Drury Lane, and later set himself up at Covent Garden as a rival.

2. This letter is in the Pierpont Morgan Library, New York. None of the letters after 27 July 1820 and before this one has been located.

3. The quotation is un-Shakespearean. John Ripley has pointed out to me that in Kemble's promptbook, act 2 scene 2 ends "On, on to the Capitol," and act 3 scene 2 has the line "Mother, I am going to the market-place / Chide me no more."

4. "*Hell*'s concave" appears in *Paradise Lost*.

5. This is the only clue that HLP left that the "castle" may have been a casket of some kind. When she first mentioned the castle in her diary, in May 1820, it was to be "inhabited" on 27 January 1821. That day was rapidly approaching, and its occupant was an annotated Bible, to be presented to its "governor" WAC. Thus "Conway's Castle" may have been inspired by Conway Castle, not twenty miles away from Brynbella. The "castle" was both a place of security and a pipedream, a "castle in the air."

6. Tulip, the flower of flowers?

7. Horace Twiss (1787–1849), son of Francis and Fanny Twiss, had just been elected M.P. for Wootton Bassett.

Chapter 19. "Sickness and Sorrow"

1. And still is.

2. Letter in Beinecke Library.

3. *Melmoth the Wanderer*—a recent novel by Charles Robert Maturin (1782–1824), who also wrote the play *Bertram*.

4. A new play by J. Howard Payne, first produced in London at Drury Lane, on 2 February 1821.

5. 21 March 1821, Princeton University Library.

6. Salusbury had refused Fellowes access to his aunt's papers, so thwarting her wish that he should be her literary executor.

7. As reported to Mangin, *Piozziana*, p. 93.

Chapter 20. "Be kind to my remains"

1. Letter dated 5 May 1821, quoted by Hayward, *Autobiography, Letters and Literary Remains*. 1: 362–63.

2. The following correspondence is in Ryl. Eng. MSS. 568/154–57.

3. The new footman, whom Mrs. Pennington had recommended. James seems to have been paid off shortly after they arrived back in Clifton.

4. In the Hyde Collection.

5. Ryl. Eng. MSS 596/12.

6. Quoted by Dorset Fellowes in some notes dated 14 February 1841, found in a volume of *Letters to and from the late Samuel Johnson* in the Beinecke Library. The verse is by Dryden, addressed to Congreve on his comedy *The Double Dealer*.

7. John Gore, ed. *Thomas Creevey's Papers, 1793–1838* (London: Penguin Books, 1948), p. 204.

8. By this time Castlereagh had succeeded to the marquessate of Londonderry, but was still foreign secretary and leader of the House of Commons.

9. Reproduced in Jerdan's *Autobiography* (London: 1853), 3:243–46.

10. Lord Henry, the only surviving brother whom WAC had not approached, was now seventy-six.

11. This part of Jerdan's story does not stand up. The third marquess, Francis Charles Seymour Conway, lived until 1842: it is more likely that he preferred not to be accountable for the follies of an uncle thirty years earlier.

12. He crossed the Atlantic fifty-three times.

Chapter 21. The New World

1. Stephen Price (1783–1840) managed the Park Theatre in New York from 1808 until his death. His policy of importing English stars was claimed to have set back the cause of the American stage for many years. Between 1826 and 1830 he contrived to manage both the Park Theatre and the Theatre Royal, Drury Lane, where his penchant for spectacle was not universally admired.

2. Odell, *Annals of the New York Stage* (New York: Columbia University Press, 1927–1949), 3: 99.

3. Odell, *Annals,* 3: 101.

4. Ripley, *"Julius Caesar" on stage,* p. 107.

5. *The Albion,* New York, 21 February 1824. This newspaper addressed itself to the expatriate British.

6. Kendall, John S. *The Golden Age of the New Orleans Theater,* Baton Rouge: Louisiana State University Press, 1952. p. 40.

7. Later the *New York Dramatic Mirror,* 17 February 1827.

8. Macready based his *Reminiscences* on his diaries, but did not live to see the work published; it was edited by Sir Frederick Pollock in 1875. Volume 1 ends just before this joint engagement, and volume 2 resumes in 1836. Unfortunately, there is also a gap in the diaries from January to September 1827.

9. Posterity's verdict, as expressed by Thomas Allston Brown, dramatic editor of the *New York Clipper* from 1864 to 1870, was kind. "He was well proportioned and possessed great muscular strength, and a masterly command of his countenance, which seemed to have been formed to express the passions of his soul and to delineate the characters of Shakespeare." (Bordman, *Oxford Companion to the American Theatre,* p. 163)

10. Quoted in chapter 7. Original in Harvard Theatre Collection.

11. Cooper's London engagement was not a success. His style was long outmoded. Anna Maria Tree had been a member of the Bath company before moving to Covent Garden in the 1820s. The scurrilous James Winston recorded that Miss [Mary Ann] Paton "drinks and sometimes gets tipsy." The former actress Harriet Mellon (1777–1837), widow of the banker Sir Thomas Coutts, married the duke in 1827.

12. 8 February 1828.

Epilogue

1. Lester Wallack, *Memories of Fifty Years* (New York: 1889).

2. Richard Savage (1697?–1743), an English poet who claimed to be the son of Lady Macclesfield and Richard Savage, fourth Earl Rivers.

Bibliography

Balderston, Katharine C. "Johnson's Vile Melancholy," in *The Age of Johnson: Essays Presented to Chauncey Brewster Tinker*. New Haven, Conn.: Yale University Press, 1949, reissued 1964.

Bate, Walter J. *Samuel Johnson*. New York: Harcourt Brace, 1977.

Beloe, William. *The Sexagenarian; or, The Recollections of a Literary Life*. 2 eds. London: printed for F. C. and J. Rivington 1817 and 1818. Chapter 47 is devoted to HLP.

Bloom, Edward A., Lillian D. Bloom, and Joan E. Klingel. "Portrait of a Georgian Lady: The Letters of Hester Lynch (Thrale) Piozzi, 1784–1821." Bulletin of John Rylands University Library of Manchester 40 (1978): 303–38.

Bloom, Edward A., and Lillian D. Bloom, eds. *The Piozzi Letters: Correspondence of Hester Lynch Piozzi, 1784–1821*. Vol. 1 (vols. 2–6 forthcoming). Newark: University of Delaware Press, 1989.

Boswell, James. *Life of Johnson*. Edited by R. W. Chapman. Oxford: Oxford University Press, 1980.

Bunn, Alfred. *The Stage: both before and behind the Curtain*. 3 vols. London: Richard Bentley, 1840.

Cockayne, George E. *The Complete Peerage of England, Scotland, Ireland, Great Britain and the United Kingdom*. 2d ed., rev. and enl. Edited by Vicary Gibbs et al. 13 vols. London: St. Catherine Press, 1910–59.

Clifford, James L. *Hester Lynch Piozzi: (Mrs Thrale)*. 2d ed. Oxford: Clarendon Press, 1987.

Genest, John. *Some Account of the English Stage, from the Restoration in 1660 to 1830*. 10 vols. Bath: Printed by H. E. Carrington and sold by Thomas Rodd, London, 1832.

Hayward, Abraham. *Autobiography, Letters and Literary Remains of Mrs Piozzi (Thrale)*. 2 vols., 2d ed. London: Longman, Green, Longman, Roberts, 1861.

Hazlitt, William. *A View of the English Stage*. 1st ed. London: Printed for Robert Stodart, Strand; Anderson and Chase, West Smithfield. Edinburgh: Bell and Bradfute, 1818.

Hyde, Mary Morley. *The Impossible Friendship: Boswell and Mrs Thrale*. Cambridge: Harvard University Press, 1972.

———. *The Thrales of Streatham Park*. Cambridge: Harvard University Press, 1977.

Ireland, Joseph. *Records of the New York Stage from 1752 to 1860*. New York: 1866.

Jerdan, William. *Autobiography*. 4 vols. London: 1852–53.

Knapp, Oswald G., ed. *The Intimate Letters of Hester Piozzi and Penelope Pennington, 1788–1821*. London, and New York: John Lane; Toronto: Bell and Cockburn, 1914.

Love Letters of Mrs. Piozzi, written when she was eighty, to William Augustus Conway. London: Printed by John Russell Smith, 1843.

McCarthy, William. *Hester Lynch Piozzi: Portrait of a Literary Woman*. Chapel Hill: University of North Carolina Press, 1983.

[Mangin, Edward] *Piozziana; or, Recollections of the late Mrs. Piozzi, by a Friend*. London: Edward Moxom, 1833.

Merritt, Percival. *Piozzi Marginalia* (includes extracts from HLP's "Commonplace Book" and marginalia written by her in WAC's copy of *Observations and Reflections*). Cambridge: Harvard University Press, 1925.

———. *The True Story of the so-called Love Letters of Mrs. Piozzi*, "in defence of an elderly lady." Cambridge: Harvard University Press, 1927.

Nicoll, Allardyce. *A History of English Drama, 1660–1900*. 6 vols. Cambridge: Cambridge University Press, 1955.

Odell, George C. D. *Annals of the New York Stage*. 15 vols. New York: Columbia University Press, 1927–49.

Oxford Companion to the American Theatre. Edited by Gerald Bordman. New York and Oxford: Oxford University Press, 1984.

Oxford Companion to the Theatre. Edited by Phyllis Hartnoll. 3rd ed. Oxford: Oxford University Press, 1967.

Penley, B. S. *The Bath Stage: a history of dramatic representations in Bath*. London: W. Lewis, 1892.

Piozzi, Hester L. *Anecdotes of the late Samuel Johnson, LL.D., During the Last Twenty Years of his Life*. London: 1786; Edited by S. C. Roberts, Cambridge: Cambridge University Press, 1924.

———. *Letters to and from the late Samuel Johnson, LL.D.* 2 vols. London: Printed for A. Strahan and T. Cadell 1788; Edited by R. W. Chapman, 3 vols. Oxford: Clarendon Press, 1952.

———. *Retrospection; or, a Review of the most Striking and Important Events, Characters, and their Consequences, which the last Eighteen Hundred Years have presented to Mankind*. 2 vols. London: Printed for John Stockdale, 1801. The copy that HLP annotated for WAC is in the Beinecke Library, Yale University.

———. *Observations and Reflections on a Journey through France, Italy and Germany*. 2 vols. London: Printed for A. Strahan and T. Cadell 1789. The copy that HLP annotated for WAC, including the MS of "The Abridgment," is in the Hyde Collection, Somerville, New Jersey.

Pollock, Frederick, ed. *Macready's Reminiscences*. 2 vols. London: Macmillan, 1875.

Prior, J. *Life of Edmond Malone*. London: 1860.

Ripley, John D. *"Julius Caesar" on stage in England and America, 1599–1973*. Cambridge: Cambridge University Press, 1980.

Tearle, John L. "An Interpolation in 'Julius Caesar,' " in *Theatre Notebook*. Vol. 35. London: Society for Theatre Research, 1981.

Thraliana: The Diary of Mrs Hester Lynch Thrale (later Mrs Piozzi), 1776–1809. Edited by Katharine C. Balderston. 2d ed., 2 vols. Oxford: Clarendon Press, 1951.

Trewin, John C. *Mr. Macready. A nineteenth century tragedian and his theatre*. London: Harrap, 1955.

Who's Who in the Theatre. Edited by John Parker. 11th ed. London: Pitman, 1951.

Wraxall, W. Nathaniel. *Historical Memoirs of his own Time, from 1772 to 1784*. 2 vols. London: 1815.

———. *Historical and Posthumous Memoirs*. Edited by H. B. Wheatley. 5 vols. London: 1884.

———. *Posthumous Memoirs of his own Time*. London: 1836.

Newspapers and Journals
(Published in London unless otherwise stated)

The Athenaeum
The Bath and Cheltenham Gazette
The Bath Herald
The Bath Journal

The Birmingham Chronicle
The Birmingham Gazette
The British Stage
The Boston Statesman
The Chester Chronicle
The Courier
The Era
The Gentleman's Magazine
Irish Dramatic Censor (Dublin)
John Bull
St. James's Chronicle
The Morning Post
The New Monthly Magazine
The New York Albion
The New York American
The New York Clipper
The New York Dramatic Mirror
The New York Herald
The New York Times
The Literary Cadet (Providence, R.I.)
Theatre Notebook
The Theatrical Inquisitor
The World

Index